The
EVERYTHING
Home Storage Solutions Book

Dear Reader,

When I told people I was writing a book on home storage solutions, the reaction was universal: "That's exactly what I need!"

Why is it we routinely step over, around, and occasionally on our accumulated treasures instead of finding a proper home for them? Writing this book allowed me to test out plenty of clutter-busting strategies and experiment with lots of different storage products on the market. Even the most organized among us—Did I mention I'm also an inveterate list-maker?—sometimes needs an organizational overhaul now and then. It doesn't matter if you live in a studio apartment or five-bedroom home. There never seems to be enough space for all we accumulate. In my "research," I managed to fill dozens of trash bags, giving the sanitation crew a workout (an extra Christmas bonus awaits, guys). Local charities got a windfall, too. I streamlined the clutter and reduced the paperwork. Ahhh, finally I'm in control, and it feels really good.

I hope this book helps you gain control. And I really hope it doesn't wind up among another ever-growing pile of books on your coffee table.

Iyna Bort Caruso

The EVERYTHING® Series

Editorial

Publishing Director	Gary M. Krebs
Director of Product Development	Paula Munier
Associate Managing Editor	Laura M. Daly
Associate Copy Chief	Brett Palana-Shanahan
Acquisitions Editor	Lisa Laing
Development Editor	Jessica LaPointe
Associate Production Editor	Casey Ebert

Production

Director of Manufacturing	Susan Beale
Associate Director of Production	Michelle Roy Kelly
Cover Design	Paul Beatrice Matt LeBlanc Erick DaCosta
Design and Layout	Heather Barrett Brewster Brownville Colleen Cunningham Jennifer Oliveira
Series Cover Artist	Barry Littmann
Interior illustrator	Kathie Kelleher

Visit the entire Everything® Series at *www.everything.com*

THE

EVERYTHING®

Home Storage
Solutions Book

Make the most of your space with
hundreds of creative organizing ideas

Iyna Bort Caruso

Adams Media
Avon, Massachusetts

To my parents, who always led by example.

An Everything® Series Book.
Everything® and everything.com® are registered trademarks of F+W Publications, Inc.

Published by Adams Media, an F+W Publications Company
57 Littlefield Street, Avon, MA 02322 U.S.A.
www.adamsmedia.com

ISBN 10: 1-59337-662-6
ISBN 13: 978-1-59337-662-8
Printed in the United States of America.

J   I   H   G   F   E   D   C   B   A

Library of Congress Cataloging-in-Publication Data
Caruso, Iyna Bort.
The everything home storage solutions book / Iyna Bort Caruso.
p. cm. -- (Everything series)
Includes index.
ISBN-13: 978-1-59337-662-8
ISBN-10: 1-59337-662-6

TX309.C37 2006
648'.8--dc22
2006028209

This book is available at quantity discounts for bulk purchases.
For information, please call 1-800-289-0963.

Contents

**Top Ten Ways You Know You've Got a 911
   Storage Emergency / x**
Introduction / xi

Containing Yourself / 1
Living in the Material World **2** • Organized Grime **5** • Clutter-Busting **6** • Fill 'er Up **8** • Purge and Resurge **10** • Up, Up, and Away **12** • Swept Away **14**

If You Can't Stand the Heap: Kitchens / 17
Out in the Open **18** • Taking Stock **20** • Cold Storage **26** • The Kitchen Sink and Everything under It **27** • Cooks and Crannies **30** • Baker's Dozen **34**

Bed, Belongings, and Beyond: Bedrooms / 37
Out of Sight **38** • Segregate, Donate, Eliminate **40** • Habit Forming **42** • Quick Drawers **44** • Taking a Stand **47** • Incredible Convertibles **48** • Have a Seat **49** • Kidding Around **50** • Be My Guest **51** • The Great Escape **52**

Closet Confidential / 53
Tug of Wardrobe **54** • Repeat Offenders **55** • Suit Yourself **56** • Hanging On **58** • Walk Right In **61** • Shoe-Ins **62** • Hook, Line, and Sneakers **63** • The Linen Closet **64**

En Suite Success: Bathrooms / 69

Shower Power **70** • Console Yourself **75** • Wall-to-Wall Solutions **77** • In a Lather **78** • Big Ideas for Little Spaces **79** • Bathrooms to Spare **79**

It's Showtime: Media Rooms and Home Theaters / 83

That's Entertainment **84** • Media Madness **85** • TV or Not TV **90** • Hide and Seek **90** • Out of (Remote) Control **93** • Multiplexed, Not Perplexed **94**

Home Sweet Home Office / 95

Over, Under, and Out **96** • Broken Records **98** • Divide and Conquer **99** • Piles of Files **101** • Mail Call **103** • Table Talk **104** • Book Smarts **107** • Letter Perfect **108** • Digitize to Downsize **109** • How Suite It Is **111**

Child's Play: Playrooms / 113

Toy Stories **114** • Toys R Everywhere **117** • Changing Times **118** • Age-Old Issues **120** • Think Small **121** • Fun and Games **122**

Sub-Floor Décor: Basements / 123

Down in the Dumps **124** • Getting Started **126** • A Cellar's Market **129** • The Finished Line **129** • Laundry Lists **131** • Crafty Ideas **132** • Good Sports **133** • Down and Out **134**

Lofty Spaces: Attics / 135

States of Disgrace **136** • Thinking Outside the Carton **137** • All about Eaves **139** • Zoning Out **141** • Leader of the Pack **142** • The Finishing Touch **143** • Book It **144**

Grand Entrances: Hallways and Mudrooms / 147
Enter at Your Own Risk **148** • Front and Center **149** • Best Foot
Forward **152** • Mudroom Makeovers **152** • Pet Projects **156** • Secret
Spaces **157** • Over and Out **158**

The Great Outdoors: Backyards and Gardens / 161
Cleaning Up Your Act **162** • Out and About **163** • Turning a New
Leaf **164** • The Plot Thickens **166** • Tooling Around **167** • Plants and
Planters **168** • Garden Parties **169**

Park Place: Garages / 171
Car Wars **172** • Central Park **173** • Getting in Gear **176** • Stalled Plans
178 • Haul Ways **179** • Getting the Most Mileage **181**

Thanks for the Memorabilia: Collectibles / 183
Amass Appeal **184** • Crazy for Collectibles **184** • Controlling the
Volume **185** • Cent-amental Value **187** • Aging Gracefully **188** • Heir
Conditioning **189** • Out of Sight **191** • Handle with Care **192**

It's Only a Paper Boom: Ephemera / 193
TeXt Marks the Spot **194** • Reamed Out **196** • Out, Not About **197** •
What's in Store **198** • Pulp Friction **201** • Scan Artists **202** • Under
Wraps **203**

Picture Perfect: Photographs / 205
A Photo Finish **206** • Search and Destroy **207** • Developing Ideas **209**
• Box It Up **210** • In a Bind **210** • Battle Plans **211** • Virtual Memories
213 • Big Shots **215**

Rooms and Boarders: Apartments / 217
Intimate Spaces **218** • Fit to Be Tried **219** • It's a Small World After All **220** • Clean Up Your Act **220** • Good Things, Small Packages **222** • Furniture on Overtime **223** • Kitchen Aids **225** • Slumber Parties **227** • Store and Order **228**

Party On: Special Occasions / 231
The Wrong Stuff **232** • Stock and Trade **234** • Rites and Wrongs **235** • Task Masters **236** • Serves You Right **238** • Crystal-Clear Solutions **240** • Food for Thought **240**

'Tis the Season: Holidays / 243
Christmas Past and Presents **244** • Christmas Countdown **245** • Season Opener **246** • Yuletide Wrap-Up **247** • Tailor-Made Solutions **249** • For a Holly Jolly Christmas **251**

On the Road: Travel / 253
Mapping a Plan **254** • Suit(case) Yourself **255** • Route Causes **257** • Lighten Up **258** • On the Road **260** • Leader of the Pack **263** • Auto-Matic **265** • Home Away from Home **266** • On the Fast Track **267**

Appendix A: Glossary / 269
Appendix B: Additional Resources / 275
Appendix C: Further Reading / 281
Index / 283

cknowledgments

Thanks to the many friends and strangers who opened up their closets, attics, and basements to me and let me see the places where most visitors dare not go. Thanks, too, for telling me about your bad habits and embarrassing stories. We've all got our share of them.

Kudos to Evelyn, Heidi, and Ariane for going above and beyond.

Thanks to Barry for going through this JG adventure with me, to June Clark, and the many hardworking folks at Adams Media, including Lisa Laing and Jessica LaPointe. I would also like to thank my fantastic copy editor, Virginia Beck. Thanks most of all to my husband, Jay, who put up with my many months of clutter-busting fanaticism with his typical humor, grace, and unconditional support.

Top Ten Ways You Know
You've Got a 911 Storage Emergency

1. Your car hasn't seen the inside of the garage for years.

2. The Stairmaster is covered with clothes waiting to be ironed.

3. The ironing board is covered with barbells.

4. You've got to take a running leap at the closet door in order to shut it.

5. The median expiration date of food in your pantry lands smack in the middle of the Jimmy Carter administration.

6. The junk in your basement is so old it's now considered vintage.

7. You leave your clothes in the dryer. After all, it's like an extra drawer.

8. You still have warranties of long-discarded appliances.

9. Showers of plastic take-out containers rain down on you when you open your kitchen cabinet door.

10. You don't just have a junk drawer. You have an entire junk room.

Introduction

▶ What's your breaking point? When do the piles of paper get so high, the old exercise bicycle in the basement so dusty, the toys in the playroom so trip-worthy that you reach the end of your rope?

Everyone's got a story, and there are no urban legends among them. There's the businessman whose slim closet couldn't fit another item. Rather than sort through his clothes and get rid of his never-wears, he came up with an ingenious solution—or so he thought. You decide. He hung his excess shirts off ceiling fans throughout his home.

The tales of an exasperated spouse going to extreme measures are endless. Many are variations on the "while you were out" theme. The guilty party leaves for work and the Salvation Army truck parks in the driveway.

There's the story of one particular woman who got fed up with her husband's stockpiling habits. Their basement and garage looked like a thrift store exploded. You name it, they had it; piles of magazines dating back years, broken luggage, outdated TVs, ancient audio equipment, empty computer boxes. Driven to take extreme measures, she spent several hundred dollars to rent a commercial dumpster. It took the two of them an entire weekend to fill it up with a decade's worth of useless, busted, and forgettable items that should have been discarded long ago. By the way, it's been two years, but she still hasn't tossed out the business card of the carting company—just in case. Old habits die hard.

Plenty of us could take her lead. It's more than just the unsightly mess that gets to us. Clutter and disorganization first nag at us, then overwhelm us. It makes us frustrated and irritable. It eats away at our time and our sense of control. It also affects our health in ways you might not have considered.

It wasn't always like this. There's no question that we're accumulating things at a greater rate than ever before. Just visit an older home, built in the 1920s or 1930s, and you'll see that closets are narrower and fewer. "Where did they put all their stuff?" you'll wonder. Well, they just didn't have so much of it. We live in a time of excess, graduating from bigger to better to best, and hold on to stuff from all the stages in between.

There's a saying that work expands to fill the time you have to finish the task. That holds true for storage, too. The more space you have, the more things you'll find or buy to fill it up, if you're not careful. People who move from apartments to homes wonder how they'll ever be able to fill all those drawers, closets, and pantries. Check with them a year later, and no doubt you'll find their closets bursting.

But you're ready to tackle the clutter zones in your home, so congratulations! You've made a great start. *The Everything® Home Storage Solutions Book* offers you real-world strategies for getting your home back under your control, one room at a time. You'll find space you didn't know existed, even in the smallest of apartments. No need to be a professional contractor or pony up the big bucks to hire one. Each chapter gives you easy-to-implement ideas, many of which won't cost you anything more than your time and some sweat equity.

Getting organized is also a matter of getting into good habits. Let's face it. Sometimes it's just easier to pile the laundry on the guest bed "for the time being" instead of putting it away in its proper place, or to jam the golf equipment into the already overstuffed closet instead of dedicating a proper space to it. *The Everything® Home Storage Solutions Book* equips you with a game plan to manage it all. Plus, you'll get insider information on great products on the market that can change your lifestyle and transform your outlook.

When you streamline your living space, the ripple effects are astounding. Relationships improve, productivity soars, and serenity reigns.

Let's get started.

Chapter 1

Containing Yourself

Want to live a clutter-free life? Who doesn't? But it's tough when we all seem to be battling a case of affluenza—too much affluence, which usually translates into too many things. If one of something is good, two must be better, right? Look around and you'll realize how counter-productive that thinking really is. So let's create a system to prevent stuff from overwhelming our homes, our relationships, and our lives. In this chapter, you'll learn the basics of culling, sorting, and organizing, and you'll explore the pleasures of clutter-free living.

Living in the Material World

Death and taxes may be inevitable, and plenty of people would add some degree of clutter to the list. There's a reason that there's a national Clutter Awareness Week (the third week in March, by the way). Even neat and tidy types have hot spots in their homes, places that seem to attract a mess. No doubt you have a few, too. Perhaps it's by the front door where you put your keys and dump the newspaper and mail. Or is it in the kitchen, the whirlwind spot of family activities? How about the master bedroom, one of the last places guests see, making it an easy place to let things go?

Every Felix Unger has a bit of inner Oscar Madison in him. You can figure out exactly how much Oscardom by the state of your domain. There are plenty of red flags: Mislaying mail. Having to scavenger-hunt through closets for something to wear. Noticing in August that your Christmas lights are still hanging on the windows. Realizing that nothing in your house has a dedicated home of its own. What often starts out as a messy drawer or two turns into a carton or two full of junk. Then, before you know it, you're renting a self-storage unit in town to house your overflows.

FACT

Need proof that we're busting out of our homes? The self-storage industry is a $15 billion business. There are nearly 50,000 self-storage facilities nationwide. The Self Storage Association, the trade organization and official voice of its global membership, celebrated its thirtieth anniversary in 2005.

Clutter's Causes

So how did we get here? The core issue is overconsumption. Barry Izsak, president of the National Organization of Professional Organizers, says consumers are being bombarded with messages from the media, and the message is: *Get more stuff.* Americans have more disposable income than ever, so it's easy to heed the messages. We're acquiring stuff without thinking what we're going to do with it, how we're going to use it, or where we're going to put it.

And, frankly, who's got the time to figure it out? We're busier than ever. Chalk it up to work, family, school, hobbies, or usually, all of the above. Our complicated lives are catching up to us. Add to that the recent trend toward nesting, spending more time indoors, embarking on more household projects, and doing more in-home entertaining, and you've got lots of good excuses to let things spiral out of control.

Ready to purge, but want someone else to handle the heavy lifting? A company called 1-800-GOT-JUNK (*www.1800gotjunk.com*) took the idea of the old TV show *Sanford and Son* and professionalized it. It's the first branded, full-service junk removal service. Two people will show up at your door and cart away just about anything they can lift—as long as it's not hazardous.

In some instances, though, it's not a matter of schedule overload. It's a matter of stopping to consider where we are in our lives and if the trappings that surround us still fit, still make sense. Now that the kids are grown and out of the house, do you really need all those extra place settings, towels, and linens? If golf is your sport of choice, can't you get rid of the in-line skates, step exercise videos, and tennis rackets in your basement? Storage spaces are needlessly junked up because we don't stop to reevaluate our changing lives.

Hoarding for Practical Reasons

Then there are the people who've been trained at the waste-not-want-not school of housekeeping. They've lived through the Depression years, or at least some very lean times, and they wouldn't consider throwing something out. The thinking goes that if it still functions, it stays. After all, you never know when you might need it. That perfectly good alarm clock is impossible to part with even though there are clocks on your VCR, cable box, microwave oven, and computer. These tend to be the same people who amass accidental collections. You know, like the plastic containers from Chinese take-out, plastic cutlery from fast-food restaurants, and the glass vases from too many floral deliveries to count. Trashing these things somehow seems extravagant, so they go on shelves or in drawers, where they stay put. And it seems many couples have passed this mindset onto their children.

Professional Help

Clutter comes in every size and degree, from mild to severe, from annoying to debilitating. At the extreme end are folks who suffer from what some call disposophobia—fear of disposing. In other words, they hoard. According to one report, nearly a million junkaholics suffer from this psychological disorder, and the proof is in the piles. They don't buy, they stockpile, forming an emotional attachment to their things and becoming anxious at the thought of discarding them. A national support group called Clutterers Anonymous models itself after the twelve-step format of Alcoholics Anonymous. They hold meetings in towns across the country. Some experts believe clutter in the extreme may be tied to obsessive-compulsive disorder, attention deficient disorder, or depression. Believe it or not, control freaks can be the messiest. They concentrate on trying to control everything around them, and since they're unable to keep up with their own messiness, they believe they're in control as long as no one is allowed to throw their things out.

QUESTION?

How can I tell if someone is a compulsive clutterer?
According to the group Clutterers Anonymous, there are twenty warning signs, including these. You miss deadlines because you can't find the paperwork to finish the project. Your clutter is starting to affect your personal relationships. You bring items into the home without a place for them. You have difficulty disposing of things, even though you haven't used them in years. You possess more things than you can comfortably handle.

Most people, however, just need a little help strategizing their living space and optimizing their storage capabilities. The fact is that previous generations simply didn't have all the stuff we have today. They never had to contend with overflowing closets and burgeoning basements, even the annoying mailboxes full of junk mail. Generations from baby boomers to millennials may have it all within reach, but most haven't learned how to keep it in balance. Our homes continue to grow fuller, even as our households grow smaller. It's easy to internalize and say that a cluttered home is the result of a personality flaw, but in most cases it's simply the case of never having learned the right organizational skills.

Easy Does It

There's no need to get fanatical to get efficient. In fact, extreme methods don't stick. The simple fact is that when you decrease the number of items in your house, you free up a surprising amount of space, possibly enough space to abandon the need for a storage rental unit. And that's not all. Along with that comes peace of mind. Professional organizer Ariane Benefit of Bloomfield, New Jersey, says she's seen dramatic transformations in her clients once they've conquered the clutter. Some have been able to go off anti-depression medications, others have seen their marriages improve. All have gained a sense of pride and self-respect.

Organized Grime

If you're embarrassed to invite company over and cringe at the thought of an unexpected drop-in by a neighbor, you're ready for a change. Sometimes it takes seeing your home through someone else's eyes to get a reality check. The look in a visitor's eyes can say it all. There's the story of one woman whose situation came home to roost in the most ironic way. Fed up with the chaos, she remembered a home organization book she had bought years earlier. Trouble was, she couldn't find it under the mess!

Living in clutter is more than just a matter of aesthetics. Clutter is an energy-sapper that takes its emotional toll and steals domestic joy. If home is where the heap is, you'll be more stressed, less productive, and pretty grumpy, too. Suddenly things start feeling out of control. "Where's the remote?" "This aspirin is expired." "I can't find my argyle socks!" Sound familiar? And it can get even worse. Clutter can cause tension and lead to disagreements in relationships, even with friends and business associates. People are chronically behind schedule because they can't find their car keys or they're unable to sift through their closets for a complete outfit in the morning. And children can suffer as well. Some youngsters experience problems at school because they're routinely late for class or underprepared for assignments. Home, a place that's supposed to be a haven, turns into one of high anxiety. And trying to avoid the issue actually adds more stress to your life. It's a vicious cycle of self-deprecation. Is it any wonder why more and more people are retreating to day spas to get a little rest and relaxation?

E
ALERT!

> There's such a thing as visual clutter, too. When you have a room with too many disparate objects on the walls—shelves, pictures, bulletin boards, decorative plates—it can create a crowded, overwhelming effect. That's especially counterproductive in bedrooms, the place people typically want to be a room of refuge and serenity. Try to strike a design balance.

There are plenty of times when closet and cabinet doors seem like a godsend. They make it easy to keep clutter out of sight. On the other hand, they can be a crutch that enables us to continue bad habits. Envision what your space would look like neat and streamlined. How would you feel? More relaxed? In a better state of mind? Would you be proud to invite people over? The benefits of putting a storage and organization plan into play are transforming. You feel cleansed, calm, and accomplished. You may think you've reached the point of no return, but in fact, big returns are coming your way by investing time and employing a few simple strategies. You can do it.

Clutter-Busting

Getting organized is a little like dieting. There are a lot of ways to accomplish the goal, and some systems work better for some than others. Ellen keeps herself on the straight and narrow by hiring a weekly cleaning service. It forces her to tidy up, clear off the tabletops, and scoop up the piles on the floor on a regular basis so that the cleaning service can actually get in there to dust and vacuum. Jane, a single working mother, devised a ten-minute-a-day system knowing she doesn't have huge chunks of time to devote to organization. Then there's Mindy, who always thought she had to de-clutter her whole house all at once. She says she didn't sign onto the "one area at a time" approach until she was so overwhelmed that it was the only way possible to handle her situation. And it worked.

There are, however, some basic habits everyone can adopt that will make a big difference. Think in terms of economy of motion and time. Take off your coat and hang it up in one fell swoop. Undress near your closet so that you automatically hang up your pants instead of tossing them on the bed. When you open your mail, read it and decide if it should be torn and trashed or filed right then and there. And then do it. Keep trash containers handy so there's no excuse to let unwanted things lie around. Sure, you have to allow for life's realities, but a good rule of thumb is to deal with something once. And remind yourself to take an inventory of your changing needs from time to time. Dispose of the items that no longer fit your lifestyle.

Organization has to be based on the personality, environment, habits, and usage of the individual or household. A one-size-fits-all solution won't work. Trying to force-fit answers may work for a while, but sooner or later, anything forced is doomed to fail. Make sure your clutter-busting solutions fit your lifestyle.

A Place for Everything

Another important ground rule? Never buy anything unless you have a place to put it. One newly purchased painting was designated for duty in the communal storage bin of a condo complex after the homeowner was unable to find the wall space on which to hang it. Another individual bought a mahogany antique icebox thinking she could convert it into a funky bar for her den. Turns out the icebox didn't fit in the den. But it does fit in her unfinished basement, where's it been collecting dust ever since. And that goes for storage containers, too. Ariane Benefit says disorganized people tend to have more organizing products than their shipshape counterparts.

The containers actually add to the clutter problem because they were purchased without a specific purpose in mind. Plan first, buy second.

What works? What doesn't? Every item needs a home, and the home must suit the need. For instance, things you use every day should be stored in accessible and intuitive places. Toothpaste in the medicine cabinet is a no-brainer. But what about your house keys? Is searching for them part of your morning out-the-door routine? That's because you haven't designated a permanent and appropriate spot for them, which, in this case, would be on a hook or in a drawer right by the door. Similarly, there are times when people see an open space in a drawer or cabinet and find it impossible to resist filling it with items that don't belong. They'll put photographs in a night-table drawer or toys in a home office closet. That only starts the snowball effect of creating a storage nightmare. Take a look around your rooms, and you'll discover this is where many clutter problems originate.

A Family Affair

Take a holistic approach to organizing your home. Involve each family member in the planning and process. Make sure everyone knows the end goal and what is expected of him or her. Start with a needs assessment. Who does what in which room? Do you need to carve out a crafts area? A play zone? A quiet zone for homework? A makeshift home office? How will the rooms have to be rejiggered to support these various activities? Put a budget together for shelves, bins, and other storage supplies. Then, get everyone's input and buy-in to the plan. When family members understand how integral they are to the endeavor and the benefits they'll reap, you'll have taken a major step at the outset to reaching your goals.

Fill 'er Up

There are hundreds of products and services available to help you meet whatever specific storage challenges you're about to face. Almost any piece of furniture can be designed for functionality. There are ottomans with beneath-the-seat storage, pop-up television sets that won't commandeer surface space, and double-duty armoires. Products range from inexpensive Rubbermaid bins to top-of-the-line custom-built solutions with stratospheric price tags to match. Budget limitations are no excuse to keep the status quo. Even if you're on austerity, you can repurpose existing furniture and organizational aids in ways that don't break the bank.

The least expensive way to get more storage space, of course, is to donate, sell, or throw out. According to one report, 80 percent of what we have we never use.

FACT

The week between Christmas and New Year's Day is the biggest selling period for storage containers. The reason? Consumers need them to store their holiday decorations and to hold all their newly received gifts. Other peak selling times are back-to-school season and Halloween. Chances are you'll be able to find some good storage bargains if you time your purchases just right.

You can find storage products at hardware stores, storage specialty retailers, even museum shops. Visit the storage section of your local department store, and you'll get a good idea of just how widespread a problem clutter is these days. The aisles are packed. It's like going to a supermarket the day before Thanksgiving.

The biggest thing you'll have to cough up is not money but time. Finding long-term storage solutions is not a matter of neatening up the piles on your office desk. It's a commitment to eviscerating them. It's not hanging the clothes that sit on the foot of your bed. It's going through every scarf, pair of pants, shirt, and hat and committing to a take-no-prisoners approach.

Let's face it. It took weeks, months, maybe even years of neglect for your home to reach the state it's in, so it's only fair it'll require a little bit of elbow grease to undo the damage. Amazingly, you can even make money out of the deal. As you go along, you'll discover a mountain of items you no longer need. Sell them. Have a garage sale, list them online with eBay, bring them to a consignment shop, or take out a classified ad in your local paper. It's a great way to free up space and put money in your pocket. And, if you're like most people, you'll also discover items you forgot you even had, like a brand-new shirt stuffed in the back of the bedroom closet. Then again, nothing quite makes you feel as good as donating your unwanted items to a good cause.

When buying storage products that require assembly, be sure to check the label for information on installation hardware. Sometimes the hardware is included with the product. Other times, you'll need to purchase it separately. Also ask the sales representative how difficult the product is to assemble. If you're an all-thumbs type, you may need to make arrangements for professional installation.

You may come up with another discovery—that you might not be storage-deprived after all. A whole-house purge can result in big chunks of newfound space. Imagine finding an extra 25 or 50 percent more space you didn't realize you had. If that doesn't motivate you, nothing will.

Purge and Resurge

In the chapters that follow, you'll learn about the specific storage challenges and opportunities in each room of the house. The problem area will determine what supplies you'll need for a clean sweep. Generally, you should have the following on hand:

- Cartons
- Markers (A label-maker is even better. As your third-grade teacher stressed, neatness counts.)
- Labels
- Trash bags
- File folders
- Binders

Solving your storage problems entails getting to the heart of the matter: stuff. To know where to put it, you need to first determine if belongs in your home. Do you use it, need it, or love it? Be prepared to assess each item. There's no easy way around this job. As standard operating procedure, you'll need to remove everything from closets, drawers, cabinets, and pantries first. It'll force you to take an inventory of what you've got and, more importantly, what you can get rid of. Make sure that as you go along you take pains to put your possessions on a weight-loss program.

Here are four principles to discern junk from valuable, usable belongings:

- If you can't remember the last time you used, wore, or played with something, it's time to get rid of it. That "someday I might need it" philosophy is what got you into this situation in the first place.
- When evaluating items that hold sentimental attachments, try to segregate the object from the memory.
- If it's broken, and you're not the handyman type, let it go.
- If you uncover multitudes of an item, do a good deed and donate your extras to others.

Brian Scudamore, founder and CEO of the 1-800-GOT-JUNK trash-removal service, says that his employees have found their share of oddities while hauling away garbage from customers' garages and basements. Among the weirdest? Prosthetic legs, 18,000 cans of expired sardines, thirteen porcelain Buddha statues, 19,000 pounds of frozen animal carcasses, and a defused bomb from World War II.

You can only deduct donations to organizations that the Internal Revenue Service qualifies as nonprofit. Ask the charity if it qualifies, or check the IRS Web site at *www.irs.gov*. For furniture and clothing donations, the IRS will allow you to deduct the fair market price of your contributions. Always ask the agency for a receipt.

Now if your refuse is anything like that, you may need to hire a hauling service or rent a commercial dumpster. Look in the Yellow Pages and compare prices and terms.

In the case of home organization, parting is all sweet—and no sorrow. When you pare down, you automatically make your living space more breathable.

Up, Up, and Away

Putting everything away takes a little bit more thought than yanking it off the shelves. It's crucial to have a dedicated home for every item. The alternative is quiet chaos.

Store like items together so there is an inherent sense of order. Keep serving utensils all in one drawer, for instance, and athletic equipment all in one area. What happens when items scatter in a diaspora? Two words: junk drawer. The reason junk drawers are unruly is that they're a dumping ground for every miscellaneous "orphaned" item in your home. If you define your space and start thinking in terms of designated zones, you'll spend a lot less time hunting things down in places they don't belong.

FACT

Today, the average house size is 1,700 square feet. That's about the same as a decade ago. So while home size remains the same, Americans are accumulating more stuff at faster rates, which is one big reason for all the clutter.

Twenty-three percent of adults say they pay their bills late—and incur late fees—not because they don't have the money but because they lose the statements. When you don't assign a place for something, you give yourself carte blanche to keep an inefficient system going.

If, after all your purging, you still need to rent a storage unit, shop around for price, and carefully consider size. You don't want to pay for space you don't use. Accessibility and security are a couple of other issues to investigate. And before you sign, check the facility out with the Better Business Bureau, online at *www.bbb.org*.

Process Makes Perfect

Recognize that solving your storage dilemmas is a process that takes planning. Take it a room at a time. If necessary, take it a few minutes at a time, if that will prevent you from becoming overwhelmed. Otherwise, you'll be tempted to call it quits. It could take the better part of a day to do a top-to-bottom sweep of a bathroom and the better part of a month for a really huge undertaking, like a kitchen or home office. Don't rush it.

Clutter comes in all forms, including online clutter in your computer's inbox. Get around it by opening up a free e-mail account and use it exclusively for online purchases. Yahoo! and Gmail from Google are just two of the many providers. It'll help reduce spam to your primary account.

You can get through some of the smaller jobs faster if you're the multi-tasking type. Sorting through old photographs or reviewing files of paperwork are perfect jobs to do while watching TV or listening to the ballgame. Start by choosing a target that will let you see the immediate results of your work. Instead of a drawer or closet, pick a tabletop or desktop. The results will instantly enhance your functional space and give you all the incentive you need to keep moving forward.

Setting the Date

So now that you've got a plan, it's time to set a date. Grab a calendar and create a schedule. If you want to get your kitchen in primo shape for a party, allow enough time to turn it inside out and upside down. Factor in the configuration of your home and the climate, too. If you live in the north, bedrooms, kitchen, and bathrooms make good projects for the winter months. Shift your schedule if you live in a hot and humid environment.

Save noninsulated areas of your home for spring or fall. If your attic needs attention and it's neither heated nor air-conditioned, avoid a major re-org during the dog days of summer. For garden and outdoor areas, pick a beautiful day when you'll want to be outdoors anyway, enjoying fresh air and sunshine.

ALERT!

The International Association of Professional Organizers, a nonprofit association, provides free and anonymous support groups for chronic clutterers, hoarders, and packrats. Group teleconference calls are held the first Monday of every month from 7:00 to 9:00 P.M. Eastern Standard Time. Visit *http://organizingtheworld.org/chronicclutterer.htm* for instructions on how to dial in.

Enlist family members or friends. They'll help you to look at your possessions with a discerning eye and keep you on task. Sometimes we become so used to having a piece of furniture in a certain place or used a certain way, we can't imagine anything else. A yin to your yang will challenge you to rethink your design room by room, section by section. If the task still seems daunting or the situation has gotten a bit too out of hand, consider hiring a professional organizer, someone who'll come to your home to help you prioritize and systematize. The nonprofit group National Association of Professional Organizers can help you find an individual in your area who'll come to your rescue. Visit the group's Web site at *www.napo.net* for details.

Swept Away

Disorganization isn't tied to a particular gender, age group, geographic area, or socioeconomic class. It's an equal opportunity offender that casts a wide net. Today the organization business is a $7 billion market. Professional Organizer Barry Izsak says organization is learned behavior that, unfortunately, is never taught. Be patient. It's not realistic to think you're going to tame one, five, or twenty years of clutter in a day, so set practical expectations. Baby steps or giant steps, either way you're moving forward.

Clean House, Clear Mind

When you rework the space you have, assigning a function to every area and optimizing its efficiency, you'll find you have more room than you thought possible. Americans are converting their garages into living spaces and renting off-site storage units more than ever before, but realize this: Eighty percent of clutter is the result of disorganization, not lack of space.

More important, you will have created a sane and soothing environment worth all the blood, sweat, and tears. Your days will be clearer because you'll have eliminated those frustrations blocking your mission to get things done. You can move through the paces of your day more quickly, freeing up your time to do more of the things that you enjoy.

Stay on Track

Keep in mind that organization is not a one-shot deal. It's a lifestyle. You need to sustain it. The National Association of Professional Organizers says it's important to think not just in terms of *getting* organized but of *being* organized and *staying* organized. There are bound to be a few days of backsliding here and there, of course. Life gets busy. But there are two keys to avoiding a major relapse. First, it's necessary to employ a program of ongoing maintenance so that cleanup occurs while clutter is still in the minimal—not mountainous—stage. Second, it's important to take an inventory of your organization and storage strategies from time to time to ensure they're still meeting your current needs and lifestyle. Today's solutions may be tomorrow's problems, warns pro organizer Ariane Benefit.

Albert Einstein once wrote that there are three rules of work:

1. Out of clutter find simplicity.
2. From discord find harmony.
3. In the middle of difficulty lies opportunity.

Today, the kitchen; tomorrow, the world.

Keep It Up

Once you've completed the hard work, don't fall back into bad habits. Maintain the effort by always putting belongings back in their proper places. Shortcuts will only undermine your efforts. An investment of ten or fifteen minutes of daily touch-ups is all it takes to keep you clutter-free. When tidying up, ask yourself if you really like it, use it, or need it before putting a thing back in its place.

A home that looks good helps us feel good. In her book *House Thinking: A Room by Room Look at How We Live,* author Winifred Gallagher says no matter what its price tag or cachet, a house or apartment that fails to provide enough physical or psychological support can't be a true home.

If you need an extra incentive, remember that good organization reduces stress and saves time. When you know exactly where your things are, you put an end to hide-and-seek expeditions. And many people say the process is a cathartic one that will reward you with a sense of accomplishment, self-confidence, and empowerment.

Chapter 2

If You Can't Stand
the Heap: Kitchens

2

Ah, the fantasy of a dream kitchen—one of those tricked-out numbers packed with techno-wizardry appliances. You know those kinds—their instructional manuals have the girth of a Manhattan telephone book. (Oh, and where to file all those instructional manuals? More on that to come.) We seem to have an insatiable appetite for high-tech devices, even if they're designed for extremely niche purposes. Have no fear. Here are lots of space-saving solutions to the rescue.

Out in the Open

Is your kitchen the gathering spot for family meals, projects, and meetings? Do you have more gadgets than the local electronics store? Do you super-size your grocery shopping at a discount warehouse club? Chances are you've got kitchen creep, the pesky phenomenon that occurs when items start busting out of their designated spaces. The cabinet doors don't quite shut all the way; the freezer door needs an extra good push to cement the seal. And with kitchen creep inevitably comes the dreaded kitchen heap.

The kitchen is a very difficult place to keep clutter-free because it's filled with all the things you need for the smooth operation and functioning of your household. The more stuff you have, the more you need an adequate storage plan. The key is designing one that fits your lifestyle. What works for a single person will likely be inadequate for a couple and fail miserably for a family.

FACT

Every year, the U.S. Postal Service holds its annual Stamp Out Hunger food drive. In 2006, letter carriers collected 70.4 million pounds of non-perishable donations that were delivered to local food banks, pantries, and shelters for the needy. It couldn't be easier to give. Once you get a card notifying you of the date, all you have to do is leave your donations outside your front door.

It's a fact that people are making more demands of their kitchen nowadays and forcing homebuilders, manufacturers, and contractors to meet the challenge. Time was when looking for a home, folks asked how good the schools were, how big the garage was, how old the oil burner was—all important matters, of course. But they didn't give much consideration to the kitchen. It was almost an afterthought. They never asked themselves, "Can this kitchen work for me?" Here's the good news. It *can* work, no matter what its size. We can't all have mega-square-foot kitchens with home-magazine centerfold allure. And we really don't need countertops the size of hockey rinks—at least not if we can slim our possessions down to size.

The best approach is to start at square one by taking an inventory of everything you've got in there and, essentially, turn your kitchen inside out. Think spring cleaning with a vengeance. You can dedicate small chunks of time to the task by carving out an hour here for, say, the pantry and an hour there for the refrigerator. Better still, bite the bullet and tackle the entire room all at once. It's more time efficient in the long run. What's more, it's smarter to take advantage of your let's-do-it attitude when the adrenaline is running high. An average-size kitchen might take three to six hours or more with an assistant—but only if that assistant helps you stay on task. Whatever you decide, the strategy is the same. Clear each of these areas out:

- Pantry
- Cabinets
- Under-the-sink area
- Refrigerator
- Drawers
- Broom closet
- Open shelves

Then turn into a drill sergeant. Inspect each item and be merciless. Any chipped, broken, or outdated items go straight to the trash. If you find yourself hemming and hawing over something, throw it out. Ask yourself when you last used your strawberry huller, apple corer, or hard-boiled-egg slicer. If you can't remember, you've got your answer. And don't hang onto things because you just might need them one day. Our drawers and closets are stuffed to the gills with "maybe-one-day" gadgets. Anything that's outlived its usefulness in your home might just find a purpose in someone else's, like that old set of plastic tumblers from your kids' sippy-cup stages.

Don't hold onto food items you're not likely to use, either. Making a pumpkin pie may have seemed like such a good idea when those cans of pumpkin mix were on sale, but now they're oversized paperweights that are simply wasting valuable pantry space. Don't overstock, no matter how tempting the price, especially on perishables. A bag of lemons is no bargain if the whole lot of them goes bad before you've had a chance to use them.

Donate dishware, pots, and small appliances to thrift shops or local charities, and drop off unopened food items to soup kitchens and food pantries. As they say in philanthropic circles, give generously.

What's left in your cabinets? If you've done your job well, it shouldn't be much. Only the ingredients you'll actually be turning into meals before too long and the glassware, dishes, cleaning supplies, and appliances that are part of your day-to-day survival gear should remain. A no-frills approach can yield high returns.

Now it's time to restock the shelves and fill—not fill up—the drawers. Well, almost.

Taking Stock

Before you put things right back where they were, take a moment to consider if the old space is still the best place. In the kitchen, you can opt for an open storage plan, closed storage, or a combination of both. Open storage is common in older homes, especially those with farmhouse kitchens. Having exposed jars, bins, and dishes can make a dynamic design statement. The downside is that this style can look messy in a hurry if you don't maintain it. With closed-door storage, you don't have to give it much thought. Closed storage is also the answer for those who like clean, minimal lines.

As an overarching philosophy, you're better off storing items closest to their points of usage. Easy access translates into good kitchen organization. Cooking gear, for instance, makes the most sense if it's by the stove. Dishes and glasses should be proximate to the sink and dishwasher. And you'll save yourself a few extra steps if you stack microwaveable containers near the microwave oven. Group countertop items by use, too. Put all your breakfast appliances in one spot, for example, like the coffee maker and toaster.

ALERT!

Keep herbs in tightly closed containers and store them away from heat, moisture, and direct light. Most herbs should keep about a year. Then it's time to replenish your stock. Over time, herbs lose their potency and wind up adding very little flavor or even visual spark to your dishes.

Cluster cabinet items in the order you use them. The most commonly used ingredients, like spices, should go in the front and at eye level so there's no noodling around when you need to locate something quickly. Store the gourmet (and rarely used) items, like mulling spices and edible decorating confetti you only use for special entertaining or holiday baking, in the back or on top shelves. A modest investment in stepped-up tiered-rack shelving will keep items in your line of sight and top of mind. Reserve tall cabinet shelves for oversize boxes. Set aside lower shelves for heavier items. It's more secure.

When storing glassware, think like a bartender and line them up in columns by size instead of in rows. That way you're not reaching around the juice glasses in the front row to get to the water glasses behind them in the second row. Lighted shelves make it easier to spot what's in your cabinets, especially in those hard-to-see corners. Paul Radoy, manager of design services for Merillat, one of the nation's largest cabinet manufacturers, says if you install glass shelves, a low voltage ten- or twenty-watt light positioned behind the frame on top can illuminate the entire cabinet.

Fully Baked Ideas

Store baking items all together. When it's time to bake a cake, having a single cabinet shelf dedicated to flour, sugar, baking soda, baking powder, and the like will help you avoid the door-slamming cacophony that goes along with ingredient-hunting expeditions. Set aside another area for canned goods and organize them by contents: soups on one side, beans on the other. Store pasta and rice on another shelf. You get the idea. Consider transferring store-bought containers of cookies, bread crumbs, and cereals into stackable airtight containers or a vacuum food storage system like Seal-a-Meal pouches. You'll be amazed how much space you can free up by removing products from their original, bulky packaging.

Plastics

Is there a better kitchen organizer than plastic? But in moderation, please. A familiar slapstick scene played out in kitchens far and wide is opening a cabinet door and being awash in a shower of tubs and lids. A couple of pointers will keep the situation under control. First, buy plastic containers in a single shape. Go for square or round, but don't have both. Mismatched shapes will take up extra cabinet space and prevent you from stacking to the max. Mount a separate rack for lids inside the cabinet door and your shelves will look department-store neat. Are you still squirreling away the plastic tubs and containers from cottage cheese, margarine, and Chinese take-out? Do you really need to save every last one of them? You may think you're doing your part for the recycling effort, but they're pantry-hoggers that aren't even practical. How many times did you store, say, tea bags in an opaque margarine tub and then completely forget what was in there because you just couldn't see into it—and, of course, didn't bother to label it?

Before you head out to go food shopping, take an inventory of what you've already got on your shelves and in your refrigerator to make sure you don't already have some of the items on your list. More money is wasted by buying perishables unnecessarily.

Speaking of packaging, don't forget to check food expiration dates on a regular basis. It's not just that foods lose their flavor after their end dates. They can turn your stomach—or worse. So many people underestimate the health aspects, and particularly the health risks, of a poorly managed kitchen. Foodborne illnesses can result from eating food that's contaminated with bacteria, viruses, or parasites. Harmful bacteria are the most common cause. Contamination can occur at any point in the farm-to-fork food cycle, including preparation and storage.

Heart of the Kitchen

Keep in mind that the heart of every kitchen is the culinary work triangle, or the triangular alignment of the refrigerator, cook top, and sink for food preparation. Making sure the layout dovetails with your food prep and storage areas makes for a smooth-operating kitchen and a happy chef. It also saves you time in cleanup. And let's face it: Who wouldn't want to spend less time wrapping up the leftovers for another day?

Storage solutions work best when they add order to the workspace and pretty up the site. In other words, aim for form *and* functionality. One way to blend possessions into the overall design theme of a kitchen is to make productive use of otherwise wasted space. The areas under your shelves and cabinets are prime real estate.

Got decorative tea cups and coffee mugs? Screw in some hooks and show them off. Installing small under-counter appliances can free up counter space. There are more electronic options than ever before. Drop-down television sets, for instance, that flip back up and disappear when not in use are growing in popularity. Miele makes a sophisticated built-in coffee-making system that whips up espressos, cappuccinos, and lattes in no time. Of course, you'll have to think about whether you really need all those gizmos in the first place.

FACT

Protect your fine, hard-to-replace china from chips and scratches. Buy some felt pads and nestle them in between plates and bowls to act as cushions when you're stacking. Old cloth napkins and even inexpensive coffee filters will do the job, too. And never clean delicate china with harsh abrasives or steel wool pads. The harm you do may be irreparable.

Bins, tins, and canisters on top of the refrigerator make stylish stow-aways for unwieldy itemettes like twist-ties and chip clips that usually clutter up junk drawers. Some soups and sauces comes in jars too pretty to toss in the recycling container. Rinse off the labels and reuse them. Clear jars combine personality with peek-a-boo practicality.

Look up! Don't see anything? Well, there's an opportunity. Overhead pot racks suspended from the ceiling are a creative use of air space. Make sure the rack is securely bolted in place and up to the task of handling a heavy weight load. Before going this route, however, consider the condition of your cookware. You want your display to enhance your kitchen aesthetic, which means your collection needs to be in spit-shine shape. Pots with scorched bottoms, dull copper finishes, or chipped surfaces are better left in cabinets.

Hanging pot racks run the gamut of styles, from ornate ironwork to thin minimalist wooden strips, to match just about any décor. Some have built-in shelves for lids or additional display storage. Creative homeowners have been known to turn some of these racks into conversation pieces. One homeowner converted a cast-iron register grill into a pot rack with stunning results. Another installed an antique wooden ladder and hung pots off the rungs.

Wine refrigerators are perfect for sommelier wannabes, but if you imbibe only now and again and can't justify the investment, here are a few tips for storing your bottles. Keep wine in a dark place, free of vibrations (read: not in your exercise room or woodworking shop). Make sure the room is at a relatively stable humidity level and at a consistent temperature. About 55°F is ideal.

Another overhead option is a suspended stemware rack. What an elegant way this is to display wine, champagne, and stemmed cordial glasses that are too attractive to hide behind closed doors. You can also reclaim air space by installing wire baskets from the ceiling. They can hold everything from fruits and vegetables to coupons. But here's a caveat: Don't overdo it. Too many ceiling danglers can quickly make a kitchen feel cluttered and closed in, distracting from its streamlined appeal.

When your goal is efficiency, every item in the house needs to be looked at with a discerning eye. Do you really need this? Would you really miss that if it were gone? Cast that discriminating eye on your kitchen table. How often do you really use it? Is it just a place to gulp down a quick bowl of cereal in the morning? It might seem sacrilege to part ways with a kitchen stalwart, but a multipurpose island could be the smarter solution. Imagine replacing an ordinary tabletop with a unit featuring drawers, shelves, and even a few cabinets or a wine rack. Throw in some barstools, and you've got a clever place to eat, prep, and store.

Confiscate a corner of floor space for a magazine rack to hold cooking and home design periodicals as well as coupons and Sunday sales circulars. Don't think of it as a stagnant pile, though. Make sure you go through it regularly and purge. Paper, in all its many forms, is the biggest clutter perpetrator of all.

A system of modular bookcases can hold your cookbooks, display dishes, and collectibles. The best part is that you can tailor it according to your needs by adjusting shelves, adding new ones, or adding inserts for such things as wine bottles.

Virtually every kitchen is equipped with those tippy-top cabinets out of easy reach—that is, unless you're the forward of the New York Knicks. Those shelves are the Siberia of the cabinetry world, the place where lesser items are exiled. Well, not so fast. Here are a couple of options to make that space more user-friendly. If you've got a tall ledge in a walk-in pantry, a sliding library ladder can make those oh-so-high shelves a problem of the past. Not so steady on your feet? Try a telescoping rod with a graspable handle. But don't chance it with anything too fragile or too heavy. A box of cereal, yes. A Tiffany crystal wine glass? Uh-uh. Use a good old step stool, instead.

FACT

Hoosier cabinets were manufactured in the early twentieth century and featured everything from built-in flour sifters and breadboxes to chopping blocks and cookbook holders. In 1920, a study commissioned under U.S. Secretary of Commerce Herbert Hoover on the efficiency of the American kitchen declared that the American housewife could save 1,592 steps of the 2,113 she took in her kitchen every day by utilizing a Hoosier cabinet.

If you've got a nice sliver of space, off-the-shelf rolling pantry shelves are available, and the nice part is that you don't need to renovate, reconfigure, or even call in the carpenter to build them. These "thin-man" pantry caddies fit into the narrowest of spaces—even that slice of space between the refrigerator and cabinets. They roll in and out easily on a set of casters and come with a set of six fixed shelves.

Cold Storage

If at some point you upgrade your kitchen, consider holding onto the old refrigerator and storing it in the basement or even the garage. It'll come in handy when you need the extra fridge space for entertaining or stocking up on sale items.

Stackable fridge trays can double your storage room by utilizing the full vertical space between shelves.

When storing leftovers in the freezer, label the items and jot down the date. Even frozen foods have a limited shelf life. The taste of freezer burn won't win you any culinary compliments, and, more important, languishing leftovers might be hazardous to your health.

ALERT!

> Putting food in the freezer preserves it, but not forever. Frozen foods have a finite shelf life. Be on the safe side and label anything that's not on the menu in the upcoming week. Fresh fruits and veggies can last for up to a year in the freezer. Limit uncooked meats to six to twelve months. Figure on about three months for fish.

In many homes, refrigerators wind up becoming giant, messy canvases for magnet collages. Do your magnets multiply like rabbits? It might be handy to have the phone number of your favorite pizza delivery service, but you can put the refrigerator's magnetic properties to better use. Consolidate it all with a Fridgefile (*www.fridgefile.com*), a vertical filing and dry-erase message center that can hold menus, homework, or coupons. Small magnetic shelves are a good idea for spices, paper towels, or hooks for utensils and potholders. But don't go overboard. Refrigerators dominate a kitchen and can get cluttered in no time.

When you come home from the store, try to keep plastic grocery bags out of landfills as long as possible. According to the Green Guide, a newsletter covering health and environmental issues, Americans throw away 100 billion plastic grocery sacks a year. Use them to line small trash baskets in your home. If you can't use them, bring them back to the supermarket. Many grocery chains have plastic bag recycling bins right by the checkout counter. You can also do as many Europeans do and bring your own reusable bags to the store. It's an Earth-friendly thing to do.

The Kitchen Sink and Everything under It

Open up your under-sink cabinets and you'll probably find some extra room down there. Take advantage of the space by investing in adjustable-height shelving that slides out along rails and is specially designed to fit around awkward drain pipes.

QUESTION?

How do I dispose of household cleaning products?
Some of the household products stored under your sink may be toxic and fall under the classification of hazardous waste. Don't pour them down the drain or throw them in the trash. Contact the appropriate environmental agency for your area or call your town hall to find out how to dispose of chemical cleansers properly and safely.

In most homes, the cabinet under the kitchen sink is brimming with household cleaners. It's hard to resist sampling a new product when the manufacturer promises its newest glass cleaner, stainless steel polisher, lemon oil, and detergent will make your life easier. So what do we do? We fill up buckets with soaps of every conceivable kind for every different surface. But are they all necessary? Imagine how much space you could free up if just a handful of cleansers served multiple functions. There are a few multitasking products on the market. A product called Holy Cow, for instance, can clean your walls, grout, and granite, and even your jewelry and shoe leather.

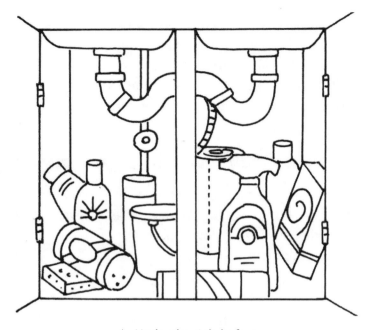

▲ Under the sink, before.

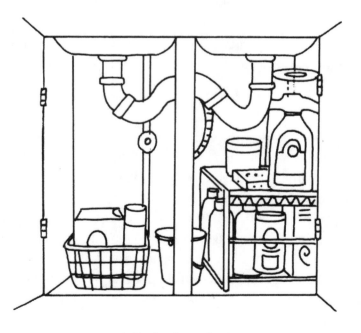

▲ Under the sink, after.

Cabinet Space

Inquiring minds want to know: Who exactly was Susan? And why was she so lazy? Theories abound, but the important thing is that her laziness led to an invention that makes our lives easier. The turntable action of the lazy Susan offers up 360-degree access to stored items with size-specific models on the market to match just about any space requirement. Give it a spin, and items come to you. Hard-to-reach items? Problem solved. Add a few wedge-shaped plastic containers and you'll have the perfect complement of optimal storage and convenience.

◀ A lazy Susan

And don't forget about the cabinet door itself. Make it do double duty. Even a small door can play host to your plastic wrap, tin foil, and baggie boxes with an easy-to-install plastic or metal shelf bracket. Store food products elsewhere, though. Food and household chemicals such as bleach and cleansers don't mix.

ALERT!

Experts recommend having a three-day supply of food and water on hand in case of an emergency. Put aside a gallon of water per person per day, a stash of nutrition bars, high-protein canned shakes, and dried fruit. Add to your kit fresh batteries, a flashlight, a solar or crank-operated AM-FM radio, duct tape, a compact multitool unit, a first-aid kit, and unscented bleach.

Making a (Back) Splash

A wire wall grid or attractive peg board (No, not your father's workshop peg board) can transform a bare stretch of wall into a kitchen tool center. A hanging organizer system can do a good job of helping you keep supplies at hand—and do it handsomely at that. It's strong enough to support spices or those eye-catching bottles of oil and vinegar. Sleek, stainless steel versions are available to flatter the most modern of kitchens. Or consider a rail system that allows you to add on such accessories as a cookbook rack and utensil basket. Use wall hooks or magnetic hooks for aprons and towels and potholders. They're old standbys, sure, but they never go out of style, because they work.

Cooks and Crannies

Everyone's got one: a junk drawer, that is. Its very name almost encourages the abuse of space. Call it a junk drawer, and that's what's going to go in it until it becomes a pit of bottomless excess. How many corncob holders and apple corers do you have jammed in there, under warranties of appliances you no longer own? It's also the collection depot for all the little things that don't have a defined home, like batteries, playing cards, and take-out menus. Using this space as a catchall will catch nothing of value in the long run.

Dump out the contents and start anew. Find the most appropriate storage place for each item. Send playing cards packing for the den, for example. Then give the drawer a purpose. Dedicate it to a single function such as serving utensils, vitamins, spices, garnishing, or decorating tools. Inserting an organization tray or custom-fit divider strips can help subcategorize the drawer even further and keep items from jamming up. If there's extra room, resist the urge to fill the drawer to the brim. And remember to go back and evaluate the contents from time to time.

Chances are you can ditch all those appliance manuals that clutter up your drawers. Virtually all manufacturers have toll-free customer service numbers and representatives on call to answer any questions or troubleshoot problems during business hours. In addition, you'll usually find around-the-clock help online at manufacturers' Web sites.

Utensil drawers are traditionally one of the most problematic areas of the kitchen. Most people don't just have a single set of utensils. They have them in duplicate and even triplicate. Here's an idea: donate your extras to a high school grad about to set off for college.

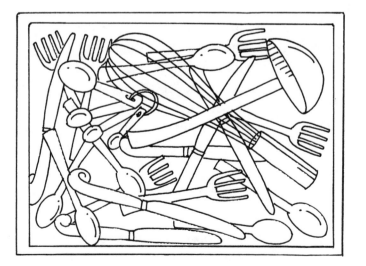

▲ A silverware drawer, before.

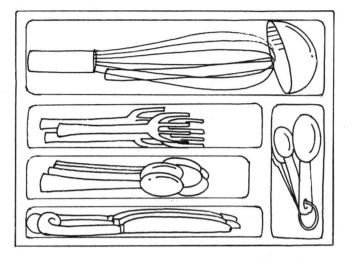

▲ A silverware drawer, after.

Get Creative

Joe, a self-described junk enthusiast and avid antiques collector, moved into an actual antique: a home whose foundation dates back to the 1850s, when it was originally a Pony Express stop. Needless to say, the house has a few quirks—namely, no drawers in the kitchen. One solution Joe came up with was to keep his flatware in attractive FireKing glass containers. They add colorful accents to the kitchen and are faithful to the vintage aesthetic of the home. Another plus is that when Joe hosts a dinner party, he just grabs the flatware jar and brings it to the table for easy place setting.

Let yourself be unconventional. One owner of a space-deprived villa in Florida never uses her dishwasher, at least not for its intended purpose. Instead of letting all those juicy cubic feet go to waste, she uses it to store her clean kitchen utensils.

Use That Space

Check around your kitchen for opportunities to convert idle space into workable storage. What's below your lower cabinets, near the kick-toe area? Nothing? Good. Retrofitting that gap might be all you need to store those no-good-place-for-it items like recyclable newspapers and pet bowls.

Full-extension pullouts in cabinet drawers make pots, pans and serving dishes easier to get to and offer up the ability to stack items more efficiently—and higher. Pullouts make reaching for items easier on your back, too.

You'll make the most out of limited space by keeping like items together. Store dishes with dishes, pots with pots, and serving trays with serving trays. Stack saucepans by size. The difference between neatly nestled and clumsy clutter are the lids, so install a separate rack for them. Pick up pullouts with wire shelf sides to prevent smaller items from falling out and causing drawer jams.

Swing-out shelves from a corner cabinet will help you exploit every spare inch. Even seemingly little add-ons—like a tilt-out sink tray for your sponges and steel wool pads—can make a marked improvement. Drawer dividers, easily found at home goods stores, keep flatware in ship-shape. Steal a wedge of space in a base cabinet and use vertical dividers to organize baking sheets, muffin pans, trays, oversize serving platters, and cutting boards in size order. The setup keeps items tidy and prevents dishes from getting chipped. Speaking of cutting boards: You can look for one that has a drawer built right in to store knives, or you might choose to have a custom version built that's set right into a cabinet drawer.

FACT

Some bulky kitchen utensils are available in easy-to-store form. You can find flexible muffin pans, molds, and colanders made of silicone that flatten for easy storage and then spring back into shape.

In his own home, Merillat's Paul Radoy built a pantry cabinet with slide-out shelves and built-in power strips expressly to hold small appliances. When he needs to whip something up in the blender or pop some bread in the toaster, he just slides out the shelf and uses the appliances right where they are. It's less cumbersome, more utilitarian, and very time efficient. Paul stores his most-used appliances like the coffee maker and juicer on the most accessible middle shelf. Less used items, like the popcorn maker and blender, go on higher and lower shelves.

Baker's Dozen

Housewarming gifts. Birthday gifts. Anniversary gifts. We love to exchange presents, and the result is an abundance of riches—or is that dishes? Count the coffee mugs in your cabinet. You've probably got more than the neighborhood coffee shop. Be vigilant and make a promise to yourself to evaluate what items are actually being used. You may use what you have but may not need as many you have. As Thoreau wrote, "Simplify, simplify." Duplicates should be inventoried on a regular basis and then given away or donated. If you don't know anyone who could use your spares, find a charitable organization that accepts donations of glassware, dishes, and small appliances. Not all do.

And don't hold onto the plastic cutlery or chopsticks that come with your usual Friday-night Chinese delivery. Yes, you may think that stuff will come in handy at some point, but that point never comes.

ALERT!

Rethink all your one-trick-pony items, especially bulky, oversize ones like salad spinners and waffle irons. It's human nature to respond to the latest and greatest come-ons. It takes willpower to resist. If you have a hard time, turn off the infomercials, skip over shopping channels, and avoid sale days at the mall.

Americans spend billions of dollars a year renovating their kitchens, turning them into status symbol jewels of the home. And then, poof! The sleek and streamlined super-kitchen façade is lost under a poor storage system. Clutter influences not only the kitchen but the adjoining rooms as well. With open floor plans featured in so many homes these days, a cluttered kitchen can affect an entire suite of rooms. Then look out. Clutter is contagious.

Need a couple more entries to add to your "Reasons to Get Organized" list? When you put things in order, you can save money. How many times have you come home from the supermarket only to discover you already bought three of those things (whatever they are) the last time they were on sale? Better still, by getting rid of stuff, you cut down on housework. It's true—up to 40 percent, by one study.

The best habit you can adopt when organizing your kitchen is to give yourself regularly scheduled reality checks. What do you use? What do you need? Is an item worth the counter space or cabinet space it demands? Keep in mind that the best clutter-buster is the ability to Just Say No.

Chapter 3

Bed, Belongings, and Beyond: Bedrooms

Bedrooms are the marriage of practicality and sanctuary. They've become the go-to place to escape the stresses of everyday life. That holds true for kids, 'tweens, teens, and adults. The bedroom is the nap center, the reading room, the music salon, and, for many, the TV room. But where does the stuff for all those activities go? How do we squeeze it all in one place? We want it all, but having it all creates clutter zones in our sweet retreats. Wake up from the nightmare with easy-to-implement ideas.

Out of Sight

Ah, pity Karen, a harried homeowner in Myrtle Beach, South Carolina, who wishes her bedroom could be an oasis of tranquility. You've heard of junk drawers? Hers is a junk room. The thing is that she's honest enough to admit it's the very definition of disorganization. A jumble of clothing is the main offender—and not just her clothes and her husband's. Their teenage daughter's jeans and T-shirts have managed to migrate into the master bedroom, too. And that's not all. The room is filled with unwanted Christmas gifts that still need to be returned, plus fabric scraps, wrapping paper, party decorations, even bubble wrap. It has all the makings of a craft room—but in the wrong room. Karen says with an exasperated sigh, with all that clutter, it's not easy to dust or vacuum. Her husband, Paul, is not much better. He empties his pockets out every evening, piling receipts, business cards, gum wrappers, and who knows what else on the dresser rather than in the trash. Paul is her buddy in grime. Every weekend, Karen promises herself she'll tackle the mess, but then she gets so overwhelmed by not knowing where to start that she doesn't start at all. Sound familiar?

Reclaim Your Sanctuary

It's easy enough to shut the door on an untidy den or ignore the five-cart pile-ups in the basement, but it's impossible to dismiss the room you spend so many waking hours in, not to mention all your sleeping hours. If you're routinely stepping over clothes to get from one side of the room to the other or peeling evidence of the day's activities off your bed before tucking in for the night, it's time to stop the madness. Close your eyes and take a minute to imagine how you would feel about your bedroom if every article of clothing was in its rightful place, every ragtag trinket had a home, and every loose piece of paper was neatly tucked away in a folder where it belonged. Even if your bedroom took months or years to get into the dire shape it's in, it only takes a heavy-duty roll-up-your-sleeves session or two to convert bedlam back to bedroom.

How do you *use* your bedroom? Is it strictly for sleeping, readying for work, and personal time? Is it the place you while away the hours watching TV? Does it stand in as spillover for the kids' playroom? Masters of multi-tasking find it hard to set limits and form boundaries. If the latter describes your room, no doubt your décor reflects that, too. Look around. Could your interior design style be described as "Disney vacation meets office supply store"? "Romantic chic meets Main Street Dry Cleaners?" And if the answer is yes, is that really the aesthetic you want to have in your haven?

ESSENTIAL

> According to Ariane Benefit, professional organizer and president of OrganizingforHealth.com, one key to clearing out clutter is to devise storage solutions that are every bit as easy to use as no solutions. In other words, you can remedy the problem by making it just as convenient to put your clothes away as it is to throw them on the floor.

The most important reason to make your bedroom a refuge is to give you a place to unwind, meditate, pray, sleep, and relax—in other words, to make it the place you shake off the anxieties and pesky irritations of the day. If your bedroom is a jumble of disorder, it stands to reason your equilibrium will be undermined. You roll over in bed, and piles of unpaid bills are staring you in the face shouting Pay Me! Pay Me! Overdue work evaluations on the dresser are joining in the deal-with-me chorus. Feel-good books and inspirational reading is fine. Business manuals? There are more appropriate places for them. Is it any wonder why 35 million Americans complain of chronic insomnia? Don't let the world come knocking at your bedroom door. If you're surrounded by clutter, it just follows that negative energy is going to interfere with relaxation.

To Your Health

One thing all health professionals agree on is the importance of a good night's sleep. Even exercise machines like treadmills and stationary bicycles can attract the wrong kind of energy that can sabotage rest.

Everything in the bedroom should be geared to support sleep. Get rid of the phone, or at least turn the ringer off at night. If you're the kind of person who stays up nights running the same thoughts through your brain over and over again—What am I going to wear to work tomorrow? What time is that staff meeting?—prepare the night before. Make a to-do list, and lay out your clothes. Do whatever it takes to get the worries off your mind so you can unwind. A serene, relaxing bedroom setting helps you end the day with ZZZZZs instead of GRRRRRs.

According to organizer Ariane Benefit, bedroom clutter can impact your health in other ways, too. For one thing, if surfaces are covered, chances are any cleaning effort is going to be cursory at best. Many people have symptoms of chronic sinus conditions that can be traced to the fact they're spending seven, eight, nine, or more hours sleeping in a dust-filled environment. Dust bunnies, balls of cat hair—some rooms are a virtual menagerie of irritants.

QUESTION?

What is feng shui?
Feng shui is the ancient Chinese practice of living harmoniously with the natural elements and forces of the Earth. Practitioners believe that orienting and arranging objects in certain ways can enhance the positive energy flow of a given space, promote health and prosperity, and result in a clutter-free environment.

Segregate, Donate, Eliminate

The plan to master your master bedroom is easy. If you start by tackling stuff on surfaces—floors, dresser tops, night stands—you'll see immediate improvement that will encourage you to keep moving forward.

To conquer the clutter, start by lining up four good-size boxes. Label them like this: KEEP, DONATE, TRASH, and MOVE.

Start in one corner and work your way around the room. Do a quick once-over and decide what box each item will go into. The "move" carton is for items that have wandered—things like shopping bags, overcoats, business cards, and toys—and don't belong in the bedroom. Place them in the box during the sorting process and let the box stay there until the room is done. If you stop to move things to other locations as you go along, you'll only get distracted from the real task at hand—getting the bedroom into shape.

Want to a turn dresser-drawer purge into a party? Have a used clothing swap. Invite friends and family members over and ask them to BYOB—bring your own bag—filled with clothes and accessories they no longer wear. One person's castoffs might be another person's trendy treasures.

Be aggressive, and let your donation and trash heaps trump the keepers. The items you hold on to should be the ones you genuinely use, the items that make you feel good about yourself and enhance your environment. Keep these guidelines in mind as you move along.

In the keep box, place only the following:

- Clothing you've worn sometime in the last year and only garments in good condition. No tears, stains, or button-missing sweaters you'll never get to repairing, please.
- Collectibles that mean something special to you. Don't hold on to things out of obligation or guilt. Instead of making you feel good, bedrooms decorated in sentiment can contribute to unrest.
- Books and magazines you actually read in the bedroom. Avoid letting periodicals pile up or using shelves for reference or business materials.

In the donate box, place only the following:

- Clothes that are in truly wearable condition
- Electronics that are in good working order
- Objects (like vases, cups, and plates) that are free of chips, cracks, and blemishes

In the trash box, place only the following:

- Broken and tattered costume jewelry
- Vanity clutterers like years-old colognes, perfumes, lotions, and powders

- "Roving" items like expired medications, no-longer-used hair care products, and broken toys

And don't let furniture off the hook. Decide whether you really need that Parsons chair or free-standing jewelry armoire. Excess furniture has a way of making us feel closed in.

When it comes to the donation and trash piles, don't look back. Bag up the items and clear them out. It's a good idea to put the bags slated for donation in your car immediately so you're not tempted to second-guess your decisions. The next time you get behind the wheel, drop them off at a donation bin or charity. And it doesn't hurt to keep a spare garbage bag or box dedicated squarely for donations always at the ready. The fewer excuses you have to expand your bedroom inventory, the better.

Even if you've done a bang-up elimination job, you'll probably still be surprised by how much is left. The million-dollar question is this: Do the remaining items relate to activities that will take place in the bedroom and enhance the ambiance? Simply put, does it pass the sanctuary test? If so, then you're off to a good start.

Habit Forming

As you make headway through the clutter, try to figure out what behavior led you to this point. Ask yourself, "Why are these papers here instead of in the office?" and "Why aren't these clothes in the closet or laundry basket where they belong?" Bad habits are tough to break, but realize you can just as easily get yourself into good habits, too. Start by focusing on the productive outcomes that are the consequences of positive behavior. What does all that mean? Put another way, it means concentrate on the actions that reap rewards.

Tackling the Clothes Pile

When it comes to bedroom disorganization, one of the most prevalent self-sabotaging practices is changing clothes and leaving the old ones on the floor, on the bed, or draped over the footboard. Are you nodding your head in agreement? As soon as you throw that shirt down, that little mound is almost guaranteed to grow. There's something about seeing that first item that encourages us to keep piling on, like adding to the ante of a poker game. Do the math. You come home from work and change into casual attire. That's two outfits a day, seven days a week. Figure in the "contributions" of your spouse or significant other, and it's no wonder you're knee-deep in a quagmire of cotton and wool.

FACT

The organization Vietnam Veterans of America (*www.vva.org*; 800-775-8387) will pick up items right from your front door. The group accepts clothing, small appliances, bric-a-brac, small furniture, televisions, lamps, bedding, and more as long as it's in good, workable condition.

Paint a giant circle-and-slash across the whole messy heap. It takes hardly a moment's more time to drop your clothes in the laundry basket, hang them in the closet, or put them back in the drawers where they belong. Any garments that need special attention, such as mending or ironing immediately, should go to a designated spot. Just remind yourself that the fraction of time it takes to hang things up will prevent a huge buildup at the end of the week, when you'd rather be doing something else a lot more fun than straightening up.

A Call to Order

Consumer mistake numero uno: Buying storage containers first and figuring out how to use them after the fact. If you think you can't get started toward your organizational goals without them, you're putting the cart before the horse. Too many people buy bins, boxes, and stowaways thinking they'll surely be able to use them somehow, some way. As the Gershwin brothers might have put it, "It ain't necessarily so." Purchasing unnecessary storage units is not only a waste of money; ironically, it adds to the clutter. Before you run out to a department store or specialty shop with credit card in hand, evaluate what your bedroom really needs to get organized.

Quick Drawers

Dresser drawers serve their purpose best when designated for specific roles. Store lingerie, socks, and underwear in one drawer; sweaters in another; sleepwear in a third; and workout clothes in a fourth. You get the idea. Without a system of organization, items just get thrown around without rhyme or reason. In short order, they get out of order. Sweaters, jeans, knitwear, and other items not prone to wrinkles are well suited to drawers. Hang garments made of rayon, linen, and cotton in closets, as well as pleated and creased items that need to keep their shapes.

Sweeten up your drawers and closets. Scented drawer liners are a nice touch. For a stronger scent, throw in those perfumed sample cards that come in department store catalogues and magazines. For something a bit subtler, toss in a small bar of fragrant soap or a sachet of fresh lavender.

To squeeze more into your drawers, roll up garments instead of stacking them. It's easier to see what you've got that way, too.

One more way you can help yourself keep things in check is also arguably the best way. If you buy something new, throw something out. Once you pare your wares down to size, this one-in, one-out philosophy ensures your possessions never get out of balance.

Check under the Bed

Think about drawers on the floor. If you've got a nice chunk of space down under the bed, exploit it. If you don't have the space, inexpensive bed-lifters are available that snap onto the legs of your bed to give you a few more inches of height. Made-to-fit roll-out drawers and plastic containers come in handy. Just make sure the plastic ones are see-through so you know what's in it without wasting time playing guessing games. Those heavy-duty plastic zip bags that blankets come in can be repurposed for storage, too. Consider using under-bed areas for seasonal items. Make sure whatever storage option you choose is airtight to keep out dust and pests. It could be weeks or months before you need to use those items again. Pass on storing things you use every day under there. It's just not practical. You don't want to have to get down on your hands and knees to search for commonly used items.

Vanity Fair

Don't forget to consider what's on top of your dresser. Wrist watches, earrings, and on-again, off-again rings? Tidy up the tabletop with a handsome jewelry box, just big enough to store your everyday gems. For men, a compartmented valet will hold the day's loose pocket change, keys, and watch. Dedicated watch valets can cradle multiple watches, protect them from scratches, and keep them dust free.

Instead of putting loose change on your dresser at the end of each day, toss your coins into a jar and watch your money grow. Automatic coin-rolling machines like the ones offered by Coinstar (*www.coinstar.com*) will tally up your totals for a small percentage fee. You can pocket the cash, donate it automatically to charity or, at certain locations, use the proceeds to purchase a no-fee gift card. Coinstar machines are available at retail outlets throughout the country.

Sock Therapy

Ah, the bane of our existence—the mighty sock. Or, more typically, the missing sock. Before you have to issue an all-points-bulletin, pick up plastic or cardboard organizer inserts to keep the sock drawer orderly and matches easy to find. Sock organizers also give drawers a custom-designed look at a bargain price. Sort socks by color. Is there anything more frustrating than trying to figure out in the dim light of morning if a pair is black, charcoal, or dark navy? Drawer organizer inserts, now commonly available, come in a variety of sizes, not just for socks but also for underwear, gloves, and lingerie. For pantyhose, some women swear by all-purpose zip-close baggies as an effortless and inexpensive way to arrange hose by color and protect them from snags.

▲ The sock drawer, before.

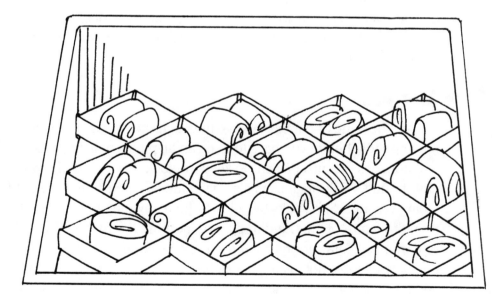

▲ The sock drawer, after.

Taking a Stand

When it comes to the furniture in your bedroom, make sure you're getting the biggest bang for your buck. Nightstands will serve you better if they offer more than just surface tops for a lamp and alarm clock. Plan it right, and you'll be amazed at the difference even a single drawer or cabinet can add to your organizational efforts. At the same time, be sure that you relegate only bedroom-related items here. Sleeping mask, yes. Reading glasses, sure. Hot glue gun, absolutely not. For stowing bigger, bulkier items, opt for an inexpensive round tri-legged table, throw a floor-length tablecloth over it or a skirt around the perimeter, and you've got instant storage under wraps. If floor space is at a premium, a wall shelf mounted at tabletop height could serve the purpose.

Bed Storage

Then there's the bed itself. How about a model that lets you store things *in* it, instead of all *over* it? It's a great solution, particularly when a room is too small for a nightstand. A number of retailers sell nifty storage headboards in which upholstered pillow-top doors lift up to stash essentials. Other headboard models can give you a few choice shelves or cubby holes for displaying your most precious keepsakes and enhancing your bedroom's aesthetic. Some headboards are even available as stand-alone units. The nice thing about that is you can simply move the ready-made shelf system into position at the head of the bed. No nails or hammer necessary.

ALERT!

To ensure you get a good night's sleep, the National Sleep Foundation suggests you maintain a regular bedtime and wake-up schedule. Stick to it even on the weekends. To create a sleep-conducive environment, make sure your bedroom is dark, quiet, and cool. And avoid caffeine, alcohol, and nicotine too close to bedtime.

Hot Pockets

Nighttime readers aren't the only ones who love having books at their fingertips. Everyone from list-makers to poets can appreciate bedside pockets that tuck under the mattress and hang flat against the bed to create reachable storage. The saddle provides convenient pocket space for books, tissues, lotions, magazines, eyeglasses, and water bottles—in other words, all the usual stuff that ordinarily clutters up the night tables.

One gorgeous, albeit pricy, solution for the space-deprived is pop-up television technology. Furniture makers are integrating ultra-thin LCD and plasma monitors right into footboards. Even dressers are being custom-designed to conceal TVs. When you're ready to watch your favorite show, simply push a button on your remote control. The set pops up and even swivels so you can see the screen from any angle in the room. When it's lights-out time, a motorized system lowers the unit back down and out of sight.

Incredible Convertibles

Never underestimate the power of the imagination to drum up clever storage options. Some of the best-dressed rooms are the result of a serendipitous fusion of creativity with utility. Often all it takes is looking beyond the original intended use of a given piece of furniture. Take, for instance, the case of a midcentury, intricately carved, walnut linen closet. It was sold at an auction house in Racine, Wisconsin, for just over $100. The successful bidder used the piece as it was originally intended and then, over the years and through a number of cross-country moves, he converted it into several different types of storage holders as his household situations demanded. It may have started out as a linen closet, but it's had more disguises than a Halloween trick-or-treater. The linen closet was transformed into a stereo cabinet, file cabinet and, most recently, an extra sweater armoire.

Stand-Alone Storage

Armoires are probably the most adaptable piece of furniture you can own. These days they're often sold as entertainment units, but you can easily retrofit them for added closet space.

Vintage leather suitcases can also double as funky, retro-style storage for bulky handbags, hats, gloves, or can't-part-with mementos that don't need to be displayed. They're practical, stylish and, best of all, stackable. Hat boxes, new or antique, do the trick, too.

Armoires are great for keeping items behind closed doors when not in use. Today's armoires are more versatile than ever. You can buy models that open up to reveal baby layettes, wine closets, shoe racks, desk space, and even exercise equipment.

Storage on the House

Along with old furniture and accessories that can be repurposed for new uses at no cost, free storage solutions abound. There are the heavy-duty plastic bags from blankets, mentioned earlier, that are too good not to reuse. Window curtains and bed sheets often come in similar salvageable packaging. Boxes from stationery and greeting cards can be inserted into drawers to hold scarves and other small items. Even the tops of jewelry boxes can come in handy. Use them to create a patchwork of shallow containers to hold rings, earrings, pins, and bracelets instead of having your bling tossed all together in a single jewelry-box drawer.

Have a Seat

In the good old days, there was a chest for every use: silver chests, blanket chests, map chests, and, of course, hope chests for a young lady's trousseau. Today's array of storage chests is more of the fill-in-the-blank variety. You get to decide what goes in your chest and how it's used. Just like the heirloom styles of yesterday, however, chests continue to make a design statement. Velvet, tiger stripes, or postmodern sleek—there's a pattern, style, and size of chest to fit every room. In the bedroom, they make a practical storage spot for bed linens, pillows, and extra blankets. Storage benches often fit comfortably at the foot of a bed.

Place a wooden storage chest by a window, throw a couple of cushions or pillows on it, and you've got the makings of a lovely window seat. A word of caution: Tempting as a flat, unclaimed surface may be, avoid using the bench as a temporary staging area to pile up stuff. Whatever your best intentions, history proves that such "temporary" uses rarely are.

FACT

Hope chests were traditionally used by young women to fill with clothing, linens, and household items in anticipation of marriage. Some chests were hand painted or intricately carved, making them works of art in their own right and highly prized as family heirlooms.

If you're still leaving the back of your bedroom door bare, you're losing out on a big chunk of some red-hot property. Knobs, pegs and hooks are easy answers for bathrobes, hats or handbags. Dress it up by utilizing antique doorknobs and crystal drawer pulls instead of ordinary, ho-hum hooks.

Kidding Around

Basic bedroom clutter-busting strategies also apply to children's and teens' rooms—to a point. Today's youngsters have so much more than kids of even a generation before them. Once, the biggest storage challenge might have been keeping stuffed animals in check. Now kids' rooms need separate zones carved out just for computers and high-tech digital entertainment.

To have any hope of keeping order, on a regular basis you should evaluate which toys, clothes, and games your kids have outgrown. Try not to get too emotionally attached. Quite often, the kids are ready to let go while mom and dad are guilty of holding on tight to items for sentimental reasons. Once a child is old enough to put things away for himself, allow him to be part of the vetting process. Otherwise, reorganize younger children's rooms when they're not around to avoid a thankless tug-of-war session. If you're lucky enough to have the space for a separate playroom, you should be able to keep the bedroom relatively clutter-free. Allow the playroom to be the activity center for toys, schoolwork, and craft projects while letting the bedroom remain a place of sanctuary. For more on playroom organization, refer to Chapter 8.

To cut down on the sheer quantity of toys, games, and gadgets in the bedroom, move out anything your child isn't old enough to play with to a long-term storage area in your home, like the basement. You should also limit the number of toys that are in the room at any given time. When a new toy comes into the house, an old toy should go to make room for it. Replace, don't augment. Make sure storage containers are age-appropriate and match your child's level of dexterity. Open baskets are easy for little ones to comprehend and access. Forget the lids. They just contribute to the clutter. Use clear plastic bins and shoeboxes for art, crafts, and science projects. If your child can see what's in it, she'll use it. Also, banish any containers or bins from the bedroom that are less than 100 percent sturdy.

By exposing your children to strict anticlutter practices, you not only have less clutter today, you also set them up for a better shot of developing organizational habits that will carry them through to adulthood.

Be My Guest

Unless you're running an inn or have a family the size of the Waltons, you probably have a "hyphenated" guest room, meaning it's got a shared purpose. Perhaps it's also your home office or yoga studio. If guests are few and far between, think about opening up floor space with a pull-down wall bed or a futon instead of a full-size bed. And don't let the dresser drawers in the room go to waste. Sure, you should keep some space free and clear for the occasional overnighter, but don't feel bad about using the rest for your own necessities. Again, give this space a specific purpose. It might be the perfect place to dedicate to, say, your gym wear. If you start mixing and matching personal gear in two different rooms, in no time you'll have the makings of a sad state of the union.

The Great Escape

Remember, the hardest part of straightening out your bedroom is making the commitment to do so. Be inspired by the "after" picture in your head of a beautiful, streamlined room by taking charge of your stuff. Bedroom organization is all about balance and maintenance—not extremes. No one wants a bedroom that resembles an army barracks. This private space, separated from the communal areas of your house, is where you can feel the power of place. If you take a holistic approach, you'll see the benefits rippling through into other areas of life. Less household clutter leads to more effective cleaning, and that can lead to better health. Less mental clutter can lead to better sleep and enhanced vitality.

Once you start to see the top of your dresser again and the pattern of your carpeting, you know you're well on your way to having a room you'll no longer want to escape from, but a refuge you'll want to escape to.

Chapter 4

Closet Confidential

Does your clothes closet look like a department store sales rack the day after Christmas . . . you know, where everything's in a kind of helter-skelter, nothing-quite-makes-sense disarray? Do you need to send in a search party to find your favorite shirt? Instituting an organizational system beefed up with a few space-saving solutions can bring order and breathing room to even the smallest of closets. Even if you think there's just not enough room, a few nips and tucks can result in a streamlined closet makeover.

Tug of Wardrobe

Was there ever a closet with room to spare? Well, there are at least a couple. There's the closet of a Long Island, New York, woman, a clotheshorse for sure, who had a two-story closet built in her new home. It's hard to imagine what bells and whistles would need to go with a double-decker closet. Perhaps a library ladder or elevator to access the garments? Maybe even one of those electric merry-go-round contraptions you find at the dry cleaner's. Then there's the 250-square-foot closet of a Manhattan businessman. A walk-in closet? This one's big enough to live in! His cabinet doors are made of mahogany; the drawers are lined in cashmere. The closet is even decorated with a pair of nineteenth-century urns.

Push and Pull

And then there are the rest of us. Most of us will never need to worry about tracking down a suit in a closet bigger than some apartments, but that doesn't mean we don't have trouble finding what's in there, anyway.

How much time do you spend hunting and pecking around your closets for a complete outfit? Pushing the clothes back and forth on that overly jammed rod of yours is not quite the bicep-building exercise your personal trainer had in mind. Still, you just *know* those black slacks are in there somewhere, so the frustrating search continues. Then, at last, success! There they are, only now the pants are so scrunched you need to schedule in an unplanned ironing session. It may be a brand-new morning, but when it comes to the frustration of staring down an overinflated closet, it's the same old thing, every day.

Breaking Out of the Rut

Facing a dysfunctional closet every morning is a bad way to start the day. Life is filled with anxieties, many of which are out of one's control. This is one that's definitely *in* your control. Purging your clothes closets of unworn and unwearable apparel and ridding your hall closets of rarely used gear gets at the heart of your home's storage capabilities. Tackle it, and you'll not only maximize your space, you'll feel empowered as you face your day.

FACT

According to California Closets, the cost of custom storage system can range in price from $400 to $30,000, with the average sale around $2,900. California Closets has installed more than 4 million custom-designed storage systems around the world since its founding in 1978.

Repeat Offenders

So let's get down to the biggest offenders. At the top of the list: adding a new item of clothing or pair of shoes without purging any of the old ones. It stands to reason that you'll max out your capacity in no time. And one more thing: When you've got so much packed in, it's impossible to keep track of what's there. So what happens? You wind up buying multiples of what you've already got.

Emotional Reasons

Then there are the shoes, an obsession that's gotten the better of plenty of women. Can you say "Carrie Bradshaw"? As the lead character of *Sex in the City* once famously said, "I rationalized that my new shoes shouldn't be punished just because I can't budget." Some women could say their shoes shouldn't be punished just because they have no place to store them.

Another reason closets tend to be a problem is that shopping for clothes is a national pastime. There's a reason it's called retail therapy. It's fun and, hey, it makes us feel good—up to a point, that is. When the shopping bags come home and there's no place to put the goods, those feel-good moments turn into stressful ones.

Finally, the closet winds up being the place most frequently used to throw stuff into when we need to quickly tidy up for company. But when company's gone, the closet catch-all is never "undone."

Special-occasion clothes like formal suits, gowns, and party dresses might stay in your closet for years without getting a wearing. It's a good idea to try on these outfits at least once a year to make sure they still deserve a place in your closet. Fashions change, weight shifts. It may no longer be the great number you remember.

Professional organizer Heidi M. Gaumet of HMG Organizing in Bellport, New York, ran into a client whose clothing was overrunning her entire house. The client, a woman in her early seventies, refused to get rid of anything. She also bought multiples of each item of clothing because she had multiple homes—but all that space didn't help. The woman had a thousand pairs of shoes. In a desperate search for space, she had even stored some of them in the wine cellar. Clothing racks lined every hallway. Her clothes even crept into the master bath. How bad did it get? Her husband built an entire addition onto the house, including two huge walk-in closets, just to regain control. Now that's someone who needed the help of a pro.

Straighten It Out

Fashionistas rejoice. Putting a clothes-storage system in place is easier than you think, no matter what size closet you've got or how busy it is. Some people might argue that small-closet organization is an oxymoron. Rest assured there are entire businesses created around the concept of decluttering closets, and size is no barrier. You don't need to break down walls and make a bigger closet when you could make a smarter closet. Closet pros are available and happy to turn your muddled mess into a designer showcase with generous built-ins that look like fine furniture. Or you can make it a do-it-yourself project with a game plan and the help of a few space saving devices. So let's find out exactly what's going on with—and what's going into—those closets of yours.

Suit Yourself

Remember the scary childhood tales of spooky closet doings? It's always the stuff you can't see that's most frightening. If you open your closet doors and don't like what's going on, then it's time to get down to business and assess the mess. Take out each and every item from your closet. If you're like most people, you'll uncover things you didn't even remember you had, maybe even a couple of brand-new items with the price tag still on them. And if you're really lucky, you might be like the Los Angeles actor who decided to tackle his closets and found a windfall of $80 in the pocket of an old sports coat.

Is that really your Class of '86 prom dress? Sorry, you just don't have the luxury of waiting for it to become a vintage classic. And that polyester leisure suit? *Starsky and Hutch* might have been your favorite childhood show, but that is *so* not coming back in style. Sometimes we hold onto items for the wrong reasons. It was a favorite years ago or it reminds us of a fun time in our lives. Face it: Unless you're the lucky owner of that two-story closet, your closet is no place for nostalgia.

ALERT!

Remember that before donating worn pants, skirts, coats, handbags, and wallets, you should check every pocket and zipper compartment to make sure each one is completely empty. A couple of years ago, a British man discovered he was out of luck when he accidentally left the equivalent of more than $2,000 in the pocket of a donated jacket.

While you're at it, chuck the motivational mini that's supposed to lure you into losing those extra ten pounds. How long has it been hanging there, anyway? Nice thought, but it's taking up unnecessary room. Besides, some motivational experts will tell you it often has the opposite effect. Those size sixes, eights, and tens are constant reminders of goals you're not achieving. (You look great the way you are, by the way.) When you drop the weight, then you can feel free to treat yourself to a shopping spree. If you haven't worn a shirt, sweater, skirt, dress, or suit in a couple of seasons, chances are you won't be wearing it again. And don't be dragged down by an item you know you'll never wear, even though it still has the price tag. It has happened to everyone. Allow yourself to ditch the inappropriate getup you bought at the hands of an overzealous salesperson. It's a little like buying a losing stock and holding on to it even as the price continues to sink. You want to get your money's worth. But accommodating unworn and unwanted items means that pair of pants or the denim jacket you really like may wind up as orphans in another room of the house. And how's this for a reality check: 80 percent of the time, we wear only 20 percent of our wardrobe.

Now, get ready to prepare your piles. You'll make one for keeping, one for donating, and a third for the dumpster. Check all your garments for rips, holes, loose threads, and stains. Mend it, fix it, or deep-six it, and don't put it back in your closet until you've taken action on it. Reach out to a charity like Big Brothers Big Sisters (*www.bbbs.org*) for a clothing pick up, or donate castoffs to a local homeless shelter or soup kitchen. You get a tax deduction and free up lots more space. Everyone wins.

Hanging On

Now that you've done away with the most egregious closet-hoggers, it's time to put a system in place. First, make sure you've got adequate lighting. If you can't see it, you won't wear it. No need to call in a professional electrician. Go to your local hardware store and buy an easy-to-install battery-operated closet light. Be sure to give your closet a thorough cleaning, too. Wet-mop floors and wipe down shelves. Dirt and dust balls work their way in and wind up on your clothes. Unknowingly, you may be aggravating your allergies by stopping housecleaning at your closet door.

Older homes are notorious for having small closets. In fact, some oldies-but-goodies have none at all. Before the late nineteenth century, cupboards, cabinets, and stand-alone wardrobes kept belongings in check. Then again, most people had relatively few possessions, especially compared to their twenty-first-century counterparts.

Sometimes older homes lack closets by design. New owners of prewar homes have been known to take out the lowly closets altogether in order to get more floor space out of small master bedrooms. In the old days, armoires were freestanding closets of choice. You can still eke out prime acreage in a narrow closet. Take a good look at its depth. Is there room to have one rod up front and a second rod behind for the clothes you don't wear as often? Perhaps it's the place for storing off-season gear.

FACT

It wasn't until around the 1850s that people started using hangers to store clothing in stand-alone wardrobes and closets. Before that, clothing either hung on hooks or lay flat in trunks.

The truth is that the standard closet design of any size, with just a single rod and a shelf above it, utilizes space very inefficiently. If you're willing to invest $2,000–$4,000, you may want to investigate a custom closet system, especially if you're planning to stay in your home for the foreseeable future.

Custom Closets

Custom closet designers typically charge a design fee and are better suited for larger closets. If you have a small closet with one rod and a shelf, a customized closet is not going to do you a lot of good. Many people think that a closet designer will find a way to create enough space to fit everything they own into a closet when most of the time the problem is that the client has too much clothing. If your closet is full and there are piles of clothing outside its doors, a customized closet is not the solution.

That doesn't mean there aren't good do-it-yourself alternatives. Install another bar and you'll double your storage space. A big chunk of vertical space is lost above the shelf and below the rod. The best solution is to reconfigure a closet so that it's customized to your needs with a variety of rod heights as well as shelves. If you opt for this route, you'll probably need to reposition the top bar a bit higher. The clothes in your closet will dictate space requirements. Suits, blouses, and folded slacks require thirty to forty inches of clearance. For long dresses, figure on about fifty to sixty inches.

If the prospect of breaking out a toolkit is enough to make you break out in a cold sweat, fear not. A no-installation alternative is a hanging rod doubler. It's a device that attaches to an existing clothes rod, instantly doubling your storage capacity. It works best for shorter pieces such as shirts and skirts and transforms all that wasted space into easy-to-access storage. The investment pays dividends. Items like rod doublers and hanging closet shelves that store sweaters and shirts can follow you to all your future homes. To avoid sagging rod syndrome, you may need to beef up the bar.

In some closets, double barring of any kind isn't practical, but you can still maximize the space beneath hanging clothes with low, two- or three-drawer clear plastic cabinets. They are the perfect storage answer for handbags, scarves, and sweaters because they're lightweight and see-through. Select a model on wheels, and you can scoot it out easily instead of ferreting through to the back of the closet.

▲ A tidy closet.

Stacked Up

Think vertical when it comes to maximizing space. Can you replace the existing shelf above the rod with one that's a bit deeper? Shelf dividers, which are widely available at do-it-yourself centers, not only keep clothing piles from toppling over but adjust to the exact width you need. It's also a great way to segregate little things like hats and scarves. Take a look and see how much space is wasted between the shelf and the closet ceiling—space you could be taking advantage of. So what's your option? Consider installing a second shelf midway up the wall. It'll be a bit harder to access, so use it for your less frequently worn items, like formal shoes or out-of-season attire. Clear acrylic drawers, which interlock for stable stacking, can be purchased in a variety of sizes, as well as canvas cases with "picture windows" for easy clothing identification.

One desperate housewife admits her small closet is filled with several purses that should rightly be in the trash. She also uses her little bit of space for items that are best stored elsewhere, like gifts she has bought on sale and is saving for Christmas. One wire shelf was so overloaded, and so haphazardly stacked with items, that it came right out of the wall. Needless to say, months later that shelf still hasn't been fixed or replaced.

Walk Right In

As you return your garments to the closet, line them up with a sense of order. Sort shirts and blouses by color and formality so that dress shirts are separated from casual weekend wear. Ditto for skirts and dresses and suits. Function and usage should determine location. Keep the things you grab daily closest to the closet door.

If you think hangers are just an afterthought, think again. In *Mommy Dearest*, Joan Crawford permanently gave wire hangers a bad rap, but it was well deserved, anyway.

Don't throw away those flimsy wire hangers you get from the dry cleaner. Local recycling plants will take them off your hands, and dry cleaners love to reuse them, too. You can also drop them off at thrift shops and homeless shelters or save them for the kids' school projects.

Wire hangers simply aren't constructed to keep the shape of your garments. They add shoulder lumps and give slacks awkward creases. Wood or padded hangers keep your clothes in shape by maintaining the contours of garments and add to their longevity. The sturdier the hanger, the better.

Sweaters, by the way, are better off folded. Folding sweaters over a sturdy hanger bar, dry cleaner–style, is also fine. As a rule of thumb, hang garments made of rayon, linen, and cotton, as well as anything that's prone to wrinkles or needs to keep its shape, such as delicate fabrics, pleated skirts, or creased slacks. Use dresser drawers for knitwear, sweaters, jeans, pajamas, and sportswear.

Have hangers facing in the same direction, and use a complete set of uniform hangers. Your closet will look better that way. Who cares about looks? You should. When you open your closet doors to find your clothes looking like the inside of a Rodeo Drive boutique, it'll go a long way in helping you keep the momentum moving.

Shoe-Ins

Shoes are the most problematic part of our wardrobe, at least from a neat freak's perspective. According to a survey by the American Apparel and Footwear Association, in 2005 Americans purchased more than 2.15 billion pairs—that's 7.4 for every man, woman and child. On average, women own something like thirty pairs of shoes, and most aren't likely to forsake their mules, pumps, sandals, and loafers for any extra closet space. Even when it comes to athletic footwear, we've got one set for tennis, another for walking, a third for jogging. Banish the thought of an all-purpose multisport sneaker, even for the most nominal of exercisers.

The answer isn't a high pile of shoes in their branded shoe boxes, even if the boxes are stacked neat as a pin. Unless you've got Superman's X-ray vision, it's a good bet you don't even know what's in each box. Instead of ready-to-wear, you've got a mountain of forget-to-wear.

If you fancy yourself the arts-and-crafts type, you can snap a picture of the shoes and tape it to the outside of the box for identification, but let's face it. That kind of uber-organization takes ongoing commitment. Nice to think about, but who's got the time? Purchase plastic see-through boxes, instead. There's no guessing involved. And keep those piles of shoe boxes low. Otherwise, reaching for a pair way down on the bottom will set off an avalanche. Can the inside of your closet door or a section of interior wall accommodate a hanging shoe organizer? It's a great way to keep footwear orderly, accessible—and in pairs. How many times have you found yourself stumbling around for a renegade shoe that fell somewhere deep in the back of the closet floor?

FACT

Shoes will look good and feel good if you keep them in tip-top shape. Always use a shoehorn to protect the integrity of the heels. Shoe trees will help hold the shape and can prolong their life; cedar trees will absorb moisture. Allow shoes to breath between wearings—try not to dress in the same pair on consecutive days.

Revolving shoe carousels take up minimal floor space, though you'll need to clear about three feet of height for an eighteen-pair revolving system. Boots are always a bit clumsier to manage. Boot trees will help them hold their shape better, keeping them upright and more neatly aligned. Clear boot boxes are a better idea if your boot collection numbers more than a few.

Hook, Line, and Sneakers

Kids usually won't complain about their own unruly closets, but that doesn't mean the clutter doesn't take its toll or set youngsters up for a lifetime of bad habits. Start them on the right track by employing a system that gives little ones the basic foundation tools for closet organization while providing easy accessibility.

Think small. Place rods low for everyday clothing. Install a second bar above for off-season wear. Don't let outgrown clothes take root. As soon as an article of clothing no longer fits, save it elsewhere as a hand-me-down for another child or donate it if it's still in good condition. Buy sturdy hangers specifically designed for children's clothing. Full-size hangers are difficult for little fingers to manipulate. Clothes will wind up on the closet floor instead of on the rod. For sweaters and shoes, hanging organizers are no-fuss, barrier-free answers. Keep your system simple. Organize clothes by type—pants, shirts, and so on. It'll give your child a blueprint to follow so he'll be able to figure out where things go when it's time to put items away.

And be sure to reevaluate storage accessories annually, if not more often, to make sure they continue to meet the needs of your growing child. For ideas on kids' playrooms, see Chapter 8.

▲ A child's closet.

The Linen Closet

When you open a door and see an impossible stack of fabrics, you know it could only be the linen closet. Though linen closets have always been where all the bedsheets, towels, and tablecloths are stashed, it may be time to rethink the old ways. All it gets you is sky-high towers instead of a solid organizational strategy that won't result in an all-comes-tumbling-down ending.

Despite the name, is the linen closet really the best place for bedding? Wouldn't having sets stored in each corresponding bedroom be more convenient on sheet-changing day? If the bedroom closet allows, reserve a space on a shelf or consider stowing them in plastic containers under the bed. Put extra coverlets inside pillow shams, if you have them.

ESSENTIAL

Here's a cheat sheet on bed linen care. Remove sheets from the dryers while they're still warm to keep wrinkles to a minimum. Store sheets in sets. Folding is easier if you work on a large table or flat surface. Lay the sheet right side down, elasticized corners facing up. Neatly turn in corners and edges so they're straight. Then fold in thirds. Rotate sheets regularly for even wear.

A more practical spot for commonly used tablecloths, napkins, and placemats is in the kitchen or dining room. Can you squeeze out space in your sideboard or china cabinet? Or, if you've got space in your closets, consider hanging these items up over heavy-duty hangers. It'll keep them crease-free. You can also roll them around the tall cardboard tubes that come with wrapping paper rolls for another wrinkle-free solution. Towels and washcloths are better left in the bathroom. If cabinets are full, roll towels up and put them in pretty, oversize baskets.

If the linen closet really is the most practical place for your sheets and towels, use shelf dividers to keep piles in place and add more shelves to keep stacks low. If you do add shelves, be sure to paint the wood. Unfinished timbers can stain fabrics.

Coat Closets

Coats are tough to part with. They last years, but before you know it, you've got an accumulation for every occasion. There's the special dress-up coat for celebrations, the everyday jacket, and the weatherproof utility number for nor'easters. Pare down and donate the ones you haven't worn in a while. Instead of storing gloves in coat pockets, scarves around the hangers, and hats who knows where, use the vertical space above the rod. Mesh or clear bins are perfect ways to keep accessories accounted for and dust-free. You can also nail small baskets to the inside of the closet door and allocate one basket to each family member's accessories. Install a few hooks for grab-and-go items like umbrellas, purses, knapsacks, and gym bags.

QUESTION?

Why is cold storage recommended for fur coats?
Heat and humidity can dry out the oils in furs and leathers. Professional cold storage in temperature-controlled vaults during the warmer months will increase the life span of your fur and maintain its peak condition.

It's likely that coats are not the only things in your coat closet. In many homes, coat closets are a catchall for a growing collection of shopping bags, wrapping paper rolls, and cleaning appliances. You're better off not jamming the closet to the gills. Coats need to breathe, and you need to see exactly what's in there. If you're going to turn it into a multipurpose closet, create zones.

Addition by Subtraction

By weeding out your clothes, linen, and hallway closets, you free up space and reduce a source of stress and tension. Though it seems counterintuitive, by sorting through your clothes closets and getting rid of idle garments, you may actually discover that your wardrobe has grown in size. That's because some favorites may have been hidden under mounds of sweaters or secreted deep in the recesses where garments were all but inaccessible. It's addition by subtraction.

ALERT!

Always use sturdy hangers for outerwear. They'll help to better hold the shape of coats and jackets. Store coats in a well-ventilated closet—they need to breathe—and away from access to sunlight that could cause colors to fade. Before packing them away for the season, have coats cleaned according to manufacturer's instructions. Soiled coats can attract pests.

Once you do a thorough job of exorcising your closet, it should only take periodic tune-ups to keep it organized and working for you day after day. Schedule the tune-ups for spring, summer, winter, and fall. Do it at the same time you change your wardrobe and before you go shopping for the newest seasonal fashions. It's easy to forget what items you have from one year to the next, and you don't want to end up buying duplicates.

Abandon the idea that a closet is a static storage center. Think of it, instead, as an ongoing tool used to support your lifestyle and enhance your daily routine.

Chapter 5

En Suite Success: Bathrooms

Utilitarian and utopian. Can a bathroom really function as both? It's the place of prework traffic jams, where the inevitable time crunch forces us to play beat-the-clock every morning with the efficiency of an office manager. In a perfect world, it's also the place to unwind at the end of the day with, perhaps, a long soak in a spa-like ambiance. That's asking an awful lot of a single room, especially when you add in all the stuff we need to keep the place spic 'n span.

Shower Power

Hard to believe, but indoor plumbing wasn't common in homes prior to World War II. As late as the 1940s, more than a third of U.S. homes still didn't have flush toilets. Even more lacked a bathtub or shower. These days, that same percentage of homes has at least 2.5 bathrooms. They're bigger, too. Still, with all that we ask them to house, it's little wonder why so many bathrooms are teeming with toiletries, towels, and Tylenol. (The Tylenol is for the headache you get trying to make your way through the clutter.) The smallest room in the house is standing storage for the stuff that pretties us up and restores us to health. But how much is too much? Do you have shampoos, conditioners, and soaps multiplying in the corners of your tub like wild mushrooms? Is your medicine cabinet jammed with old prescriptions for illnesses you don't even remember suffering? Does your hamper double as a tabletop for cosmetics and toiletries? Something's gotta give.

FACT

According to the National Kitchen & Bath Association trade organization, some 8 million bathrooms were remodeled in the United States in 2004, and there were about 4.5 million new bathroom constructions. Remodeling totaled more than $23 billion, with about half of those jobs coming in under $1,000.

Buying too much before using up what we've got is the curse we bring upon ourselves. We love trying out new products, even if the old favorites still do the job. That's why there's a shelf displaying a dozen half-empty jars of hair gels and facial masks. You know that twelve-roll pack of toilet paper you just bought on sale this week? Well, just stack it on top of the twelve-roll of T.P. you bought *last* week. Call it the "just in case" mindset. It's one of the habits that prevents us from gaining control of our environment. Keep items to a minimum, and you'll know exactly what you've got. What's more, you won't wind up buying products unnecessarily. That's especially good advice for one retired couple, empty nesters, who insist on doing their weekly grocery shopping at a discount warehouse. Their purchases are so disproportionate to their needs that they've had to carve out a section of their basement for storage, a section they've nicknamed "the pharmacy."

Be sure to use childproof containers and keep drugs on high shelves out of children's reach. When you dispose of drugs, don't throw them in a trashcan where youngsters might be able to get their hands on them. Increasingly, pharmacies are taking back medications to ensure proper disposal. Contact the Poison Control Center at 800-222-1222 to find out the best way to discard expired medicines in your area.

When you see an item on sale, remind yourself you don't *have* to buy it. There are only so many boxes of cold medication you actually need to have on hand. One backup is fine; two are overkill. An item can very well expire before you have a chance to use it. There's the story of one man who cleaned out the drawers in his bathroom vanity to discover not one or two hairdryers but four. Maybe it was wishful thinking on his part, considering the extent of his male-pattern baldness.

Getting a Grip

In theory, bathrooms should be relatively easy to tame because the basic items they house are very specific. So what is the big-picture approach to getting clutter under control in the bathroom? How do you get down to the business of determining how much you really need to keep in order to reclaim your bathroom from the mighty grips of drugstore central?

You'll need to clear things out first in order to clear things up. Grab a beach blanket or old bed-sheet to put down on the floor. That'll be your temporary staging area. The guck from medicine cabinet and bathroom closet potions is laden with oils and syrupy goos you don't want to have to scrub up from your floors after your purging is done.

Starting with one section at a time, clear out your medicine chest, drawers, bathtub area, shelves, and so on. Inspect each item carefully. Have a supply of giant trash bags on hand for refuse, not the little supermarket bags. Think *big*.

Look for expiration dates on medications and discard any drugs beyond their dates. You may be tempted to eke out another dose, but expired medicines can lose their potency or, worse, make you ill. Add to your discard pile leftover antibiotics and medicines that aren't clearly labeled. This is one area where you don't want to take chances.

ESSENTIAL

Two-in-one and even three-in-one personal care products can free up space in your medicine cabinet. You can pick up razors with built-in shaving cream dispensers. Shampoo and conditioner combos have been around a while, but now you can add in body gel to the mix for a one-size-washes-all cleansing solution. A multipurpose body moisturizer can also be used for baby bottoms, cuticles, and calloused feet.

Open up any opaque containers to see exactly how much product is left inside. There's no reason to hog up a lot of shelf space if a jar or bottle has only trace amounts left. Transfer remainders to smaller containers or consolidate half-empties of like products together. Along the same lines, if you're a warehouse club shopper, transfer titanic-size products into more practical slim-down sizes that don't take up so much space. A mega bottle of mouthwash, for instance, can unnecessarily dominate a valuable chunk of your vanity's countertop.

Throw out any items you've tried and nixed—colognes, hair gels, makeup. You're not going to recoup your investment by having these things sit around collecting dust. Face it: The money's already gone.

Trash any products that are impractical for your lifestyle or just more trouble than they're worth—to wit, that face mask that promises fountain-of-youth results if you wear it an hour a day, three times a week. It ain't gonna happen.

Discard old makeup that's been junking up your cosmetic bag forever. Its purity may be compromised. Liquid makeup stays good for about a year, but figure on six months for eyeliner and three months for mascara. Otherwise, you run the very real risk of serious eye infections.

Get rid of that collection of makeup bags that come "free with purchase" at the cosmetic counter.

Be realistic about how many different products you need lining the tub. Are all those shampoos, conditioners, hair masks, and body shampoos really necessary? Wouldn't one of each suffice? Back brushes, pumice stones, loofahs, nail brushes—use 'em or lose 'em. One woman came face to face with a little compulsion only after seeing the stockpile of moisturizers in her collection. Apparently, she never met a lotion she didn't like.

FACT

The Freecycle Network (*www.freecycle.org*) is an online grassroots organization made up of communities around the globe that allow individuals to recycle their no-longer-wanted goods by offering them free to other members. The Web site was started in 2003 to promote waste reduction. Post details on the items you want to get rid of, and chances are you'll have an enthusiastic taker before you know it.

What can you do about an overabundance of products that might someday, in the distant future (when you have more time), improve your life? If you have more than you can realistically use, consider making a donation to others who can use the product right now. Homeless shelters can use shampoos and toiletries all the time, so bag up all that extra stuff and drop it off at your local shelter!

Time to Regroup

There's an old joke that goes something like this. A gentleman has about six items in his bathroom arsenal: a toothbrush, toothpaste, shaving cream, a razor, a bar of soap, and a towel swiped from the Holiday Inn. The average number of items in a typical woman's bathroom is 437—most of which a man wouldn't even be able to identify.

We all know, however, that clutter is an equal-opportunity offender. Before you start putting items back in their old places, stop and consider the best way to reorganize. In your medicine chest, keep the items you use regularly, as well as some first-aid products you might need to get to quickly.

If there are children in your household, make sure all medications are in childproof containers and stored on high shelves for extra measure.

For medicine chests, a good storage solution is to use small plastic baskets that can neatly hold several small items. Store all like items together (e.g., medicines in one basket, hair clips in another) and put first-aid items in a spot where they will be easily accessible, even in the dark.

E ALERT!

The Red Cross suggests having a well-stocked first-aid kit on hand for emergencies. At a minimum, the kit should include adhesive tape, bandages, a cold pack, pain reliever, antiseptic ointment, and sterile gauze pads. Be sure to tuck in a small first-aid booklet for quick reference, too.

Take boxed items out of their original packages, where appropriate, to free up space. One imaginative homeowner reduced packaging bulk by using collectible jars and bottles to stow small items. Individual-size milk containers stored her manicure items, bandage strips, and cotton swabs.

◀ A medicine cabinet.

Find a home other than your medicine chest for suntan products, cough drops, and the stack of mini soaps you took from your last hotel stay. Reserve these shelves for the products you use on a daily basis, such as toothpaste, dental floss, eye drops, hair care products, and so on. Don't stock multiples of anything in the chest. Relegate backup inventory to a storage closet or a secondary cabinet. If yours is a shared bathroom, give each person her own shelf or let everyone carve out a zone for personal items.

It's a good idea to go through your medicine chest thoroughly at least once a year to make sure all the items are still being used.

Console Yourself

The choice of vanity is the most important decision you'll make in the bathroom. The fixture defines the room. Understandably, many people are reluctant to compromise looks for practicality, even if it means more storage space. Fortunately, manufacturers are ahead of the game with beautiful models that don't sacrifice their functionality. If you love the graceful lines and retro looks of a pedestal sink, you no longer have to forsake storage capacity. Showrooms are filled with pedestal sinks that sit atop cabinetry to give you the best of both worlds. In fact, more and more people are saying goodbye to standard consoles altogether and opting to move honest-to-goodness furniture from the dining room and bedroom into the bathroom. Dressers are being outfitted into vanities. High cupboards are being recycled for towel storage duty.

QUESTION?

What is a cosmeceutical?
The cosmetic industry coined the word "cosmeceutical" to refer to cosmetic products that have medicinal or therapeutic effects on the body. Cosmeceuticals represent the fastest-growing sector of the beauty industry, although the classification is not officially recognized by the U.S. Food and Drug Administration.

A word of caution: Some woods (such as African mahogany) lend themselves to high humidity conditions, but for the most part wood and water don't mix. Furniture placed in the moist environs of a bathroom will need a good protective coating of polyurethane.

If your vanity has drawers, pick up a few small baskets to keep things from getting tossed and tangled. Baskets, drawer dividers, or mesh trays work especially well for organizing combs, hair clips, cosmetics, and cotton swabs and keeping drawers from becoming free-for-alls.

◀ A towel basket.

Stackable plastic drawers are space-enhancers under the sink. Lazy Susans are useful for toiletries, too. No, they're not just for the kitchen. In fact, many kitchen aids can be incorporated into the bathroom, such as simple mounted, pull-out shelving.

Looking to free up floor space? A wall-mounted sink is your answer. You can make up for the lack of under-sink storage by using attractive covered baskets to hold beauty and cleaning products. As much as possible, buy all-in-one cleansers that work on multiple surfaces. You really don't need separate cleaners for mirrors, countertops, shower, and floors. Adding a skirt to an older, existing wall-mounted sink will give you a place to hide those items away, while still keeping them accessible.

Wall-to-Wall Solutions

If you're feeling constrained by the four walls of your bathroom, push back. Literally. Use a stud detector to determine how much space is between your wall studs. There might be enough to create niches for stylish recessed shelving.

Bathrooms are often a patchwork of skinny open spaces. Even just a foot of wall space could be enough to house a freestanding open shelf tower, plenty big for soaps and bath oils. Many products nowadays come in attractive packaging, elegant enough to make a design statement of their own. Got vaulted ceilings? A stretch of vertical space might be a good spot to install upper cabinets—but not too high or they'll be impractical. Bathrooms are not the place for long-term storage because of their high humidity levels.

FACT

While the trend in bathrooms is toward personal spas, it takes careful planning to reinvent the space. The average bathroom size is five feet by nine feet in suburban homes and much smaller in apartments and townhouses.

What about your windows? Glass shelving offers up the perfect place for sunlight to sparkle off pretty decanters. Shelving above the window frame and door are often overlooked areas. Since it's out of easy reach, reserve it only for items you don't need to use on a daily basis. Before you go for the hammer and nails, here's a tip. With the relatively tight spaces of bathrooms, make sure shelves don't interfere with traffic flow or with the opening and closing of medicine chest or cabinet doors.

Above the sink, suction cups are a great way to declutter the vanity area without leaving lasting marks on your walls. Many renters employ this trick. You'd be amazed at the range of specially designed suction cups available to hold razors, washcloths, toothbrushes and glasses.

In a Lather

All the bath and beauty products in your bathroom should be limited to the ones you use on a regular basis—keep all the sometimes-used extras in a plastic bin in a closet, and remember to pitch the ones you no longer use! You can store the bath products you use daily on a shower rack. Choose either the kind that hangs over the showerhead or the suction-cup version. Many bed and bath shops have interesting and fun options for shower storage—it doesn't have to be boring or plain.

Corner shelves in the tub area help you to recoup lost space and maintain clean lines. No-tool stacking systems and over-the-showerhead shelving units are other ways to streamline the parade of plastic bottles that give even the cleanest of bathrooms a sloppy look. Besides, bottles that sit on a damp tub ledge encourage the growth of mold by trapping water underneath the containers. House them on higher, drier ground and you'll head off the problem.

Make the most of your shower time. Water-resistant radios are now all-purpose information stations for the bathroom, giving you not only tunes but weather-band radio as well as TV audio so you can listen to your favorite morning shows while getting ready for the day.

Increasingly, twenty-first-century wizardry is finessing its way into bathrooms and turning them into resort spas. Sound systems and TVs aren't anomalies anymore. A company called Aquavision produces waterproof flat-panel TVs especially designed for the shower and other wet environments. The set resembles a standard mirror until you turn it on. Presto. It's HBO. Then there are the hands-free sinks that use motion detectors to trigger the flow of water, as well as gas fireplaces and telephone communications centers.

Speaking of state-of-the-art, are you ready for a novel way to free up that space devoted to cleaning products? Be prepared. You'll need to reach deep into your bank account. The Shower-Shower, an automatic shower-cleaning system from Intelligent Consumer Products of Arizona, is a kind of washing machine for the bathroom. By touching a button or using a remote control, jets installed on your shower will actually shower cleaning fluid to eliminate soap scum and mildew. With the price of this convenience in five-figure territory, however, most of us will just have to make do with a bottle of bleach.

Big Ideas for Little Spaces

Over-the-toilet shelving is a solution for ultra-tight spots. And think of the toilet tank as an extra shelf, too. Apothecary jars are great places to store items that don't have a logical home, such as manicure items, cotton balls, and dental accessories. Add a few hooks to the underside of a standard shelf and you have a place to hang hand towels. Install a peg or two on the wall by the sink for hairdryers and curling irons. They take up way too much space in a drawer. Wall-mounted hairdryers, often seen in hotel rooms, are another alternative.

Have multiple bathrooms and minimal space? You don't need to keep a complete set of cleaning supplies in each bathroom. Instead, pick up one all-purpose carryall to hold your cleansers and, on cleaning day, simply tote the lot from one bathroom to the other.

Depending on your space, a rolling rack with open shelves and drawer options can give you added flexibility.

E ALERT!

If you're considering a bathroom renovation, your designer may be qualified, but ask if he's also certified as a CBD (certified bathroom designer), an AKBD (associate kitchen and bath designer) or CMKBD (certified master kitchen and bath designer). That will let you know he's passed muster with the industry's stringent professional requirements.

Bathrooms to Spare

For a children's bathroom, those whimsically decorated, over-the-door shoe holders with plastic pockets are ideal for holding washcloths, powders, and bathing products. Put up a few attractive hooks on the back of the bathroom door for bathrobes, pajamas, and wet towels. Hooks make it easier for kids to hang things up, which gives them less of an excuse to toss items on the floor. Dedicate a place for bath toys. Covered baskets work really well. Otherwise, toys wind up underfoot and are liable to become potential hazards. Speaking of hazards, childproof any cabinets you don't want your kids to access and use only unbreakable containers—never glass—in the bathroom.

Guest Bathrooms and Powder Rooms

Guest bathrooms can be used to keep extras of what we use, but not at the risk of making them look like a stockroom. This is really the place to keep things simple. Since the guest bath typically gets much less use than other bathrooms, take inventory, especially before company arrives, to make sure there's enough soap and toilet paper on hand along with a fresh guest towel.

Room to Roam

In many cases, dysfunctional bathrooms are the product of time management, or rather time mismanagement. It's being in so much of a hurry that you change your clothes and leave the old garments on the floor. If you don't want to break your old habit, adopt a new support system. Keep a laundry hamper right there.

Avoid buying toiletries on impulse. Sheer volume is the biggest problem in bathroom clutter. Got a product you don't use? Toss it.

If you're having overnight guests, be a good host and put together a pampering basket that includes sample-size products of everything your guests could use for a comfortable visit. Include soap, shampoo, towels, toothbrush, and toothpaste. Be creative. Toss in a few extras such as postcards, a local map, a reading light, the latest bestseller, and a water bottle. Just be warned: They may never want to leave.

Today, homeowners have their pick of bathroom storage options. But very often off-the-shelf products just don't do the job. Standard lipstick holders are too small to accommodate your favorite brand. Toiletry kits are a smidgeon too small to house all your lotions and clippers. The answer? Go tailor-made. Use spring-loaded drawer dividers to customize your drawer space. Take advantage of deep jewelry boxes, tea boxes, and even sturdy card boxes you have lying around the house to contain frequently used medicines and personal care products.

As for shelves, closets, cabinets, and carts, there's the danger of implementing too many solutions. They can overwhelm a small room mighty quickly. Where's room for you? There's such a thing as solution confusion. Use organizational aids to solve your storage problems, not to aid and abet the clutter.

Chapter 6

It's Showtime: Media Rooms and Home Theaters

DVDs, CDs, HDTVs. Our homes are filled with all kinds of electronic wizardry designed to inform us, educate us, and, most of all, entertain us. Whether you call it a home theater, media room, or just the room with the TV, aim for high tech but keep it low maintenance. On the following pages, you'll find smart ideas for getting the techno gadgets under control and that muddle of videos, music, and games out of sight.

That's Entertainment

Once upon a time, high-end electronics were the domain of a select group of gadget-happy enthusiasts known as early adopters. These are the people who buy an item the very first day it comes on the market. By the time the product goes from prototype to mass market, these early adopters are already on to the next new thing.

Well, today's alphabet soup of audio-video equipment—DVD, HD, LCD— has entered the language of the masses. Media rooms are now as ubiquitous as iPods. So . . . how big is your plasma? Homeowners are re-creating the movie-theater experience by reconfiguring their dens or living rooms. Meanwhile, home buyers are building new residences with state-of-the-art theater environments. That means cushy cinema seating, automated lighting, and acoustic paneling, as well as top-of-the-line audio and video components. The National Association of Home Builders' "Housing 2005: Facts, Figures and Trends" report found that an emerging movement in higher-end markets is the advent of a "flex" or "bonus" room that homeowners can use for a variety of purposes. Many homeowners are opting to flex theirs into media rooms.

The best setting for a home theater is the room with the least amount of light. That's why many finished basements are prime candidates for reconfiguration. You can obtain the same low-light effect in a main-floor room by facing the TV away from the windows and using lined window treatments to prevent the picture on the screen from washing out.

Even if your version of a home theater is more of a souped-up den than something that rivals the screening room of a 20th Century Fox executive, you'll need to take a look at how you use the room as the first step in strategizing a plan of action.

How many people in your household spend time in the room? Are there any serious movie buffs or audiophiles in the mix? Is your home the spot where the whole neighborhood gathers to watch the latest home video releases? Or is it the place for game-of-the-week football parties? What about the kids? Do they use the room for Xbox and PlayStation? If that's the case, are the video games strewn all over the floor?

Media Madness

While we're mired in movies, the movement toward hard-drive–based products like personal video recorders is gaining speed. Think of it as "Me TV." TiVo-ing your favorite show is nothing new, but now media storage units allow you create a virtual digital jukebox out of your personal DVD collection in order to access selections on demand. In the mood for *Gone with the Wind*? It could be as close as a button on your remote control.

QUESTION?

What is a personal video recorder?
A personal video recorder (PVR), also known as a digital video recorder (DVR), is a device that lets you record and time-shift TV broadcasts on a hard disk drive for later viewing. TiVo first introduced the technology in 1999. PVR service is also available through most cable operators.

Meanwhile, though, we still have plenty of physical media to contend with in the here and now, and in large part, it's that media that makes the mess. Big-time clutter comes from too many videos, DVDs, CDs, and games, and no good place to contain them. Take Charlie, a sound-hound in New Jersey. In the TV room of his pretty Dutch colonial home, he's got a hamper, a wicker chest, and an entire breakfront filled with compact discs. That's not all. He also has a bookcase crammed with old record albums. Talk about mass media! Charlie admits he probably listens to less than a third of the music in his collection, but discarding even a few? That's a thought too horrible to contemplate, and so the vinyl and discs continue their domestic incursion.

The most important element of a streamlined media room is managing your music and video collections, and that starts with triage. Haul out four boxes and mark them KEEP, DONATE, DISCARD, and PRESERVE.

Save Your Special Memories

The box marked PRESERVE is for all videos and music with special meaning. Make sure each is clearly labeled. How many times have you heard about someone accidentally taping over a precious graduation ceremony or once-in-a-lifetime music recital? Remember that classic episode of *Everybody Loves Raymond,* when Ray inadvertently tapes a football game right over his wedding video? In a real-life scenario, a surprise sixtieth-birthday party for one special grandmother was videotaped for posterity. Well, at least that was the plan. But days later, when the birthday girl herself needed a tape to record her favorite show, she grabbed the nearest—unmarked—one. You guessed it. Goodbye, surprise birthday party; hello, *Law and Order.*

FACT

According to the Consumer Electronics Association, the average household is stocked with 100 CDs, more than forty DVDs, and sixteen video games. How does your home compare?

On VHS cassettes, there's a tab you can pop off so that the tape can't accidentally be recorded over. Even with such preventative measures, it's a good idea to have a duplicate copy made. All media has an army of adversaries: fingerprints, scratches, heat, dust. If a recording is really important to you, don't take chances with it. Make a backup and transfer it to the most up-to-date format available. Put old music cassette tapes on CD, videotapes onto DVD, and so on. Segregate these special tapes, CDs, and DVDs, and keep them together for safekeeping.

Make sure to safeguard your precious videotapes by following a few guidelines. Never touch the tape itself, only the external cassette casing. Be careful where you keep them in your home. Humidity and dust are your enemies. Rewind tapes before you put them back on the shelf, and store them vertically. Don't leave tapes sitting in a hot or cold car for prolonged periods of time. Cassettes are extremely sensitive to the elements. And because tapes are magnetic, don't leave them lying around on your stereo speakers.

Decide What to Toss

Now that you've put aside the things with sentimental value, everything else is up for grabs. In with the new? Then it's out with the old. Take a fresh look at your entire entertainment library, from your old super-eights to your eight-tracks to the boxed DVD set you bought and never watch. Keep in mind that your collection is always going to grow. There will always be a new movie to buy, a CD you've got to have, and a new format coming down the pike that will make you want to go out and start your collection of all-time favorites all over again. With those things in mind, review your stash and ask yourself how you can start whittling it down to a manageable size. Here are a few ideas:

- Donate all redundant copies. If you have *The Godfather* on DVD, lose the VHS version. Ask a senior citizens' center if it might want a few additions to its video library.
- Find new homes for those movies you received as gifts and never liked. Why keep them around if you have no intention of watching them?
- Recycle all the children's movies your family has outgrown. Hospitals, nurseries, schools, and even the day-care center at the gym will be grateful recipients.
- Pass along the exercise videos you no longer use. The local recreation center could have a use for them.
- Throw out all the instructional videos and CDs that came with your ionizer, exercycle, bread maker . . . you get the point. Somehow they seem to linger on the shelves long after the products they accompanied were discarded.
- Trash or transfer everything on dying, obsolete, or inconvenient-to-watch formats, like your original home movies.

Of course, this is also the time to chuck any old electronic equipment you might have lying around the room, too. Patricia, a mother of three, tried to do just that when she put an old television set down by the curb for garbage day pickup. Before the trash collectors could get to it, a neighborhood "recycler" had loaded the set into his van and wasn't too shy about ringing her doorbell and asking for the remote!

TV isn't just for video anymore. Turn your monitor into a photo album. Plug the memory card or stick from your digital camera into the TV or connect the cable from your camera to the set's USB port, and you'll be able to view your photographs on a nice big screen.

Remember that movie your family enjoyed 300 times one summer, four years ago? Why is it still living in your entertainment center, behind thirty or forty other movies you no longer watch, and beside at least twenty-five CDs of music that no longer "sing" to you? Donate your old favorites to someone else who might not have experienced them and who can enjoy them for the first time.

Here's a note about record albums. Even if you're still playing the occasional LP on a functioning turntable, take a look at your albums, one at a time, to see if any of them are warped. If a record looks like a question mark in silhouette, trash it. Don't make the mistake of thinking it's a collector's item just because it's old. While preparing to move from his home to a townhouse, John found a milk crate full of records from the 1940s and 1950s in a back corner of his basement. He put them up for sale and then turned down the only nibble he received because he thought the offer insultingly low. What happened? Well, those records are back in the basement, only this time in John's new home. Even in the best condition, very few records are particularly valuable.

Organize Your "Keepers"

Now sort your CDs and videos using a system that makes sense for you. For some households, that might mean categorizing them by "owner," with Dad's movies in one section, Mom's favorites in another, and Junior's in a third. Or simply take a tip from your local video store and categorize them by format (video, DVD) and then by genre, like so:

- Comedy
- Drama
- Horror

- Sci-Fi
- Foreign
- Documentary
- Classics
- Children
- Instructional

Then, finally, sort videos alphabetically by title. Arrange CDs alphabetically by artist. Good job. So now where does your trimmed-down collection go? Depending on the quantity, you can repurpose a bookshelf, build shelves, or buy ready-made storage holders. Figure out if you've got a preference for opened or closed storage. Many people who treasure their collections enjoy showing them off where others can see them.

Accordion-shaped units grow as your collection grows. They're expandable, wall-mountable, and some sleek models are as much about art as they are about utility. This storage option works for many types of media and doesn't eat up any floor space, either; if you've got a small room, it could be your answer. Modular systems are another approach for using the space you have now and having a plan for adding on later. Closed-door cabinets keep your music and movies dust-free and convey a cleaner look.

Ottomans with media storage beneath the seat offer unexpected storeroom space. Some oversize ottomans can hold hundreds of cassettes and DVDs. If you want guests to do a double take, buy a piece of furniture that does double-duty. Pedestal media holders are a perfect place to showcase a sculpture, vase or plant. Better still for the storage savvy, they open up to reveal hidden shelves for all your movies.

Baskets make CDs and DVDs easy to access and, just as important, easy to put away. If you use baskets or drawers for storage, make sure the discs are stacked vertically, not on top of each other, so that you can read the titles.

You don't necessarily need to store all your media together. If you have a big collection of Christmas movies and CDs, for instance, you might want to put them with your holiday gear—as long as climate conditions are media-friendly. There's no reason the holiday classics you listen to one month a year should take up space on your shelves year-round.

TV or Not TV

When television first made its way into our living rooms in the 1950s and 1960s, it was the focal point of the home, the special guest that took center stage. TVs were housed in big bulky consoles. Clumsy antennas on the roof captured the programming of a handful of channels. Even on those, reception was marginal.

But then TVs began to shrink. They got lighter, more portable, and more affordable. And they started multiplying throughout the house, showing up on bedroom dressers, basement TV tables, and kitchen countertops. Now it's back to the future. While the average household has about three sets, big-screen numbers are once again drawing the family together in a single common area. But instead of just a big console, there's an arsenal of equipment and add-on accessories that requires the lion's share of an entire room to accommodate it all.

FACT

By one forecast, more than 50 million homes in the United States will be watching television on a high-definition set by the year 2009. According to the Consumer Electronics Association, sports broadcasts are a major driver of digital and HDTV sales, with the Super Bowl being the biggest sales booster of all.

There's no doubt about it. Home theaters are a hot national trend. According to a report in *USA Today*, one out of every four households in the United States has some kind of home theater, 37 percent have a thirty-inch or larger TV screen, and about 8 percent of new homes are being built with a home theater or media room.

Hide and Seek

Homeowners used to hide their televisions in armoires and cabinets, but the sleek good looks of ultra-thin screens have turned TVs into the stars of the room. Should these status symbols be out front and center stage? Or are they just big ugly black holes? It's a judgment call—and sometimes a bone of contention within the household. He loves the look of the set; she wants to disguise it. Sometimes, there's just no easy answer.

◀ An entertainment unit.

Yesterday's furniture wasn't necessarily made to fit today's entertainment technology. But the good news is that a thin plasma or LED monitor is a lot easier to manage than the fat cathode ray tube set we grew up watching. Professional installation of any new audio-video system is often available at a nominal charge. Installers are magicians at hiding the knots of wire and reconfiguring the room to optimize the space.

DVD screensavers, produced especially for flat-panels, can transform your monitor into a beach, rainforest, even a roaring fireplace. There's something to fit just about every mood from Screen Dreams (*www .screendreamsdvd.com*). Art Plasma (*www.artplasma.com*) has screen-savers that feature classic and contemporary works of art. DVDs are on a continuous loop, so they'll keep playing until you hit stop.

Flex Furniture

The the trend these days in TV cabinetry is future-proofed entertainment consoles that adjust to changing screen sizes. Davis Remignanti, lead design consultant at Furniture.com, reports that furniture makers are getting hip to the idea that electronic components are continually changing. In response, manufacturers are making adaptable storage units. An eye toward "flex furniture" means the unit you buy today for your TV and accessories won't be obsolete tomorrow.

Instead of fixed-size cabinetry that might lock or limit you to a certain size television set or a certain number of components, the sky's the limit. Manufacturers are designing products knowing that consumers may want to trade up to larger components at some point in the not-too-distant future. Cabinet units with an extending bridge are built in a way that the center section adjusts to accommodate even the largest projection TVs.

Today, there are plenty of clever ways to hide components without sacrificing style. One of the smartest is a TV unit with adjoining display shelves and sliding doors. If you want the TV to be a focal point, slide the doors open. They reveal the set and cover the shelves. If you want a neat buttoned-down look, slide the doors closed to hide the TV monitor and reveal the shelves.

ALERT!

When choosing a home entertainment unit, beware of the harmful effects of dust and poor ventilation. Overstacking electronic components can result in blocked vents that may reduce your system's performance. Allow enough room between shelves so that air can circulate freely, and be sure to wipe down components frequently. If your entertainment center has doors, close them when it's not in use to minimize dust.

Cabinetry maker Merillat has even designed a triple-functioning media center that handles a computer station, video game station, and family entertainment station in one super-efficient unit. Then there are slick, conceal-and-reveal entertainment units in which skinny LCD and plasma TVs pop up and swivel out of any number of different types of cabinet consoles.

◀ A multipurpose unit.

Mighty Mounts

Wall-mounted screens are the long-awaited answer for small rooms with limited square footage or an awkward layout. Many older homes that were built before the advent of television fall into this category. Homeowners have long been stymied by radiators that take up valuable floor space. A wall mount is a cleaner and leaner alternative to the standard TV cabinet. For standard tube sets, ceiling or wall platforms can hold your TV on a swivel rack along with a DVD player. No need for any kind of TV stand.

Out of (Remote) Control

A storage-friendly coffee table with drawers or shelves makes the most sense for those items you use the most in the TV room, like coasters, TV listings guides, electronics manuals, spare batteries, and remote controls. Be sure to compartmentalize, or you'll wind up with nothing but a messy junk drawer. Spring-loaded dividers by Dream Drawer Organizer install easily to corral accessories and keeps things in place.

Coffee tables are more versatile than ever. There are even coffee tables on the market with adjustable tops that lift up to seating height and then lock, making them more comfortable to use for snacking or reading. Too many remotes? Replace the ones you've got for your DVD, CD, VCR, cable, and TV with a universal remote, or pick up a remote caddy. If remote controls have a designated place, you're less likely to have to go hunting for them under the couch cushions.

Multiplexed, Not Perplexed

The big problem in home theaters and TV rooms across America is not having the proper storage containers to house a burgeoning collection of video games, CDs, tapes, and DVDs. Shelves, cabinets, baskets, and drawers are all workable solutions, but some are trickier to access than others. Let's say that to put away a Disney movie, your youngster has to put the DVD in its case and then find a place for the case in a closed cabinet—with that many steps, there's a good chance it's just not going to happen. More likely, the disc will be added to an ever-growing stack of movies and music that will wind up overwhelming the room. And that's if the discs don't disappear altogether. There's not much point investing in a high-ticket HD system if you can't find your favorite movies to play.

FACT

Theater seating is a hot home trend. Ergonomically designed loungers with cushy headrests, power footrests, built-in cup holders, and even TV speakers transform the viewing experience. Padding can even absorb sound waves and improve the room's audio quality.

Transfer chunky videotapes onto trim digital formats. It's a huge space saver, and you get enhanced quality to boot. To keep the size of your collection manageable, take a one-in, one-out approach to your movies, games, and music. Trade in or sell off your no-longer-used discs at places like Half.com and Wherehouse.com and put a few dollars back in your pocket. It just takes a few easy steps to turn state-of-the-art into a state of grace.

Chapter 7

Home Sweet Home Office

Remember the famous plaque on Harry Truman's desk in the White House, the one that read "The buck stops here"? If you're like a lot of people, it's also where the piles of paperwork stop. It's easy to get swallowed up in mounds of bills, letters, cards, and sticky notes (not to mention the electronic clutter of computer components). Take control of the white stuff with storage strategies that will help you tame the paper tiger and get you back in business.

Over, Under, and Out

If you look around at the proliferation of office supply stores, you see a clear reflection of the millions of folks with some version of a home office. So who are some of the people behind the desks? Everyone from telecommuters, work-from-home entrepreneurs, and students to those clocking in late-night overtime hours, the chief financial officers of the household, and computer game players.

It's a good guess that what all these people have in common is a big mess and a certain amount of denial. Here are a few of the little white lies we tell ourselves:

- Yes, it's messy, but I know exactly where everything is.
- I can't throw that (fill-in-the-blank) out. I might need it one day.
- I like it messy. It helps me be creative. I can't be productive in a neat environment.

Hmmm. So that's the reason your desk is cluttered with that lucky rock, toothpaste cap, and a Derek Jeter rookie card.

Reclaim Your Calm and Focus

Allison, a home-based graphic artist, says she knows it's time to get tough on paperwork when there's no more desk space left and the piles start moving to the floor. The comedian Bill Maher described his procrastination technique in the *New York Times* magazine this way: "I make piles of things and then move the piles, as if that's addressing the problem. If I put a pile on the desk, that means 'urgent,' but it can sit there for weeks."

Paper management is a learned behavior, not an inherited trait. The problem is that it's never taught. Life runs more efficiently and less stressfully when you become a paper filer instead of a paper piler.

Paper clutter drains our energy and diverts our focus. It's hard to concentrate on the tasks at hand when our peripheral vision is distracted by bank statements, tax forms, reminder notes, and grocery lists. Misha Keefe, president of Misha K, a professional organizing company in Washington, D.C. says paper management—or rather mismanagement—is one of the biggest causes of stress in the home. If there's one thing that makes her phone ring, that's it. People will try organizing their basement or attic on their own, she says, but when it comes to the office, they cry uncle.

Consider Your Office Needs

Getting your office under control starts with a question: How should your workspace be configured to serve and support what you do? Before you even think about storage and organization, think about how you use your office. Do you require a big, clear surface for working on projects, paying bills, or writing letters, for instance? Or are you a digital stalwart who rarely picks up a pen and pad anymore? If it's the latter, you might not need lots of surface area to work on, but what about all the electronic wizardry your lifestyle demands? So many home offices are designed catch-as-catch-can with a ragtag assembly of tables, confiscated from other rooms of the house. The fax machine is on a folding snack table. The scanner is sitting on the carton it came in.

▲ A desk, before.

A home office might be one area of the house that repurposed furniture is less than optimal. It can hamper efficiency and productivity; plus, bad furniture could be harmful to your health! An uncomfortable chair or a desk that's not properly positioned for a keyboard and mouse could wind up being a royal pain in the neck—and in the wrist. Carpal tunnel syndrome, eyestrain, and headaches are common complaints and yet another illustration of the relationship between good organization and good health.

Broken Records

To determine what storage capabilities you actually need, get rid of the dead weight that's been fattening up drawers, files, and shelves. Even people who pride themselves on their proficiency in filing every record in its rightful folder rarely revisit those files down the road. As a result, filing cabinets and drawers turn into one-way streets of document excess and distress.

Janis, from Wyoming, always considered herself an organized individual—until, that is, she found herself having to set up an office at home. Now, after two years, she finds herself in a tailspin, overwhelmed by clutter problems, an inefficient filing system, and the wrong kinds of storage accessories. Her in-box is a mess, and her to-do list is out of control. The rest of her house is neat as a pin, but the chaos in her office weighs heavily on her productivity—and her sanity.

QUESTION?

How can I decrease the volume of junk mail being delivered to my home?
Junk mail is an ongoing source of irritation for most consumers and a major contributor to paper pileups in the home. Have your name removed from certain mailing lists by signing up online, at *www .dmaconsumers.org*, or by writing to Direct Marketing Association Mail Preference Service, P.O. Box 643, Carmel, NY 15012.

There's no getting around it. Clearing the clutter starts with a big-time purge session. In the office, don't just focus on the piles on the floor and around your desk. Empty out your drawers, vacate your cabinets, and gut your folders. Depending on the state of the office and how long it's been since you last gave it a thorough going-over, plan to allot anywhere from four to twenty hours for the cleanup. Need some encouragement? Pick a clutter buddy who will keep you focused.

▲ A desk, after.

Divide and Conquer

For the purge session, arm yourself with file folders, markers, a few cartons for sorting, and a cache of big trash bags. Mark the first carton ACTION. Go through your paperwork, and put each slip of paper in your ACTION carton if it represents any of the following:

- A pending project
- An ongoing project
- A specific issue that requires your attention

Filling out the rebate form for the scanner you just bought or completing the application for the bank certificate of deposit you've wanted to open for a while are good candidates for your action file.

Mark another carton for FILING. These are the documents you need to save but don't necessarily need to act on. Among other things, they include these:

- Credit card statements
- Bank statements
- Cancelled checks
- Tax receipts
- Health care records
- Insurance forms

Here's where we run into the number-one clutter problem. Everyone's got files, but most people don't have a proper filing system. The one they have is outdated, underutilized, and therefore ineffective. Creating a manageable filing system is the single best thing you can do to control papers. It doesn't have to be complicated. In fact, the simpler it is, the better. Organizing authority Ariane Benefit says a lot of her clients "complexify." They create Byzantine systems with too many subcategories and then have a hard time remembering where anything is.

If you start overcomplicating your system, rather than going with a plan that's intuitive and easy to follow, you'll wind up tripping yourself up. One method is to set up files by main categories, such as Home, Automotive, Finance, Health, Insurance, and so on. You can create one file for each topic and then subdivide as needed. One automotive file might be enough for, say, maintenance records, but owning several cars might warrant a separate file for each vehicle. Try not to create too many, though. It's easier to go through twenty files than 200 when you're searching for something. For easier identification, it's helpful to code your files by using colored folders or labels. All health-related folders could be blue, for example, with bank statements red, investment documents yellow, and so on.

Another method is using a straightforward A–Z filing system. There's no one-size-fits-all way. Neither are there one-size-fits-all folders. Match the folder to fill the need. Some papers are better off in see-through folders, others, like thicker documents, in expandable portfolios. Pendaflex, a major manufacturer of office products, offers solutions and lots of sympathy at its free I Hate Filing Club, online at *www.pendaflex.com.*

Before you put anything in the to-be-filed carton, make sure you've got a reason to keep it. Conquer your fear of letting go. There's virtually no chance you'll ever need those Christmas gift receipts from three years ago. There's even less chance that you'll need that cable TV bill from 1994.

And then there's the matter of unnecessary layers of backup. You're saving your electric utility statement, plus you've still got your cancelled checks? Ask yourself why, especially considering how unlikely it is that you'll ever need proof of payment in the first place. Instead of saving it now only to deal with it later, get into the mindset of assuming that incoming papers are disposable, unless there's a good reason to think otherwise.

Piles of Files

If you have old magazines you still haven't gotten around to perusing, rip out the articles that interest you and put them in a separate, labeled folder for future reading. The near future. It's better than stockpiling entire issues. If there's a recipe that catches your eye in a cooking magazine, save it, not the entire publication. Hospitals, senior centers, and gyms are some great places to which to donate your magazines. Before donating or discarding, though, be sure to rip personal address information off the front cover for security reasons.

On the other hand, there are those who are habitual rippers. You know, the kind of person who's always tearing out newspaper articles. According to experts, newspapers are considered to be the material of choice for obsessive hoarders. One ninety-five-year-old woman yanked stories from the paper every single day with the best of intentions of reading them later on. She never did. The articles just piled up. Not only did they turn brown with age and become terribly outdated, but they practically took up more space in her little home office than the petite great-grandmother herself. If you have the scan-now, read-later mentality, don't let articles accumulate more than a week.

And all those sticky notes? America loves them but, boy, can they get out of hand. One little yellow reminder is fine. A furry wall of them? Uh-uh. For an inkling of how far they've crept into our culture: There's one artist who has created a sculpture out of the sticky stuff, which is probably not too far a cry from some home offices.

QUESTION?

How can I protect myself from identity theft?
The Internal Revenue Service recommends reducing the risk of identity theft by keeping your Social Security card in a secure place. Don't carry it around with you. And only give out your number when absolutely necessary.

What to Keep

Some documents are definite keepers. You should retain your tax records for seven years in case you're ever audited. ATM and bank statements, though, can be tossed as soon as you've noted the amounts in your records and reconciled the information with your accounts.

Make it a point to keep only the documents you need in your office space and only the current year's files. Box up any receipts, statements, or miscellaneous paperwork older than that and put it in long-term storage, perhaps the basement, attic, or a hall closet. Exceptions to the rule are medical files, veterinarian records, and car repair records. It's a good idea to keep those relatively handy, even if they're a few years old, for reference.

Go through your files once a year to determine what you still need to hold on to, what you can purge, and what you can move to long-term storage in another location. Not just your papers, either—review your address book and Rolodex, too, to keep it current.

Some individuals find that having a family journal that can be stored on a shelf is the most convenient option for frequently used information or medical records. For a reference journal, use a three-ring binder with color-coated tabs for emergency contacts, frequently dialed numbers, take-out menus, mainstay recipes—the information you use on a regular basis. For a health journal, create tabs for prescriptions, physician contacts, and medical history.

What to Cut Out

Even certain reference materials can be pared down. You may not need to store a bulky information packet when a fact sheet or business card will do. Better still, you can usually find the latest and greatest information online at a given company's Web site, including operating instructions and technical assistance for computer components. Are telephone books taking up too much space? Access phone information online instead.

Cut down on paperwork, and save yourself the price of a stamp. Virtually all banks now offer online bill payment services, some at no cost. They also make it effortless for you to transfer funds from one account to another or open up new ones. Credit card companies and utilities are also getting in on the paperless act by allowing you to get bills by e-mail.

Mail Call

Mail pileup is a clutter abettor. Unopened mail goes from mailbox to desktop, and then straight up and up. Dealing with the day's mail doesn't mean stopping everything to pay the bills or responding to an invitation or an offer. It just means quickly categorizing it all so the important stuff is prioritized and the junk mail is junked. Sort your mail over a trash can so unwanted correspondence is instantly gone. Aim for the touch-it-once approach. Read it, sort it, or discard it. Be sure to rip up or shred unwanted credit card offers and anything else that has personal data. You may want to invest in a paper shredder for extra protection from your confidential papers getting into the wrong hands. However, if after your home office purge you have hundreds, or possibly thousands, of documents that need to be destroyed, professional paper shredding services are available that can handle the task for you far more efficiently.

FACT

Identity theft affects approximately 10 million Americans each year and totals more than $50 billion. The Federal Trade Commission works on consumers' behalf to stop fraud, deception, and unfair business practices. Complaints can be filed by phoning the agency toll-free at 1-877-FTC-HELP or online using the complaint form at *www.ftc.gov.*

Keep all your mail supplies together in one central place, including stamps, envelopes, and notepaper. Date-stamped bill-paying organizers are a good way to help you keep track of due dates. Look for models with a drawer to hold pens and stamps. If you prefer paying your bills in one fell swoop rather than as they come in, pick a specific day, such as payday or the first of the month. You'll have less chance of losing track and sending in payments late if you carve out a designated date.

Table Talk

Now that your piles have gone on a crash diet, it's time to figure out where the remaining papers go. Desks have evolved from simple writing tables to storehouses for highly complex electronic equipment. Take a long hard look at your desk and determine whether it functions for you. If not, you should consider changing it for a more practical desk or slimmed-down computer system. A laptop or standard desktop computer with a flat-screen monitor will make a dramatic difference in tabletop territory. Prices continue to come down, so if you thought one of these options wasn't in your budget, it might be time to check again.

If a new computer isn't in your future, however, look for a desk that has a CPU holder. Too many people keep their processors on the desk; that's a clumsy way to work. Slide-out keyboard drawers and pullout shelves for printers and scanners keep home offices from looking like a high-tech stockroom. For big-time consolidation, all-in-one devices that scan, fax, and copy make the most sense for all but the biggest spaces.

Consider installing more electrical outlets if it will result in better, more efficient placement of your components. Code your computer cables with colored ties for reference. That way, if you need to disassemble your computer or move your equipment, you'll know exactly where every cable goes.

Today, there are more ways than ever to customize your desk. A simple tabletop can be placed over a pair of file cabinets and then augmented with a hutch to suit your storage requirements.

Armoires-cum-desks are a slick way to stow and hide a monitor, processor, and printer. But don't think because you have the ability to close the doors that you'll necessarily hide the mess. One television producer sadly admits she hasn't closed her armoire doors in the five years she's owned it. Why? Because every hinge is blocked by a stack of papers.

ALERT!

Make sure all your electrical components are protected by using a surge protector. It'll prevent damage to your equipment during a storm or voltage surge. Also take a look to see if your electrical outlets are ample for your needs. You might want to add outlets in other areas of the room to better suit your furniture scheme and hide the knot of electrical cords.

If two people are sharing one office, there's no need to get two desks. An antique partners desk is an option for tight quarters. It's an oversize desk with drawers on two sides, enabling a pair of individuals to work simultaneously, facing each other.

Don't scrimp on desk-drawer organizers for pens, clips, and the supplies you use most often. They belong to the list of little, inexpensive storage accessories that will keep you on the straight and narrow and prevent desk drawers from turning into tangled messes.

Hutches and Cabinets

A stand-alone hutch, if space allows, or an enclosed shelf unit above the desk is a wonderful way to hide extra office supplies, stationery, and CDs. Store loose items in baskets or inexpensive see-through boxes, segregating them by category. For open shelves, pay a little more attention to style. It's not an inconsequential matter. You want to feel good about your workspace. Positive energy equals a productive work environment. You can find a great selection of trendy-to-sophisticated accessories, no matter what your budget, at storage specialty shops and department stores. Keeping showcased storage accessories uniform will give your office a finished look.

As a rule, keep the items you use most often closest to you.

Mobile file cabinets are useful when you need them at your desk. Just roll them into a closet when you're done for the day. Lightweight plastic file drawers are easy on the budget. Ottomans and benches with hidden storage capacity preclude the need for additional seating. Remember, congestion is the enemy.

ESSENTIAL

Carpal tunnel syndrome affects thousands of Americans. The American Academy of Orthopedic Surgeons recommends choosing a mouse that allows you to work with an opened relaxed hand posture. Try to keep the mouse close to the keyboard, not out to the side of the desk. Don't use a wrist rest. It actually increases the pressure inside the carpal tunnel. Also, get in the habit of taking short but frequent breaks from the keyboard.

If you've commandeered a spare bedroom, you may want to yank out the wardrobe rod in the closet and reconfigure the space with shelves for bulky binders, reams of paper, and computer accessories. If books are more

CHAPTER 7: HOME SWEET HOME OFFICE

than a match for you, consider taking the door off a small, reach-in closet and converting it into a recessed bookcase.

Fitting In

Don't sweat the small stuff. Find clever places for it instead. Roll up maps, posters, and unframed prints and store them in a tall basket, oversize urn, or an umbrella stand.

Multipocket wall organizers take the "dis" out of disorder by giving office supplies a home of their own. Expandable wall-mounted CD holders grow with your collection. Mesh baskets that hook onto the edge of the desk will help you keep those mail-order catalogs off the floor. No tools required. And here's an important reminder: Anything that doesn't belong in your home office—that doesn't further your work goals or enhance your productivity—needs to go.

Book Smarts

For many people, books are difficult, if not impossible, to part with. When it comes to book collections, what goes on the bookshelf stays on the bookshelf—even if there are five reference books on the same topic and they're all out of date. We personalize them, sentimentalize them, and rationalize holding onto them. Take the case of one retiree, a voracious reader who gobbles up bestsellers at the rate of three or more a week. When she moved to a new part of town, she had no problem disposing of her knickknacks, old furniture, and excess clothing, but every last one of her books came along with her. Was she going to read any one of them again? Not likely.

FACT

Books require a little TLC. They're susceptible to mold in high humidity conditions and don't take well to the effects of direct sunlight. For longevity, stack volumes loosely so that air circulates, use bookends to prevent warping, and handle them gently. Rather than yanking a book by the top of its spine, push the two books on either side away and then grab the book around the middle of the spine.

Look hard and objectively at your book collection. If you don't read them, weed them. Libraries, schools, recreation centers, and hospitals will have a field day with your donations. Another option? Try bookcrossing. Bookcrossing.com is a free book-tracking Web site that encourages lovers of the written word to "read and release" their books by strategically placing them in public places like building lobbies, park benches, and airports for others to find, take, and enjoy.

What remains in your library should be only relevant and up-to-date reference manuals, books you definitely intend to read or reread, and those volumes with sentimental or collectible value, like a first edition or an author-signed copy. No need to go Dewey decimal on your books, but you might want to classify them either by topic or alphabetically by title, depending how you use them. Try to keep books lined up in size order. It helps prevent warping.

Letter Perfect

Keep important documents in a secure lockbox, such as a fireproof home safe. These are the hard-to-replace items you don't necessarily need to access on a regular basis. Among them are the following:

- Wills
- Title to your vehicles
- Stock and bond certificates
- Home and life insurance policies
- Contracts
- Passports
- Marriage license
- Social security cards
- Birth certificates

Having them all together in one grab-and-go box is a sensible precaution should you ever need to leave your home in an emergency. Alternatively, you might want to consider renting a safety deposit box at your local bank.

Papers with sentimental value—those important documents, cards, and letters you want to preserve for the long haul—should be stored in archival-quality boxes or wrapped in acid-free tissue instead of in standard folders. Paper is brittle and has a finite lifespan. It breaks down over time. Heat and humidity hasten the deterioration. Even everyday handling can harm it. You'll keep the decay at bay longer if you employ protective measures—more about that in Chapter 15.

Reserve a box or special envelope exclusively to hold all invitations you receive and/or tickets for airline flights, sporting events, concerts, or shows. When the date arrives, you won't waste time checking every drawer in the house wondering where you left them.

Digitize to Downsize

The best way to cut down on paperwork is to digitize it. Scan it and discard the original, whenever possible. A 100 percent paperless work environment might not be a realistic goal—at least not yet—but thinking in bits and bytes means less maintenance and easier document access. Of course, you'll need a system to back up your files, music, and pictures. A number of options are available, from external ZIP disc drives and data sticks or cards, to CDs and DVDs, to Web-based file storage programs.

At the speedy pace of technological advancements, you'll need to keep tabs on the latest platforms. If you used to back up onto floppy discs, for instance, you remember having to make the change to CDs or DVDs when you found that your next computer would not have a floppy disc drive. The solution, however, is not to keep your old equipment around to access isolated files. The answer is to transfer them from old platforms to newer, more efficient ones.

When saving files on a CD or DVD, make sure the discs are clearly labeled and placed in a plastic jewel case. Discs are best stored in a cool, dark place. Stick with high-quality brand-name CDs. If a CD becomes scratched, it can become unusable. One more thing: Avoid backing up crucial information on a rewritable CD. If you do, you might unwittingly use that same CD for another application and accidentally rewrite over your data.

Writer Moira Allen first created an archival system to back up her tax records. It's a smart idea as protection from a home emergency or disaster, but Moira had another motivation in mind. She moved nine times over the course of twenty years and was looking for any means to lighten her load. After the tax returns, she backed up all her important personal documents. Keep in mind that scanned copies of business receipts and tax records are acceptable by the Internal Revenue Service. On the other hand, scanned birth certificates, passports, deeds, marriage licenses, and the like are not considered valid documents. It still makes sense to digitize them. A scanned copy will contain all the information you need should you ever have to replace the originals.

When you're ready to upgrade your computer, avoid having your old unit wind up in a landfill. It's becoming one of the nation's fastest-growing environmental concerns. Many computer manufacturers will accept computers for recycling for a nominal fee or, sometimes, free of charge. Schools, charities, and even some prisons will accept donations of no-longer-used computers and electronics.

While you're at it, declutter your computer's hard drive, too, by defragging. Over time, files get scattered around your hard drive, causing your computer to work twice as hard to access them. By running the disc defragmenter software utility, you're simply organizing all your files in way that makes it easier for the computer to locate them. If you're the type of person who installs and uninstalls programs frequently, you should defrag every couple of weeks. Otherwise, once a month is good enough. You should see a noticeable boost in speed.

Want to cut down on all the little notes and long lists you leave for yourself to remind you about birthdays, meetings, and events? Try some of the free online date-book tools, like AOL's Remind Me, Yahoo! Calendar, and HappyBirthday.com, and you'll never have to apologize for your bad memory again.

Virtual Reality

Not everyone has the luxury of siphoning off a spare bedroom for a home office or building a home with a dedicated workspace. But even those who are a little tighter on space still have plenty of options. More and more people are creating virtual offices with nothing but a laptop computer and wireless Internet capabilities. Their "offices" are back porches, park benches, coffee shops, and sandy beaches. Yet even the most mobile need some dedicated space for record keeping, space that can often be found in bedroom alcoves, kitchen corners, basements, and dens. In fact, just about any place will work, as long as it can fit a desk or cabinet. Otherwise, paperwork gets lost, bills go unpaid, and the next thing you know, a little disorganization results in a big fat late-fee penalty from your credit card company.

If this describes your ersatz office situation, be careful how you use your limited desk area. Otherwise, pristine kitchens and bedrooms can wind up looking cluttered in a hurry. Keep paperwork to a minimum. Limit the space to a computer and a few staple supplies. Banish filing cabinets to another location of the house. If you have wall space above the desk, use it for a stylish shelf unit. Give family members an in/out box so each person can be responsible for his or her own papers. One resourceful mom gives each of her four children a three-ring binder to hold important school papers, notices, and schedules.

How Suite It Is

Thanks to the computer, today's home offices have the technological horsepower of corporate headquarters. Yet the workspace that surrounds the PC is filled with lots of old-fashioned clutter.

When a home office gets to a certain sorry state, the very idea of tackling the mess can be overwhelming. So many people simply don't know where to begin. Yes, it's a bit tedious and certainly time-consuming when you consider that each slip of paper has to be looked at and dealt with. How tempting it is to just add another piece of paper onto the pile when other duties call. But once you plow through the task and actually start seeing the color of your carpet again, your only regret will be not having done it sooner. One woman, in fact, described herself as "exhilarated" after the hard work was done.

Even after you've put a filing system in place, you're not off the hook just yet. Keep in mind that organization is an ongoing process. Once you have your system up and running, keep up with it. Ongoing maintenance, just a few minutes a day, is the answer to avoiding a relapse of the paper chokehold. Put things where they belong as soon as you're done with them. Exorcising files from folders from time to time is the perfect exercise for multitaskers. When you're watching TV or waiting for the water in the teapot to boil, grab some folders and pore through them, weeding out old documents or moving them to long-term storage elsewhere in your home. The time you devote to office organization today, even ten minutes a day, is an investment toward the hours you'll spend tomorrow.

Chapter 8

Child's Play: Playrooms

Playroom or junk room? The key is to create a kid-friendly workspace that's childproof when necessary and organized always. Mission impossible? Not necessarily. For games, toys, stuffed animals, supplies, and management of big, messy craft projects, read on for creative ideas you can deploy quickly and inexpensively.

8

Toy Stories

A playroom? You may be thinking your whole house is one big playroom. There are toys in the living room, board games in the basement, and stuffed animals on the stairs. Oh, and is that last night's science experiment on the kitchen table?

According to the Toy Industry Association, toys are a $20 billion annual business, making it larger than the video game, domestic motion-picture box office, and music industries. If you're like most parents, there may be days when you feel as though you're single-handedly responsible for keeping those toy companies afloat.

FACT

Toy industry analysts point to a trend known in the business as KGOY. It stands for "kids getting older younger." It's a theory that says kids are not only becoming increasingly more sophisticated in their use of technology, they're consuming more mature entertainment at younger and younger ages.

Having too many toys is one problem, and having too many pieces is another. A big frustration, says one exhausted mom, is that something is missing from every toy and game in her house. Pull out a Barbie doll, and she's got just one shoe. Play Scrabble, and the Z is missing. Puzzle pieces go AWOL and are never seen again. If your home doesn't have a dedicated playroom, every room becomes a playroom, and the entire house suffers. Suddenly, you feel like your nice adult habitat has been taken over by little squatters—who happen to have *big* sprawling needs. It's time to regain control.

To begin, you need to carve out a space and give the kids a home of their own. If you have a spare room in the house, great. Otherwise, think about the best spot to dedicate to a play area. Of course, that doesn't mean there won't be spillover. Kids are kids, after all. They have a tendency to spread out their toys in different rooms and leave them there. However, giving them their own place bestows a sense of ownership and permanence. It lets them know there's a place where their things belong. One family tried by dedicating a sunporch to their two daughters, but the quantity of toys got so out of hand they took up the entire room. The kids actually needed to find another room in which to play.

ALERT!

Kids love stuffed animals, but according to the *Green Guide*, the newsletter covering health and environmental issues, the cottons, synthetics, and wools used in the stuffing may contain insecticide residue and dyes, which can be carcinogenic. Toys using organic, toxic-free materials are available from a growing number of companies, including Organic Gift Shop (*www.organicgiftshop.com*) and Mama's Earth (*www .mamasearth.com*).

Here are a few possibilities for play areas:

- Basement
- Den
- Enclosed porch
- Finished attic
- Great room
- Guest bedroom

Any of these rooms can be zoned off as play areas, even if it's just a chunky, oversize corner. The trick is to make sure the area is clearly delineated. Be inventive. You can use paint, drapes, a piece of furniture, or decorative screen panels to mark the territory, or even be whimsical by using beaded curtains or a hammock filled with stuffed animals to define the space.

Don't underestimate the power of a well-decorated room to create an environment in which your children will want to work, play, and dream. A wall dominated with a blackboard or bulletin board can become an ever-evolving backdrop that reflects your child's changing tastes, hobbies, interests, and creativity.

Now, before you move all the old toys over to the new play space, give them a good looking-over. If your child has more toys than Santa's workshop, you've got your work cut out for you. The hardest part is going through all the little pieces associated with so many games. No one has to tell you how maddening it can be to match parts without mixing them all up. If you start feeling overwhelmed, take the task in small doses, a couple of hours at a time, suggests organizing expert Heidi Gaumet. But if you tackle it that way, make sure you separate out what's already been organized so you don't wind up duplicating efforts.

Keep these details in mind as you do your sorting:

- Relocate games your child isn't old enough to play with to a long-term storage area such as a basement, attic, or closet.
- Separate the toys you want to save for sentimental reasons, and store them elsewhere in a special container or chest.
- Discard all games with missing pieces, stuffed animals that have seen better days, and toys no longer in working order.
- Throw out any books with torn, tattered, or chocolate-smeared pages.
- Donate items your child has outgrown, has multiples of, or has lost interest in.

Put a limit on saving items that have sentimental value. Oddly enough, it's the parents—not the kids—who are often reluctant to get rid of old toys. One mom still saves the storybooks she read to her son when he was a toddler, even though he's preparing for college. That same mom didn't keep such a good eye on a cherished heirloom rocking horse, though. It was accidentally donated to a neighbor, and the disappointed mom wound up having to buy it back a year later for $25 at the neighbor's garage sale.

QUESTION?

What's the best way to preserve toys that have sentimental value?
You can create a memory box to hold special items and turn the production of the box into a family project at the same time. Visit your local crafts store and pick up a plain wooden box. Then use your imagination to decorate it with family photos and personal objects so that both the box and its contents can be family heirlooms.

If any items are brand new and still in their original packaging, donate them to a local children's hospital or save them for a holiday toy drive.

If you're on the fence about whether to give away something your youngster might want down the road, you can always pack it up and put it in storage temporarily. Wait about six months, and if your child hasn't asked for it, feel free to give it away.

Toys R Everywhere

Should you or shouldn't you? Let your child become involved in the weeding and sorting process, that is. The answer is a definitive maybe. You might have a clear idea about which playthings your child is using, but she might not be ready to part with any of them. Avoid putting yourself in a situation in which a sorting session can degenerate into tears and tantrums—and not necessarily your child's. Purging and organizing can be stressful enough. What's more, you and your child are likely to have different concerns. You're more focused on issues of safety and neatness. Your little one has one desire: to get at the goods.

On the other hand, if you think your child is mature enough to be part of the decision-making process, it could be a great way to introduce him to a lifelong lesson in personal organization. Incorporate him in the process, and he'll be more motivated to keep it up. It'll also show him you respect his space and belongings. Figuring out the right age isn't an exact science. Try it, but be patient. The tools you employ in the playroom might be a bit overwhelming for a young mind.

Misha Keefe, professional organizer, recommends thinking in thirds. When it comes to toys, keep a third, purge a third, and store a third. Then every few months, take out those stored toys and put them in rotation. Your child will feel like she's getting new toys on a regular basis.

As you start moving items into place, break down the area into three separate zones: one for play; another for creative ventures like art, crafts, and science projects; and a third reserved for quiet study, homework, and reading. The zones don't have to be elaborate to be functional. Keep in mind that clutter affects children as well as adults. It's distracting and stressful. The trouble is, kids can't articulate their response to a messy environment, so it's up to you to be aware.

Like father, like son; like mother, like daughter—your kids will follow your cues when it comes to organization. If the rest of the rooms in your home are cluttered and your tabletops are stacked high with messy piles, chances are your children are going to pick up your bad habits and follow suit. If you set an example, you'll have an easier time helping them keep their playrooms neat and tidy.

Changing Times

Storage requirements change from year to year as kids grow. A toddler's needs and interests are different from a kindergartener's. Fast-forward a few years, and that same youngster is now a teen whose room might very well be overwhelmed with schoolbooks, trophies, sports gear, and instruments. Keep it simple. Straightforward solutions are the easiest for kids to follow at any age. Take advantage of vertical space, but you might want to consider a youngster's perspective and arrange items in the room at a lower level than you would for adults.

There are a few storage solutions that cut across all ages. Baskets, for instance, are stylish, multifunctional, and available in a wide range of sizes to fit all needs. Never mind the lids. Open baskets make it easier to see what's inside, and lids wind up adding to the clutter. Sturdiness is always the name of the game. Make sure your containers are up for the punishment kids have to give them. Anything tippy or wobbly has to go. See-through bins will help a child spend less time hunting and more time playing and creating. Repurpose plastic shoe boxes for Barbie dolls, action figures, and model kit parts.

If there's one area ripe for innovation, this is it. Not long ago, Tupperware held its first ever Global Design contest. Entrants from the United States, Latin America, Europe, Asia, and the Middle East produced artistic and functional products out of Tupperware. One of the winners, a Tupperware saleswoman from Brazil, took a top-selling bowl and created a clown-shaped toy trunk out of it to hold toys, games, and crayons. The clown trunk was even displayed in a special exhibition at an art gallery in Manhattan.

The U.S. Consumer Product Safety Commission is charged with protecting the public from risks of serious injury or death from thousands of types of consumer products. To find out if a toy or children's product has been recalled, visit *www.cpsc.gov*. It's a good idea to keep this site on your list of Web-site favorites.

High-placed shelves are an attractive way to keep fragile items out of harm's way while giving special items like precious collectibles, awards, toy models, and even beloved stuffed animals the spotlight they deserve.

Can't control the stuffed animal population? Plush toy "zoos" are ideal solutions. Flexible bars allow kids to move their favorites in and out, and yet the collection is neatly contained in a fanciful cage.

Throw a decorative swatch of material over a worktable, and you'll have a hidden storage area underneath.

Is there a closet in the room you can co-opt? You might want to forgo the hangers and install adjustable shelving instead. Hang a shoe organizer with multiple clear pockets over the closet door, and you've got lots of pouch-size homes for everything from hair clips to vacation souvenirs.

Lots of board games come in oversize packaging that uses up unnecessary storage space. Shrink games down to size by removing the plastic, foam, cardboard inserts, and superfluous boxes. Then store game parts in small see-through stackable bins or zip-close bags.

Plan intuitively by remembering to store items closest to their points of usage. Paper, books, and stationery supplies should be near the work desk; art supplies go by the crafts table; puzzles and board games by the game table. That'll make it easier for kids to put things back where they belong when they're done. Is there a would-be Picasso in the family? Instead of burying her works of art in drawers, hang a clothesline to display them for an instant art gallery and a giant splash of color.

If you have more than one child sharing the playroom, use color-coded containers to help them find their own toys more easily and nip squabbling in the bud. You can also assign a wall per child so that each one has shelves, bins, and cabinets suited especially for him.

Age-Old Issues

For older, more independent children, nail a few hooks in the wall and hang drawstring mesh bags to hold sports equipment and bulky items like stuffed animals and pillows. It's a quick solution to getting clutter off the floor. Storage benches will do, too, but avoid turning them into giant catch-alls. It's easy to create a situation in which items are tossed into a chest, fall to the bottom, and are never seen again.

If your playroom has a bookcase, make sure books are stacked on lower shelves for easy reach. For more versatility, stackable cubbies can store books and toys. Game tables, especially built for board games and puzzles, come with drawers to keep all the pieces handy.

Use small baskets or modular boxes for CDs, DVDS, art supplies, note cards, and crafts. Tackle boxes, tool chests with multiple drawers, even zip-close bags are practical for small items.

For an open-and-shut case, use a flip-top box, like a cigar box. They're perfect for pens and markers. Old stationery boxes with plastic lids are also useful for small collections.

Childproof your playroom. Cover unused electrical outlets to head off the possibility of electrical shocks. Use child-safe locks on cabinets, where appropriate. Scan the room to make sure there are no sharp corners to endanger little ones. And tie up cords from window blinds to prevent strangulation hazards. Never hang mirrors above a crib or bed or too close to a play area.

Mobile carts with drawers and pull-out bins allow kids to be productive and tidy in their work. They can just roll the cart back in a closet or corner when they're done. And don't forget about easy-to-implement aids like Lazy Susans to bring squirreled-away items back in reach.

Think Small

What age, stage, and even what size your child is will determine how her playthings should be organized. For the preschool crowd, take the height and weight of objects into consideration when giving kids access to their things. Realize, too, that storage is a moving target. The height of shelves and storage bins this year may need to be adjusted before you know it. Storage is impractical, even counterproductive, when it doesn't fit a youngster's needs. Kids don't play with toys they can't see or reach. If you stack toys too high, they're liable to become dust collectors. Or worse: They'll become temptations. The last thing you want is your child climbing chairs, furniture, or windowsills to get at something enticing.

FACT

The popularity of some toys never wanes. Classic toys that are still on the market more than a century after they were created include Parcheesi, Lionel Trains, teddy bears, Crayola Crayons, and the Model T Ford, the first die-cast toy car. Parcheesi, by Milton Bradley, was first introduced in 1867.

To guard against a potential choking hazard situation, keep toys and games with small parts off limits unless there's adult supervision. These items should be stowed in closets on high shelves or in cabinets with child locks. Toy chests aren't always a good idea at this age, either. A heavy lid can gobble up tiny fingers.

All storage units should be clearly marked. Use identifiers that young children can easily understand. If they're too young to read labels, employ a color-coding system. Try red bins, for instance, for dolls; blue for puzzles.

Better still, create a label for each container with a picture of the item. Over-complicate your organizational system, and you'll have a system destined to stall.

Fun and Games

The core issue when it comes to playroom clutter, like other rooms in the house, is overconsumption. Get a handle on that, and you're on your way to streamlined bliss. A surefire way to maintain the momentum is to recycle toys on a regular basis. Your child outgrows toys as quickly as he outgrows clothes. Teach him to let go. Donate items or discard them, but don't let them loiter. Otherwise, the stockpiles will just continue to grow.

Stick with the basic principles of matching the storage unit to the task as well as your child's abilities. Keep up with an easy-to-master labeling system, use easy-access storage containers, make sure things are put away on a daily basis, and you'll have a proper playroom—and your tidy home back, too. The other big benefit to getting your clutter under control is the lesson you teach your kids and the good habits you instill. As with all organizational skills, if you teach children at a young age, they'll reap the benefits into adulthood.

Chapter 9

Sub-Floor Décor: Basements

The basement just may be the most unstructured, do-what-you-will-with-it room in the house. It can be the family center, gym, hobby room, office, or party place. And it could be all of the above. It could also be the dark dungeon you dread to enter. Whatever the case, finished or unfinished, chances are it's one of your home's prime storage areas. Learn how to make the best use of that utilitarian space with a host of surefire ways to keep the boxes and junk at bay.

Down in the Dumps

When people talk about being down in the dumps, they could be referring to their basements, also known as the dumping ground. If you've got a case of subterranean blues, it could be because you've taken an out-of-sight, out-of-mind approach to clearing out the clutter. You move stuff down, but never out. And out—by the curb, that is—is probably where a lot of it belongs. Some of the tidiest homes have the untidiest underbellies lurking beneath their floorboards. Like closets, basements are an easy place to let things get out of hand. Company's coming, so downstairs the clutter goes. The trouble is, it never comes back up to be returned to its proper places. The clutter just builds and builds and builds . . .

ESSENTIAL

Make it easy to part with your outgrown or rarely worn clothes. Leave a "charity" bag right by your laundry area. That way when an unwanted item comes out of the washer or dryer, it goes right into the bag, making it one step closer to finding a more deserving home. When the bag's full, it's time to call your favorite charity for a pickup.

Do any of these scenarios describe the situation in your basement?

- You moved into your new home, stored some cartons down there to get them out of the way "for the time being," and then—oops!—never looked back.
- Your son, sister, cousin, or uncle left some items down there for safekeeping—years ago. Now the area's become a multigenerational chest, not of treasures but of outgrown, worn-out, and long-forgotten belongings.
- Your basement has become the land of backups. You've got your pre-Y2K computer, first-generation scanner, sparks-ridden toaster oven, and dishes that no longer match your kitchen décor packed down there—just in case you ever need them.

- You never met an empty carton you didn't like, or least one you didn't want to hold on to. After all, you never know when you'll need to crate up that bulky piece of electronics or appliance again . . . right?
- Your basement is a tangled heap of Valentine's Day, Easter, Independence Day, Halloween, or Christmas decorations. You can't get up the energy to organize any of it, let alone actually put them on display.

And that's assuming you even know what's down there at all. More often than not, items are packed in newspaper and then socked away in unmarked boxes. Or worse. One unfortunate homeowner put out an SOS after a dreadful discovery. The home she moved into had an old, unplugged freezer in the basement. She assumed the freezer was empty and never bothered to open it. When it was time to install a new furnace, the old unit had to be moved. It was only then that the hapless homeowner opened the freezer for the very first time to discover it was filled with eight-year-old rotted meat. What will you unearth in your basement? Isn't it time you took a good look at what you've got down there?

More than the clutter that plagues any other room in the house, basement clutter can go on for years before you finally reach the "I've had it" stage. In fact, it can go for decades if you live in one place long enough. Even when people get up the motivation to reorganize their homes, the basement is the place most of them save for last when it comes to a streamlining overhaul. The turning point often comes when it's time to move elsewhere or when you start thinking about reworking the space for another use, such as converting it into a family room or home gym. Then you're left to face the music. Don't wait. Now's the time to give your dead storage a little CPR and let the space work to your advantage.

FACT

Among the different types of basements, poured concrete is the most popular. Other types are masonry walls that are made out of blocks and sealed to prevent seepage and precast panel basements in which concrete panels are poured at the factory, transported to the site, and then lifted into place with a crane.

Getting Started

The first thing you need to do is to give yourself some elbow room to work. Scan the room and set your priorities on eliminating the most obvious, aisle-jamming items: the old ice skates, the large picture frame with the cracked glass you've been meaning to replace, the ancient air conditioner you trip over at every turn. Moving them to the side to create aisles isn't good enough. Getting rid of things is the name of the game.

The basement is typically reserved for big bulky items. For that reason, when you're ready to start sorting, it often makes sense to relegate those things into piles rather than bother with cartons or trash bags. Let one area be for your keepers. You're likely to find a lot of sentimental favorites down there—photos, stuffed animals, even family heirlooms.

Weeding Out

Depending on the item, you may need to move these to more appropriate public spaces where you can actually enjoy them—but not just yet. If you stop what you're doing to relocate items to other rooms of the house, you'll get distracted from the task at hand and never finish the job.

Clear another section for your giveaways. If you're planning to hold some for, say, a future garage sale, put those items all together in one area and clearly label them so that the only other time you'll need to go through the collection again is the day of the actual sale. Your final pile is for your throwaways. Be sure to get rid of anything that's been damaged by humidity or pests. Now is also the time to dump anything that's obsolete, rusty, or not in working order. Lose the ceiling fan with the broken blade, the dot-matrix printer, and the coffee table with the bum leg. You probably have a few old cans of paint, varnish, and dried-up stucco there, too. Dispose of them, but make sure you do it in accordance with your local regulations. If your throwaways seem intimidatingly large and heavy because you've allowed the situation to degenerate for so long, you might consider hiring a trash removal service like 1-800-GOT-JUNK to do the heavy lifting and haul them out of your house for you.

QUESTION?

What do I do if my basement has a mildew problem?
Here are a few tactics you can try to rid the room of the odor. If you've got windows, leave them open to vent the room. Use a dehumidifier, and if there's carpeting, give it a good deep cleaning.

A few words about the keepers. First, don't put anything back in cartons or storage containers without making sure the box is clearly labeled on multiple sides. Clear plastic containers will help take some of the guesswork out of the process, too. Avoid making the boxes too heavy or stacking them too high. If they're too hard to move, you'll be tempted to let them stay where they are for good. Store only the items that intuitively make sense as belonging in your basement. Gardening tools, for instance, are better housed in your garage or shed. Segregate items so that like items are all in one place. Think of it as you would a retail store, keeping all kitchen items together in one spot, sports equipment in another, and so on. The best storage solutions are the most logical ones.

Keep that retail image going a bit longer as you strategize your organizational goals. Putting items on old baking racks or similar shelving units will help clear the floor space, giving you room to maneuver and the ability to access items easier. Hooks and pegboards will help, too. You can put abandoned furniture back to work down here as makeshift storage holders. Breathe new life into old lockers, pantry units, and bookcases. If you're planning a kitchen remodeling job, think about setting up your old cabinets here.

What shouldn't you keep down in the basement? Well, it depends on the climate conditions. Dampness and sweaty walls are often problems, especially in older homes. And there's always a chance of flooding, so chemicals as well as items of special value should be stored above potential flood levels. If your basement is prone to high humidity or flooding conditions, here are some items you'd be wise to store in other areas of your home:

- Precious mementos
- Books

- Photograph albums
- Artwork
- Letters and cards

When positioning items on shelves, make sure the heaviest bottles, cartons, and cans are on low reinforced shelves, close to the floor. House lighter and more frequently used items on the most accessible shelves—figure somewhere between waist high and eye level.

Good Ideas for Basement Storage

On the other hand, the basement is a fine place to store household management items like cleaning products and bulk supplies. Keep nonperishable foods, paper towels, napkins, bath tissue, and light bulbs on shelves or, better yet, in dust-free and pest-proof cabinets. Stack items in a way in which you can easily see what you've got. Then you'll know when it's time to restock. It'll also prevent you from buying extras unnecessarily.

Other items well suited for basement storage are pieces of big, bulky sporting equipment, like camping supplies and ski gear, as well as tools, holiday decorations, and party supplies.

Store luggage here, too. Unless you're a road warrior who's on a plane every week and needs to have your bags always at the ready, there's an advantage to storing your luggage in the basement rather than clogging up a high-trafficked closet. Just keep an eye on those suitcases every once in a while to make sure mold doesn't form due to excess humidity. For space efficiency, nestle smaller suitcases inside the large ones. The area under the stairs is an especially good place to stow luggage, but make sure to keep your bags away from any windows in case there are leaks.

Basements have always been a good place to store wine because of the darkness and their cool temperatures. If you have a collection, store bottles on their sides to prevent the corks from drying out. Also, make sure the bottles are a safe distance away from the furnace, hot water heater, and other heat-producing equipment. Group them by category: reds, whites, dessert wines, and aperitifs.

Mold spores require moisture to grow and thrive, and areas of the home where there's water buildup from high humidity or flooding are ideal growing conditions. If you've got musty odors or spot clusters of dark specks, both good indications of mold, it's time to take action.

A Cellar's Market

In many homes, unfinished basements are so uninviting they're downright intimidating. What could be less appealing than a place with poor bare-bulb lighting, crumbly old walls, and musty odors? It's the stuff of horror movie settings. Unfriendly environments wind up contributing to storage problems and systematic disorganization, too. You run downstairs, toss an item on the storage pile, and run right up again in order to spend as little time in the basement as possible. Imagine how much better off you'd be if you livened up the space. You don't need to sink much time or money in it. A quick whitewash would clean it up, and an upgrade to your lighting would brighten it up. A dark room is an unproductive room. Poor lighting is a hindrance to good organization. To get more light, especially in the dark corners and halls of the basement, pick up a few inexpensive battery-operated lights, often used for closets. They're easy to install and require no wiring.

The Finished Line

Having a finished basement is a bonus for any home. It's less expensive than putting on an addition, and it yields a high return on investment when you're ready to sell. Many people put it on their must-have list when shopping for a new home. Yet the space in a finished basement is often misused, a kind of a whole-room equivalent of a junk drawer. The reason? Too much is demanded of a single space without properly zoning it into dedicated function areas. For instance, the ten-pound dumbbells rest by the laundry facilities. Intermingled among DVDs on the TV set shelf are craft supplies, photographs, and Christmas decorations. Tools migrate from the workshop to the arts-and-crafts area. It's a worlds-collide scenario that throws the entire room off balance. Instead of multiple function areas, you've got a mass of no-function areas.

FACT

According to the American Society of Home Inspectors, fall is a good time to fill in any low spots that are close to your home's foundation to prevent basement leaks and flooding. A survey by the trade association reports that problems related to water, specifically in the basement, were among those most frequently cited by homeowners.

First up, to redo the space you need to define it. Sit down and figure out how you'd ideally like to use your basement. If you're like most people, in addition to long-term storage, your basement is also the place for at least two or three of the following activities:

- Exercise
- Children's play
- Hobbies such as crafts, sewing, art, and gaming
- Everyday activities like gift-wrapping and music practice
- TV viewing
- Home office
- Laundry and ironing

When you figure how you want to your basement to support you, you can then start thinking about setting up different zones. It doesn't mean launching a major construction project. You can easily zone out rooms using furniture or decorative objects instead of putting up walls.

Open-back bookcases (tip: fill shelves with vases and other ornamental objects so it's equally attractive from both sides), multipanel screens, large floor plants, area rugs, and even curtains or stained-glass windows that hang from the ceiling can demarcate one area from the other. Once that's done, employ the storage techniques appropriate for each area. Some, like TV, playroom and office areas, have been discussed in earlier chapters.

Laundry Lists

If there's one place you want to make a clean start of things and foster an inviting atmosphere, it's the laundry area. The washer and dryer used so often, it pays to make the section bright and welcoming. Don't be afraid to go whimsical. Liven up the space with fun, upbeat paint colors and colorful storage bins. It'll help take away some of the drudgery. Install good lighting, and organize storage facilities in ways that minimize stooping and reaching.

ESSENTIAL

Whirlpool manufactures Duet front-loading washers and dryers with optional storage pedestals to help minimize bending and stooping. The pedestal raises the machine thirteen inches off the floor and makes a convenient stowaway zone for laundry bottles. Visit *www.whirlpool .com* for more information.

In one of the more unpleasant tasks she had to face, professional organizer Heidi Gaumet found piles of laundry, clean and dirty mixed together, in a client's basement. Everyone in the family simply tossed their dirty clothes down in the laundry area. But when the laundry was done, it was never brought up, so both piles simply intermingled.

Create a workspace area so you can fold clothes right out of the dryer, thereby cutting down on ironing. It also cuts down on the chance that a shirt or sock will go AWOL. Portable racks can save drying time now and ironing time later on. Wall-mounted drying racks are available that won't eat up floor space. A shelf or cabinet above your washer and dryer will keep all your detergent needs within reach. But if you buy oversize products that may make it more difficult to lift, avoid straining your back. Look for a tiered rolling cart instead. Some cart models are so slim they can slip into the narrowest of spaces, even between your washer and dryer. Otherwise, think about transferring detergents and fabric softeners from big, heavy jugs to smaller, easier-to-lift sizes. Investigate whether you can use the space between your wall studs for a flip-down ironing board.

▲ A laundry center.

If your basement is like most, it's probably where all your important equipment is, like the furnace, water softener, water heater, and washer and dryer. In other words, it's the guts of your home. Remember: these areas need to remain accessible for servicing. And that's not all. Clutter around these areas could create a fire hazard situation, so make sure the areas around pipes and drains aren't blocked with boxes.

Crafty Ideas

If you enjoy scrapbooking, crafts, arts, or sewing, you know fabrics and supplies can quickly spiral out of control. Once that happens, reeling it in becomes a daunting task. Take advantage of the many storage products on the market to create an efficient workspace.

QUESTION?

Can a crawl space be converted to a basement?
Yes. A crawl space, which is a shallow space beneath the house, usually less than four feet high, can be converted into a full basement. Contact a qualified masonry contractor or general contractor to find out what's involved and if it's a cost-effective solution for your home.

Mobile carts with wide, shallow drawers are perfect for scrapbook supplies. By the way, if you have a plain old plastic or wooden cart, add on casters. Keeping supply carts close to you when you work leaves less opportunity for clutter to congregate in places where it doesn't belong. Tool chests with multiple drawers are great for housing lots of small items. Lightweight portable tool chests also make good homes for art supplies such as paint tubs, pencils, and brushes. Repurpose old spice-rack bottles and baby food jars for pint-size accessories. Otherwise, it's easy for small items to get lost in large containers, falling to the bottom, where they seemingly disappear for good. Make sure you label each drawer so there's no guesswork involved. Some items work well stored in labeled binders on bookshelves.

Good Sports

Ever notice how home-gym gear like exercise balls and weights have a way of roaming? But with the right combination of storage aids, your equipment can always be within reach and within safety limits. Purchase a dumbbell rack or weight tree sized for the number of weights you have. Pop-up mesh cubes and baskets are good for containing odd-shaped gear like yoga mats, abdominal wheels, and resistance bands. For the ultimate in home-gym storage, there's the gym-in-a-box, an armoire with a built-in home fitness center disguised as a handsome entertainment center. The doors open to reveal a treadmill and weight bench. There's even a shelf in there for a TV set. If you do watch exercise videos on a secondary set while working out, store your fitness tapes or DVDs here, where you use them, rather than in the main TV viewing room.

Down and Out

What happens downstairs affects what goes on upstairs. When you turn your basement into a storage graveyard, you bury opportunities to breathe out the living quarters in other areas of your home. Make it a point to take periodic inspections of what you've got and what you can get rid of. Then keep areas zoned out, no matter what type of basement you have, to keep the space functioning in a way that supports the smooth running of your household. With the right strategies in place in a finished basement, will you not only be able to accommodate a range of different activities and hobbies, members of your household will also be able to engage in those activities simultaneously.

Chapter 10

Lofty Spaces: Attics

The attic traditionally houses long-forgotten items and, more often than not, items better left forgotten. As a result, all that valuable space winds up becoming a holding tank for stuff that might be more appropriately housed at the curb—for trash pickup the next morning. This chapter gives you ideas on reclaiming, rethinking, and reorganizing your attic in ways that use every surface.

States of Disgrace

People should grow old gracefully. The stuff in your attic shouldn't. We allow the pointless mess to fester through sheer inertia. It's so much easier to stow it than to unload it. In fact, the only time most people ever really get a clear picture of what's under their roof is when it's time for them to move.

Let's face it. In our continuing quest for more storage space, the attic is probably the most off-putting place of all, with its creaky floorboards, spider-web décor, and dark, creepy corners. There's practically an entire genre of Hollywood movies dedicated to ghouls-in-the-attic, bodies-in-the-attic, voices-from-the-attic terror.

If reaching your attic means getting a stepladder from the basement and hauling it upstairs, chances are you're not making good use of the space. Instead, install a permanent wood or aluminum pull-down ladder. It's a do-it-yourself project that will make attic access easier and, more important, safer.

It's not only an inhospitable environment, it's a harsh one, too. For homes without tree cover, the sun's ultraviolet rays beat down and play havoc with the thermostat levels. And for homes that do have the benefit of ray-blocking branches, there's the potential problem of moss and algae developing around the puddles of fallen leaves.

Newer homes might be blessed with spacious walk-in closets, but at the same time they're notoriously lacking when it comes to attic space. Many have nothing but a crawl space. Up until a half century ago, homes were smaller, but large attics were the norm. Grandma's attic had lots of headroom, giving her ample space to move around her steamer trunks of stored treasures. But then home-builders began using stronger and less expensive trusses instead of rafters to support the roof. The construction method lowered the roof pitch and, ultimately, cut down on storage opportunities.

If you've got a hole-in-the-ceiling kind of attic that's accessible through a hatch, you've got a legitimate reason for attic clutter. Lack of access makes it difficult, not to mention precarious, to move belongings up and down, in and out. Then there's the problem of maneuverability. Steeply sloping attic walls make it a thorny, back-taxing effort to move around once you're inside.

FACT

There are several different types of attic configurations. At one end of the spectrum are limited crawl spaces. At the other are full attics that offer full headroom and can easily be converted into usable living space. If converting the space is under consideration, contact your local housing authority or town government before you make any investments. Many municipalities have strict requirements that may even include installing an indoor sprinkler system.

There's another reason why attics are often the *least* organized area of the household: because you can get away with it. When was the last time a guest paid a visit to your lofty real estate? Exactly. As a result, when you go looking for something in the attic, you know you're in for a Lewis and Clark–caliber expedition. And chances are you will come away from the experience a lot less successful than they were.

Yes, while there is a long list of reasons that make attic storage particularly challenging, it doesn't mean you've got carte blanche to keep a bad system going. Nor does it mean you need to throw up your arms and surrender. It's not a question of abandoning the attic space as much as it is bowing to its limitations.

Thinking Outside the Carton

It helps to keep a simple premise in mind: What goes up must come down. There really shouldn't be such a thing as permanent storage in your house in the first place. It's a sign your storage system has broken down. Permanent storage is dead storage. Few people can afford the luxury of giving over space without a fight when the rest of their living quarters has them feeling crowded in. If you're stowing something under the rafters and then simply forgetting about it, it's a good bet you didn't really need it in the first place.

That's not to say that attic storage doesn't have a place in your home organizational scheme. Reserve the attic for items used infrequently, as long as they can stand up to the potential of extreme hot and cold temperature swings. If you've got a four- or eight-legged critter problem, you'll need to face that situation, too. In many cases, the attic is a sound storage option for the same types of items you house in your basement, such as luggage, holiday decorations, and seasonal clothing. But leave woolen fabrics downstairs. They're like a banquet to pests. Soiled clothes and fabrics are especially attractive to vermin, so make sure you clean all items before stowing. Use canvas garment bags for clothes, and include pest control protection material, such as cedar chips.

The attic is also a good place for old files that you don't need instant access to but are still required to keep, such as tax returns, closing documents, and mortgage paperwork. Keep paperwork in a heavy-duty plastic or fireproof metal cabinet.

If you store rugs in the attic, clean them first. Then roll them tightly, secure with rope, and label.

QUESTION?

What does the R-value of insulation refer to?
The R-value is a measure that indicates how well insulation resists heat flow. The higher the R-value, the better the insulation. Insulation should be added in any area that separates a heated space from an unheated space.

In contrast to basement environments, attics tend to be dry as long as there's good insulation and ventilation. On the other hand, if an attic hasn't been properly prepped for storage use, extreme heat and high moisture conditions can be detrimental to certain items. One forward-thinking shopper bought all of her holiday cards the day after Christmas at half price and put them in the attic for safekeeping. But when she retrieved them the following December, she discovered the heat caused the glue on her envelopes to seal shut. So much for her "sale."

Other attic storage no-no's are cosmetics and food, along with most types of media like photographs, videotapes, film, and slides. They just won't hold up well under the punishing conditions.

E ALERT!

Check the labels of all items before storing in the attic. Make sure that none of the items have a label warning: "Keep away from heat or flame." You might be surprised what liquids are combustible. Summer heat could create a hazardous situation.

Be sure your attic can meet the weight demands of whatever you have stored there. The last thing you want to create is a situation in which the ceiling below the floorboards is compromised.

All about Eaves

As difficult as the thought may be, to undertake a thorough job, you've got to roll up your sleeves and find out what's there, which means emptying out the attic contents. That's right—every last carton, trunk, and cabinet. Now before you toss this book down and run, think about the upside. You'll doubtless come across items you can discard, which will allow you to relocate things from other overcrowded parts of your home. You'll probably discover some sentimental treasures, too, so get ready to be hit with a big fat wave of nostalgia. Your wedding dress, high school yearbook, maybe even your grade-school diary might just be squirreled away up there somewhere in cartons unknown. Perhaps you'll even find some investment-grade treasures. One woman had a Depression glass collection in her attic for ages. When she first stored it up there, Depression glass was considered inexpensive, run-of-the-mill dinnerware: nothing special and, certainly, of no real value. When she unwrapped it from the yellowed newspapers decades later, it had become a sought-after antique.

A whole-house attic exhaust fan works wonders to minimize extreme temperature swings and to reduce moisture levels. The exhaust fan draws hot air out of your attic and replaces it with the cooler outside air. A stable environment will add to the longevity of your stored goods.

If you access your attic via a ladder, enlist the assistance of one or two people who can take items from you without your having to negotiate an armload of stuff up and down the steps. It's a safety precaution that'll be kinder on your back and arms, too, and move the process along.

Warehousing items for friends, grown children, or other family members? Well, this is as good a time as any to remind them about their belongings and invite them to join you in the reorganizing process. Chances are they've probably forgotten about the items altogether. If you're really serious about downsizing your attic clutter, you might even want to give them an "expiration date" to take their items out of your home by—politely, of course! Set up a nearby staging area by making room for your four piles:

- **Trash:** For large items, you may need to schedule a special trash pickup with your local municipality.
- **Donation:** Before you make a call to a charitable agency, make sure your contributions are still in good condition and working order. They don't want junk any more than you do.
- **Relocate:** You may actually find a few things deserving of a second chance or—eureka!—something you've been trying to track down forever.
- **Save:** Back to long-term storage for these babies, but review them carefully to make sure your attic is, indeed, the best place for them.

Lay down a tarp or old sheet before you get going, since you're likely to kick up a lot of dust. Some people even wear inexpensive dust masks, available at any hardware store.

When taking inventory, don't just open a box, sneak a quick peek, and seal it up again. Really go through your things in detail. If you need a nudge to help you add items onto the discard pile, just think about climbing back up into the attic with those containers again. That should do the trick. The key is to be honest with yourself about what you need and what you can really live without. Don't guilt trip yourself into keeping items given as gifts that you have no use for now or in the future.

ALERT!

Squirrels can be unwelcome guests in your attic. Take preemptive measures before they take shelter. Cut down overhanging tree branches that might make it easier for them to reach your attic. Look for possible entry holes and seal them up. Install vent covers, since attic vents are also common entry points.

Zoning Out

Attics, like all good storage areas of your home, need zones of their own. Determine what categories you're working with and then assign areas accordingly. You may have:

- Housewares
- Holiday decorations
- Memorabilia
- Books
- Furniture
- Exercise equipment
- Toys and games
- Electronics

If different individuals store their possessions in your attic, carve out a section for each one.

Attics aren't the kind of places you want to linger a minute longer than necessary. Move it in or move it out. Period. When you put similar items together, you make things much easier to find. And when it's time to return them, you'll already know just where to go. It's like having a roadmap. We all know that rummaging through an attic in extreme heat or cold isn't any fun. As a matter of fact, when scheduling your plan of attack, tackle attic organization during a time of the year when room temperatures are most comfortable. No matter how much enthusiasm you might muster for the task or how much you psych yourself up for it, you won't get far if the thermometer is in single—or triple—digits.

Consider creating a simple inventory map for your attic. It'll help you locate your stored items in a jiffy. Even if you know exactly where things are, others in your household might not. Tack the map up near the attic entrance or in some other well-lit, easy-to-find location.

Leader of the Pack

If you do nothing else when you start getting ready to pack items away in your attic, re-sort them so that like items share the same containers. If you open a carton and find it stuffed with a hodgepodge collection of children's toys, kitchen utensils, and collectibles, at the very least put toys in one container, kitchenware in another, and collectibles in a third.

Containing Your Stuff

Depending on how much stuff you have in each category, you may need to subcategorize even further: for instance, girls' clothes from boys', Christmas decorations from Halloween. It'll pay off. When you do need to access things, you won't have to go digging. And if you want to discard whole categories of, say, outgrown children's clothing, you can simply grab a box instead of having to go through each container piece by agonizing piece. There are lots of storage options ideally suited to the attic, and they range in price from affordable to extravagant, fitting any household budget.

ESSENTIAL

Consider hiring a professional home engineer to inspect your attic before loading it up with storage containers. It's critical to make sure the room has structural integrity and can handle the weight demands your belongings require. You may need to add supports or reinforcements to give your attic extra strength.

As much as possible, keep your storage plan simple. Put items out in plain sight. Open shelving will allow for quick and easy access without a lot of hunting or fumbling. When choosing containers for the attic, sturdy plastic is best. Plastic provides great protection from moisture, dust, insects, and rodents. Whether you use colored containers or clear see-through ones, be sure to stick nice, big labels on multiple sides letting you know exactly what's inside.

A La Cart

Tiered rolling carts are extremely useful, too. You can stow them in the attic's recesses and wheel them out to a more convenient space as you need it. If your attic is like most, you'll find yourself doing some bending and stooping. Head off having to do any fancy footwork besides by creating clutter-free aisles. And don't scrimp on light. Have a light fixture right at the entryway both for safety purposes and to make it easier to see if any of your things have sustained damage. Flashlights aren't up to the task. To really maximize the space, right down to the little knee walls and storage alleys that run alongside exterior walls, think about having custom shelving or cabinetry built.

The Finishing Touch

In some homes, usually older ones, large attics have been converted into an extra bedroom, loft office, home gym, or play area. Many of the storage solutions targeted to these specific uses are covered in previous chapters. Finished attics have attributes of finished basements, so refer to Chapter 9 for ideas. The nice thing about finished attics, unlike basements, is that they have the benefit of lots of natural light through full-size windows and, sometimes, even skylights. Window seats with lift-up storage, built below recessed windows, are a great way to gain additional seating while making use of an otherwise awkward footprint.

Book It

If you need some motivation, the most important thing to keep in mind is that organizing your attic will make your life easier. Make a plan. Don't just tell yourself you'll get to it "one of these days." Schedule one of those days on the calendar. Be thorough in your work and, most of all, be patient. Attics are among the toughest rooms in the home to organize.

FACT

Homeowners in different areas of the country have to contend with different types of uninvited attic visitors. Some regions are prone to slithering bugs that love to munch on paper. Other areas attract mice, squirrels, raccoons, and even bats, some just looking for a warm cozy bed.

The group Clutterers Anonymous offers some positive affirmations to help its members in recovery. Some of these encouraging thoughts might help you get through this task more easily:

- I nurture my spirit by surrounding myself with beauty and harmony.
- I set reasonable goals, remembering that my first priority is my well-being.
- I schedule what I can do at a comfortable pace. I rest before I get tired.
- I allot more time than I need for a task or trip, allowing a comfortable margin for the unexpected.
- I decide which are the most important things to do first.
- I do one thing at a time.
- I eliminate an activity from my schedule before adding one that demands equivalent time and energy.
- I allocate space and time for anything new that I bring into my life or home.

- I affirm abundance and prosperity, thus I release the need to hoard.
- I am gentle with my efforts, knowing that my new way of living requires much practice.
- I do not yield to pressure or attempt to pressure others.
- I realize that I am already where I will always be, in the here and now. I live each moment with serenity, joy, and gratitude.

Once you're done, you'll be proud of your efforts and thrilled at the difference it makes in your life.

Chapter 11

Grand Entrances: Hallways and Mudrooms

A first impression makes a lasting impact, which is why an entryway sets the tone for your entire house. How do you utilize storage space in the most active thoroughfares of your home without cluttering up and obstructing foot traffic? Here's a chance to latch onto some free space, including a few unused corners of your home. Turn small areas into obstacle-free cargo zones—all the while doing it in style. Have a dog or cat? Here's where you just may find the best spot for your next pet project.

Enter at Your Own Risk

What are the first things guests see when they walk into your home? Shoes. Backpacks. Schoolbooks. Eyeglasses. Can you spell C-H-A-O-S? Serenity flies out the window with their very first steps inside. The rest of your house might be able to pass the white-glove test, but if the entryways are clogged with the daily trappings of a family on the move, the welcome mat may well look pretty uninviting.

Winifred Gallagher, author of *House Thinking: A Room-by-Room Look at How We Live*, writes that an inauspicious entry is a sad waste of the home's precious behavior capital. Ideally, the entry should be a graceful progression from street to hall to home—a near-cleansing experience, a Zen moment.

FACT

It's a widespread and deep-rooted Japanese tradition to remove outdoor footwear and place it just inside the door before entering a home. The tradition is also practiced in other Asian countries and, increasingly, is being adopted in Western households, as well.

Have multiple entrances? Then you might have a problem times two or even three.

The entryway at the front door of Japanese households is called the *genkan*. It's considered an important place, the face that shows to the outside world. It's a great concept to keep in mind as you attempt to button-up your own clutter. The challenge is to balance a need for storage without implementing so many mix-and-match solutions that they'll sabotage your efforts to streamline access.

The good news is that dejunking your foyer, hallways, and mudroom isn't a huge, clear-the-schedule undertaking. It's not as time-consuming as sorting through the old furniture in your basement or potentially back-breaking as slithering through the attic to purge years of unopened cartons. Organizing your entry points is more a matter of evaluating your needs, straightening up, and shifting things around a bit to better serve your purposes. So relax. This time around, you'll be getting a break.

Front and Center

Think of your vestibule as a point of transition, the intersection of come and go. It's where you take off in the morning and where you land at the end of the day. And if you're like most people, with you comes a pocket or pocketbook full of life's daily necessities. But then what? Where do all these pint-size items go? Though we don't exactly think of a foyer as a holding room, it's usually the most convenient place in the house for short-term storage for such personal effects as these:

- Cell phones
- Keys
- Glasses
- Handbags and briefcases
- Umbrellas
- Dog leashes
- Travel mugs
- Mail

The operative phrase is short term. Whatever is here should be in a state of perpetual—or at least imminent—motion. Halls should not be catch-alls, though sometimes they do seem to suck things in like a vortex.

If picking up a newspaper or a cup of coffee is part of your daily morning routine, keep a small jar, dish, or bowl by the door filled with spare change. Grab a handful of coins in the morning and refill the jar at the end of the day by emptying out your pocket or change purse.

An entryway is not intended for any kind of permanent storage. Nor is it a place to let piles grow, like the newspapers you haven't gotten to yet, the unopened mail, catalogs, or stacks of magazines. In some households, the foyer also seems to be the lost-in-transition point for items en route to their more suitable and everlasting homes.

A homeowner named Jose admits to amassing pens, pads, receipts, bill stubs, and even outdated coupons in his entry area. It's not until the pile reaches an unmanageable level that Jose sorts through it, either throwing things away or filing them where they actually belong. His entry is fresh, clean, and organized, though he adds a bit forlornly that it lasts just a couple weeks, until a new pile begins to grow again. What goes in your entryway? Bills? Coupons? No and no. Except for the transitional items, nothing else belongs.

Tame the Traffic

You might have a home in which more than one entryway is used. Perhaps there's a side entrance from an attached garage or a back door from a yard or driveway. If so, you're in good company. The overwhelming majority of homeowners with remote control access to an attached garage use it as an entrance every day. Consider if and how often your family utilizes these secondary entrances. You may need to set up more than one type of containment area, matched to the needs of those who use it and how they use it.

FACT

According to the ancient Chinese philosophy of feng shui, cluttered entryways block the flow of energy. A clean, inviting entryway will have a positive impact on those crossing the threshold.

Many people don't even recognize they've got a hot spot, a clutter magnet by the door. For one woman whose home doesn't have a formal foyer— you walk right into the living room—her drop-off zone is actually a deep window ledge by the door that she uses as a makeshift shelf. It becomes the dumping ground for keys, glasses, and outgoing mail. Convenient though it is, that little ledge creates one big eyesore that impacts the entire living room.

Bin There

Look around and see if you can spot clumps of clutter. They're crying out for organization. The thing is, some of the more basic storage options don't apply here. Plastic bins and rolling carts? They make poor first impressions. In hallways and foyers, seek out small, unobtrusive space-saving furniture solutions that can offer a devoted home to your everyday necessities in a way that hides the messiness.

A storage bench with easy-to-access shelves or pullout baskets below can store your clunkier items, like portable umbrellas, handbags, and knapsacks. Set up a small table with a drawer for keys, wallets, and cell phones. A night table or end table will serve the purpose. If you make a habit of parking these things here, you'll never waste time wondering where you left your essentials again. Avoid turning the drawer into a junk drawer. Once you start tossing pens, scraps of paper, and takeout menus in there, you'll discover that things will quickly get out of hand and the drawer will lose its functionality. A table with or without shelves will do the job, too, but use attractive covered baskets so you don't wind up with a tabletop of unsightly clutter.

Furniture will backfire if the area is too small to accommodate it. Scale matters. Employ size-appropriate solutions that will maintain good entry flow. You don't want to negotiate an obstacle course to get from point A to point B. If floor space is ultra-tight, improvise, and be creative with your choices. For instance, you might string a collection of pretty baskets from the ceiling to hold your gear.

ESSENTIAL

Always forgetting something when you leave the house in the morning to attend to your chores? Outgoing mail? DVD rental return? About-to-be-due library book? Here's a tip that will remind you. Set up a basket as near as possible to the front door, and use it strictly for all your outgoing deliveries. Then get in the habit of checking before you walk out the door.

Best Foot Forward

For a growing number of families, removing street shoes upon entering is a household rule. Keep a simple tray by the door to contain the collection, or purchase a flexible folding shoe rack that can be collapsed and stored away in a closet when company comes.

Install hooks for umbrellas, caps, and handbags. Unless you want your entry hall to look like a locker room, don't hang coats out in the open—at least not by the front door. If you intend to hang heavy articles from hooks, such as a bulky parka or a hefty briefcase, make sure the hooks are weight-tested to withstand the load and that heavy-duty hardware is used. If hooks aren't properly matched to support the weight, you risk doing damage to your wall. Here's another thing: Doorknobs are not a substitute for hooks. Have you ever walked into a home and noticed that every knob was looped with a baseball cap or a bag?

E ALERT!

For a healthier home, buy an antimicrobial doormat. It works to destroy microorganisms on contact and helps to reduce allergens. Before entering simply wipe your shoes on the mat to prevent pollutants, dust mites, mold, bacteria, and other potential irritants from making their way into your home.

In many homes, the front entryway opens up onto a staircase. Step baskets are a great organizational tool. They're L-shaped so they can fit neatly on a stairway step. Leave it on a bottom step in the morning and then fill it as needed throughout the day with all the stuff that wandered from its natural habitat. At the end of the day, bring the basket upstairs and return each item to its rightful place.

Mudroom Makeovers

Mudrooms are traditionally found in homes in colder climates. They're designed to prevent winter heat or summer air-conditioning from escaping when people enter or exit the house. They're seen as so practical that many home-builders in other parts of the country are adding them to the blue-print of new construction projects. Some owners of existing homes think they're a good idea, too, and are confiscating space by the kitchen or the rear door and converting it into a thirty-six- or even seventy-two-square-foot utilitarian mudroom area. If your home is lucky enough to have one, you know they can be a dream. They are an in-between area that protects your home from the harsh elements of rain, snow, sand, and, well, mud. Think of it as a kind of a quick-change staging area, the place you keep an imaginary Do Not Enter sign for dirt-spiked shoes and dripping wet over-coats. What a great luxury it is to have in a home, and even more so if you have kids. So what's the best way to maximize its use? That depends on your lifestyle.

More Than Mud

In some cases, the mudroom is given over to the washer and dryer. If so, refer to Chapter 9 for tips on the best ways to organize your laundry area. Mudrooms are also used as repositories for any of the following:

- Bulky outerwear
- School gear
- Recycling
- Pantry overflow
- Sports equipment
- Gardening tools and accessories
- Pet organization center

For stowing personal gear, consider a system of stackable cubbies. Give each member of your household a place of his own, labeled with names. Do a quick calculation to figure out how much space each person requires. Of course, where you live could make all the difference. If you're in Hawaii, you don't need to concern yourself with allocating cubby space for gloves and hats. In New York, on the other hand, room for snow boots and scarves is a no-brainer.

Given the nature of how mudrooms are used, keep a couple of safety precautions in mind. First, make sure your flooring is a nonslip surface since it's where people enter the house after rain or a snowfall. In addition, install a small bench, either a permanent or collapsible model (depending on how much room you have), so that people have a place to sit while removing their shoes and boots.

Mudroom Management

The nice thing is that you can adjust your storage needs to the season. Add modular cubbies when you need the storage room, and store them away in the basement or a closet when you don't. When summer rolls around on Long Island, for instance, you can whittle down the stackables to flip-flop and beach towel size.

▲ A hallway shelving unit.

An after-school storage locker with shelves for accessories and hooks for book bags and coats is another efficient option. Before you say "army barracks," take a look at the wide selection of handsome lockers available on the market today. They come in natural and painted woods with stylish furniture detailing.

Wire shelving offers the best ventilation for damp clothing. If you're a green-thumber who spends time in the yard, you might even want to keep a laundry basket or duffle bag in the room so that soiled clothes coming straight from garden detail can go directly into the dirty-clothes pile. The same goes for those trips to beach. No need to track sand through your house.

A high shelf is a good way to put vertical space to use. Line the shelf with attractive tins or collectible jars, and fill them with items you might not need to use on an everyday basis, like spare keys—labeled, of course.

Consider using the mudroom for your recyclables, too. A plastic unit with pullout bins is a practical solution.

QUESTION?

How does an exterior door protect elements from penetrating the home?
According to the Window and Door Manufacturing Association, doors have insulating properties in and of themselves, but on top of that, weather stripping, door frames, and thresholds work in combination to keep the elements at bay.

If you've got a sports-oriented household, folding mesh storage bags not only keep bulky equipment together in a central location but are lightweight and transportable, too. Just grab the bag and go. Some sports organizers even come with removable mesh bags for that very purpose. Many units have shelves targeted to specific sports, such as racks for in-line skates or hooks for tennis rackets. An open-grid framework makes small-size gear, like baseballs and bicycle gloves, easier to find.

A well-trafficked mudroom is also an ideal location in which to create a family communications center. It's easy to do. All it takes is a hanging chalkboard or bulletin board to keep each member of the household up to speed on one another's whereabouts.

Pet Projects

Everyone knows Americans love to spoil their animals. There's cat couture, doggy spas, birdie blogs (it's true), and even yoga for the four-legged kind. Their requirements are most easily met when they peacefully coexist with the rest of the family's needs. What does that mean? Well, try the following on for size:

- No tripping over Rover's toys
- No funny kennel smells
- No wondering who is truly Master of the House

Your pets might have the run of the house, but their toys, medications, and accessories shouldn't. In a country mad for its furry and feathered friends, the market is filled with bright ideas to manage your pet's needs and supplies, from food dispensers to travel bedding.

Dedicate a single area of your home to your pet's creature comforts and care. Depending on the setup of your home, the mudroom may just make the most sense since it's directly off an entryway and segregated from busy household traffic. Otherwise, siphon off a section of the kitchen or a pantry area.

Just like you, your pet should have its own emergency kit packed and ready to go. The kit should include medical records and medications, the name and phone number of your veterinarian, a first-aid kit, collar with up-to-date identification tag, leash, food, a feeding bowl, and manual can opener.

Food for Thought

Of course, you want to protect food from hungry pets and keep pests away. But the trouble is that those thirty-five-pound bags are real back-breakers. Rolling pet food caddies with lockable lids keep food fresh and make those bulky oversize bags easier to manage. Clear containers will let you know when you're running low. Stack-and-store bins take up minimal floor space; they're tall and narrow and can store dog chow, cat litter, or birdseed in one place, turning a small area into pet central. Wall-mounted dispensers cut out the need for floor space altogether. Push a lever and the dispenser will dole out a portion-size quantity. Get a dispenser with a tight-sealing lid so your home doesn't smell like Eau de Purina. To protect your floor from spilled water and scratches, lay down a pet placemat. It'll also help keep the feeding area neat and stable.

Toys and Treats

If you've got the room, try consolidating all your pet's needs using a single organization and storage center. Slick-looking models are on the market that accommodate food supplies and also have attractive baskets for those items that ordinarily wind up all over the house like toys, leashes, towels, and collars. You can also keep important pet documentation here, such as medical records. If you store medications, make sure they're locked up securely or at least well out of the reach of both pets and children.

On the go a lot? Roll-up travel beds take up minimal space and are easy to store. Protect your chairs, bedding, and couch from pet hair and dander by using a protective throw over your furniture. The ones that are specially designed for pets are cozy, easily washable, and made of stain- and odor-resistant fabric.

Secret Spaces

Aside from entry hallways and mudrooms, what are a couple of other oft-forgotten areas of the house that are overlooked as storage options? In many homes, there's that awkward space under the staircase. Professional organizer Misha Keefe says it's an area that often goes to waste—unnecessarily.

Add some shelving and it can hold books and decorative collectibles. Or you can transform that space into a workstation with a small desk and some built-in cabinetry.

If you've got a traditional hinged swinging door that opens up into a narrow hallway, consider changing it out for a sliding pocket door. Pocket doors disappear into specially built wall cavities, freeing up lots of floor space.

If you have long hallways, add shelves high enough that they don't obstruct traffic. Use them for open displays or stack them with attractive baskets for more functional storage.

Over and Out

When the world seems particularly chaotic, do your best to leave worries at the door, with the help of some intelligent planning. Employ no-fuss solutions. Make sure all your essentials—glasses, keys, cell phone—have a designated home. Without it, you're likely to drop stuff off on any available surface. Next thing you know, it's "Where did I leave my keys?", "Honey, I can't find my wallet," and "Where's my train ticket?" No need to beat yourself up about it. Organization is a skill like any other that just needs to be learned and put into use until it becomes a habit.

In some cases, changing behavior, yours or a family member's, may be too much to ask. In that case, put simple storage solutions in place that support the reality of the situation. For example, a storage bench may sound like a great idea, but if you're more likely to put stuff on top of it than open up the lid and put things inside, consider in-and-out lidless baskets instead.

Once you've got your entryways set up and organized, take an extra moment out of each day to keep things tidy. Think of it as you would a diet. It's one thing to shed the pounds; the real challenge comes with maintaining the success. Keep tabs to prevent your entryway, mudroom, and hallways from becoming dumping grounds. Hang things up, put things away, and keep things moving. Don't just drop and go. If your kids are leaving their books and backpacks on the floor, it's probably because you haven't given them a better alternative. Whatever storage options you employ, make sure they're user-friendly and easy for kids to access on the run.

Chapter 12

The Great Outdoors: Backyards and Gardens

How does your garden gear grow? Quite contrarily? You needn't be a green-thumber to want a four-season storage system for tools, supplies, and lawn equipment. Gardening can be a messy business, and that's part of the fun—but only to a point. In this chapter, you'll find out about the many organizational options available to you, so read it and reap.

Cleaning Up Your Act

Gardening consistently ranks among the most popular leisure activities. Some 100 million people in the United States alone consider themselves gardeners. There's something about a scenery of greenery that never disappoints.

Does this describe your situation? Your rosebushes are show quality, and your bed of annuals is traffic-stopping, but your workshop is a giant eyesore. No matter what shade of green your thumb is—novice or expert—chances are you've got lots of bags, boxes, and bottles of supplies to contend with. That's probably in addition to the not-so-tidy collection of garden gear you've built up, perhaps even in duplicate and triplicate. In gardening, as with any hobby, enthusiasts get carried away with collecting. Attractive pots are hard to resist, so they pile higher and higher. Everyone wants the newest and best fertilizer product on the market. And who doesn't get seduced by ads for the hottest gardening power tool?

ESSENTIAL

Plan ahead, and buy your gardening supplies when they go on sale. Most garden centers have huge end-of-season clearances. Stock up on items you know you've got an ongoing need for, like potting soil, wood chips, and fertilizer, but fight the impulse to buy anything that's not on your list.

One new homeowner became obsessed with gardening. It started innocently enough with a visit to his local garden center. In no time, his dropbys became routine. He'd drool at chippers, tractors, weed whackers, and the whole lot of gas-powered contraptions. Before long, there was more collective horsepower in his gardening equipment than under the hood of his car—which, by the way, was relegated to the driveway because there wasn't enough room for all of it in his garage.

Now's the time to take stock of what you've got and undertake some old-fashioned purging. First up on your to-do list is to empty the cabinets, clear off the shelves, and drag all your gardening supplies out of the dark recesses of your garage, shed, both . . . or more. One backyard devotee confessed her gardening goods were spread among three sheds, a garage, and a mud-room. Here's your game plan:

- Check chemicals, and dispose of any products that are past their expiration dates. They may have lost their effectiveness long ago. Take care to do so safely and in accordance with your local regulations.
- Get rid of pots that have any cracks or chips.
- Discard all rusty, weather-damaged, or otherwise unsalvageable tools. And that goes for the broken ones, too. If you haven't gotten around to fixing them by now, you never will.
- Throw away leftover fencing and other excess yard materials (how long ago did you put up your fence? By the time you might need to replace a section, the wood won't match, anyway).
- Ditch beat-up and moldy old chair cushions.
- Be a good neighbor and pass along multiples of tools you just don't have a use for.
- Sell or donate gear you no longer use.

Always use chemicals according to instructions on the label, and take precautions when disposing of them. Some municipalities have a hazardous-waste disposal site. If yours doesn't, contact your local government office for safe handling. Never pour pesticides in the sink, toilet, tub, or sewer. In case of an emergency, call 911 or the National Pesticide Telecommunications Network at 1-800-858-7378.

Here's another point. If you have a shed or annex, get rid of anything that's inappropriate for the space. Lots of people use sheds for storage over-flow and house items that don't belong there, such as old newspapers, toys, and even pet supplies.

Out and About

The first question to ask yourself is this: Where is the best place to store your gardening materials? Obviously, big bulky lawn-care equipment will go outside the house. You want to keep these items near where they're used. Standard places are a garage, garage annex, or shed.

If you use the garage to store the lion's share of your gardening gear, as many people do, keep it all together in a dedicated section using a combination of shelves and cabinets. Open shelves work best for frequently used items; cabinets are a better option for fragile things like pots or items that need protection from the elements. Within this section, store like categories together, pots with pots, chemicals with chemicals, and so on. Be sure to keep chemicals secure and out of reach of children and pets. For more, read up on garage organization in Chapter 13.

FACT

There are three types of sheds: vinyl, metal and wood. Vinyl composites are ready to go, preassembled right out of the box, and hold up well against the elements. Metal sheds come in kit form in a variety of styles and sizes. Wood, available either as a kit or preassembled, is known for quality and durability.

Don't leave oversize bags of gardening products outside. If they get wet, they'll be even harder to haul around. If you're considering building a shed or annex, check local statutes in your neighborhood. A permit may be needed. There's another option for freestanding storage. It's a twist on the self-storage rental concept, but in this case the storage unit comes to you. A company called PODS, short for Portable On-Demand Storage (online at *www .pods.com*), offers homeowners an on-site alterative by delivering a weather-resistant container to your door. PODS makes sense if you need interim storage, perhaps while you're building a garage, or if you rent and don't want to make a capital investment in the property.

Turning a New Leaf

If you enjoy indoor gardening, you may also want to designate an area inside your home for household plant care. There's nothing that softens and beautifies a room like plants and indoor trees, but there's nothing messier than repotting them, either. For indoor gardening, think about which area of your house is best suited to prep work. An underutilized pantry or utility closet might be a good place to designate for your small tools and supplies. If so, try to keep the closet off-limits to anything but gardening gear. Evaluate the space to see if you could add a table or flip-down shelf to use as a makeshift workstation.

Consider using a basement if there's a sink nearby, a part of your kitchen, an enclosed porch, or a mudroom. Then try to contain everything in one compact work unit. Potting benches are perfect for this application. They come in a wide variety of sizes and styles that provide work space and storage holders for small tools, gardening books, and planters. Look for models that have inset bins for potting soil and drawers for small pots and seed packets. You can approximate the functionality of a potting bench by repurposing a no-longer-used cabinet and topping it with a couple of stand-alone shelving units. Once you've got your workspace established, reduce planting materials that come in those back-breaking quantities down to manageable sizes. Transfer large bags of potting soil into smaller ones. Old Tupperware and plastic containers work great for this purpose. Just make sure they're clearly labeled.

ESSENTIAL

April is National Garden Month. For more information, contact the National Gardening Association at 802-863-5251 or visit it online at *www .nationalgardenmonth.org*. According to the association, National Garden Month is a time to focus on the essential connection between people, plants, and the environment and to make our backyards, schools, and neighborhoods greener places.

If you don't have space for a freestanding cabinet, use your sink for the messy work and go portable with the supplies. Keep all your plant-care items, like fertilizers, watering can, rooting powders, and insect sprays, in a totable utility bin. Another option is to use a rolling stainless steel utility island. That last option comes with a bonus: In warm weather, you can wheel the cart onto a porch or deck and work in the fresh air.

The Plot Thickens

Spring and fall are both excellent times to schedule your outdoor garden organization. In most parts of the country, they're the most pleasant times to work outside—not too hot or cold—but they're also good seasons in terms of garden prep. In the spring, you'll set yourself up for the busy growing season ahead. Fall is usually wrap-up time, when you're winding down and stowing things away long-term for the winter.

ALERT!

If you like instant gratification, you won't like this. Autumn, not spring, is the best time of year for planting perennials, evergreens, shrubs, and trees. Although plants might lose their leaves in the fall, the roots continue to grow.

As with most areas of your home, getting this area organized not only presents a more pleasing aesthetic and makes you feel better about your immediate environment, it helps you perform tasks more efficiently. Even for those who look at lawn-and-garden care as a necessary chore rather than a satisfying pastime, smart organization goes a long way to pruning the drudgery.

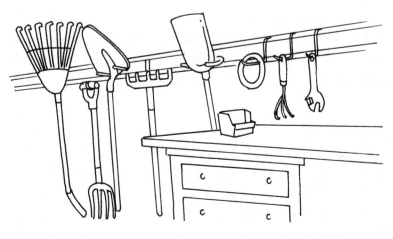

▲ Yard supplies.

Tooling Around

So now that you've whittled your lawn and garden equipment down to what you actually need and only the equipment that absolutely works, it's time to break it down into categories. These are the following:

- Manual tools, such as rakes and shovels
- Pots and statuaries
- Chemicals
- Seeds, bulbs, and other small items
- Soil, chips, birdseed, and any other materials that come in oversized bulky bags
- Large equipment, like lawn mowers and wheelbarrows

Here's the game plan. Think about how you're going to access something, not just about putting it away. Store the tools and products you use most in the front for easy in-and-out access. Little-used ones go in the back. However, seasonality will play a part. Figure on doing some rearranging at least twice a year. Snowblowers and snow shovels go to the head of the line in winter, until the lawn mower and weed whacker come out in spring.

FACT

Organic gardening is a method that uses only materials derived from living things, such as compost and manure, for fertilization and pest control. In contrast to conventional gardening, the organic approach uses no synthetic chemicals at all.

For rakes, shovels, hoes, outdoor brooms, and other long-handled tools, use nails, hooks, or handle grippers to hang them on the wall, heads up, instead of leaning them precariously against the wall, where they could become a tripping hazard. Organize small hand tools all together in such a way to let you easily grab and go. Pegboards will do the trick for tools as well as for small-handled pails. Trestles also make great utility posts. Another option for small items is to store them in convenient tote kits or hard cases, which will protect them from the elements.

Garden tools work better if they're in tip-top shape. Without proper maintenance, they can easily become caked with dirt and rendered useless. Unplug power tools before performing any maintenance or repairs. When filing or sharpening blades, be sure to wear safety goggles and leather gloves.

Hang ladders and wheelbarrows on U-hooks secured into the ceiling or on a wall using heavy-duty brackets. Get out-of-season lawn furniture out of the way by stowing it in the rafters of the garage. Another practical option is a mobile cart. For larger tools, like rakes and shovels, along with heavy-to-lug sacks of soil, rolling carts give you storage and freedom to roam throughout your property.

Plants and Planters

Nestle pots together to save space, using padding in between to prevent scratches. Stack plastic pots together and saucers separately. Terra-cotta pots can swell and crack, so it's best to lie them on their sides in a wood carton. Keep them in an area away from traffic flow. Be sure to bring pots made of clay or other fragile material inside for the winter. If you live in a cold-weather climate, you probably already know that some containers don't hold up to subfreezing temperatures. Be sure to clean and dry them thoroughly before storing to prevent disease.

Coil hoses and hang them on L-shaped hooks on the wall when off-duty for the season. Large, wide-mouthed planter containers also make handy homes for garden and soaking hoses. To avoid the "crazy coiling" syndrome altogether, buy a mobile hose cart that goes in the garage or shed in winter and rolls out and hooks up to your outdoor faucet in summer.

When storing large bags of mulch, peat, lime, and topsoil, make sure you keep them on low shelves that can sustain the weight. If you buy in bulk, try to consolidate whenever possible. It's both a matter of organization and inventory tracking. You'll know exactly what you have on hand. There's nothing more frustrating than digging into what you think is a large bag of fertilizer only to discover it's almost empty. Transfer contents of big, heavy bags into smaller, lidded containers to prevent spills. Check your local garden center or department store for durable, lightweight containers that can accommodate any size or quantity. Consider purchasing a tray with multiple drawers to store small items such as seed packets, bulbs, and work gloves.

QUESTION?

What's the best way to store bulbs for the winter?
After the season, dig up bulbs, brush off soil, and let them air dry to prevent rotting. Then store them in a bag or box with peat moss in a cool, dry place. Check them periodically for signs of insects, rot, or damage. If you spot any rot, cut away the affected section. And be sure to label the bulbs so you know what you'll be planting down the road.

Garden Parties

Cutting gardens, butterfly gardens, herb gardens. For most people, there's great satisfaction in getting down in the dirt, nurturing nature, and transforming a backyard into any number of glorious scene-stealing scenarios. Many gardeners say it grounds them and brings balance to their lives and a sense of serenity.

Plant Hardiness Zones are eleven geographic areas that help you determine what garden and landscape plants can survive and thrive in your particular climate. Zone 1 is in Alaska, for example, and Zone 11 is Hawaii. For more information, visit the U.S. National Arboretum Web site at *www .usna.usda.gov.*

Make sure to prevent winter damage to outdoor furniture. If you don't have room to bring your patio set inside a shed, garage, or basement for the season, protect it from inclement weather with heavy-gauge furniture covers. And don't forget to wrap your outside faucets with easy-to-install covers, too. Otherwise, freezing temperatures could cause water damage.

If space is at a premium, eke out some more by using outdoor storage benches that can hold patio cushions or small hand tools. If you use heavy-duty plastic tubs for storage, make sure you give each one a function. For instance, dedicate one tub to cushions, another to tools, a third to barbecue and entertaining accessories, and so on. Don't mix and match, or you'll lose track of where everything is.

ALERT!

An important issue is the safe storage of chemicals. Keep chemicals, herbicides, and pesticides away from pets and children. Poisonous items should be locked in ventilated cabinets or stored in containers on high shelves so no accidents occur. And don't underestimate the potential hazards of sharp tools, either. They should always be stowed away where they can't be easily accessed.

Once you button up your storage and have your organizational method in place, you'll discover you're spending less time in the search for things and more in the soil.

Chapter 13

Park Place: Garages

Want to actually have room in your garage for a car? For many homeowners, that's a novel notion. Heavy equipment, sporting gear, and even backup appliances have muscled their way in, leaving vehicles often literally out in the cold. In the garage, every surface is a storage opportunity. Wall arrangements don't have to be works of art. They just have to make the space tidy and efficient. Learn about nifty garage solutions that will allow you to have your coupe and park it, too.

Car Wars

Once upon a time, garages were expressly designed to house one thing: the family vehicle. But over the years, they've evolved dramatically into inexpensive yet functional workrooms and recreational spaces. Actually, in some circles they're being called "flexispaces," ready to serve any need for any family member. Some common uses of a garage include the following:

- Tool shed
- Garden center
- Workshop
- Exercise studio
- Garbage and recycling center
- Hobby and crafts workspace
- Smoking room
- Children's play room
- Sports equipment area

One South Carolina housewife, thinking about her detached garage with a second story loft, says it houses not only her husband's woodworking shop but a little mirror and basin, too. That's where he trims his beard and moustache so the whiskers don't get all over the bathroom floor!

Wonderful things have been known to happen in garages. Is there something particularly inspiring about them? Something that makes them incubators for great ideas? You'd have to think so, based on some of the fun, funky, and far-reaching concepts that were hatched in garages. Walt Disney is said to have come up with his idea for Mickey Mouse while working in a garage and watching mice at play. The theme song to the old TV show *Gilligan's Island* was recorded in a garage. A couple of Stanford University engineers, Bill Hewlett and David Packard, started Hewlett-Packard in a California garage. And that's exactly where Steve Jobs and Steve Wozniak built their prototype for the first personal computer, the Apple.

There are more than 65 million garages in the United States, according to statistics compiled by GarageTek, a New York–based garage system company. How times have changed! In 1950 nearly 60 percent of new homes were constructed without a garage. Today, garages are virtually a given, with the vast majority housing two cars or more. And like many symbols of status, the bigger the better. In fact, some super-size structures with enough stalls to accommodate multiple vehicles *plus* a golf cart *and* a boat are being dubbed "garage Mahals." The number of garages with three or more bays continues to rise at double-digit rates. The numbers are even more dramatic in those areas of the country where basements are rare and storage space is at a bigger premium.

FACT

Another popular use for the garage? Band practice. The garage rock movement began in the mid-1960s, when teenagers began appropriating their parents' garages and turning them into rehearsal studios. The term "garage rock" stuck. Bands such as Buddy Holly and the Crickets, The Kinks, Creedence Clearwater Revival, and Nirvana all got their start in the garage.

Central Park

There really is no mystery as to why a garage gets so cluttered up. The answer is quite simple: because it's there. Even for homes with basements or attics, a garage is a lot easier to access. It just calls out to be filled up! And the fuller it becomes, the less likely you'll ever want to deal with the disorganized mess. That 60 percent of homeowners admit to having a very disorganized garage shouldn't come as much of a surprise.

That's why driveways across the country are lined up with cars that no longer fit in the garage. It's no joke. According to one study, a whopping 40 percent of people who own a garage park their car in the driveway. It doesn't make much sense when you think about it. Vehicles valued at $20,000, $30,000, $40,000, or more are left out to brave the elements while beat-up lawn mowers, rarely used bicycles, and spare refrigerators get prime space.

Barry Izsak, president of the National Association of Professional Organizers and author of *Organize Your Garage in No Time*, says the American two-car has become the no-car garage. Don't know what to do with something? Put it in the garage. It's become the family dumping ground, so it's only logical that garages are the places where clutter reaches epic proportions.

There's the story of a cosmetics saleswoman who packed her inventory away in her garage and kept it there for years, even after the dates on her merchandise had long expired. Meanwhile, her husband was a livery driver who bought a new Lincoln Town car every year. The car—representing a big chunk of the couple's livelihood—sat out on the street while the garage protected a load full of useless products.

If you need extra shelter for your car, truck, recreation vehicle, or boat, a portable garage might do the trick. Choose from an all-weather model made of plastic sheeting or a metal frame covered in a form-fitting tarp.

Is your garage filled to the brim? Another woman kept an old freezer in her garage packed with meats that had been there so long, they didn't just suffer freezer burn—they were positively polar.

For some reason, we seem to have no compunction about showing our dysfunctional garages to the world. We might shut the door to a messy office or close off any views to a muddled basement, but when it comes to the garage, we open it daily for all the neighborhood to see. Then again, more likely than not, the neighbor's garage is in the same sorry, chaotic state.

The garage is one of the most difficult rooms to organize, and there's a good reason for that. When you move in, it's empty. There's no structure to follow, no blueprint to heed. Think about it. A closet at least has rods and shelves. A kitchen has drawers and cabinets. But in a garage, there's *nada*, zilch. You've got to create that structure on your own, and the fact is that few people do—or at least do it right.

Garages typically serve multiple functions for different members of the household. Sporting gear and gardening equipment are probably in every garage. That's okay. The good news is that there's room for it and more, if you plan it right. In one survey, more than half the consumers polled said they had plans to reorganize their garage. Well, as the old saying goes, there's no time like the present.

Ninety-four percent of homeowners store dangerous items in their garages. Always store chemicals in the containers they came in. Keep insecticides, weed killer, and other poisonous chemicals away from the reach of children. Move them to a high shelf or, preferably, into a locked but ventilated cabinet. For questions about the use or disposal of pesticides, contact the National Pesticide Telecommunications Network, at 1-800-858-7378.

▲ The garage, before.

But to get from here to there, from clutter and chaos to order and organization, you'll have to roll up your sleeves, don the work clothes, and determine exactly what you've got. Yes, that means it's inventory time again. The key is not to defeat yourself before you get started. You might have five, ten, maybe twenty years or more of accumulated clutter behind those great big garage doors. So set realistic expectations. Pick a nice day, and get down to business.

Getting in Gear

Enlist a friend or family member to lend a hand with heavy-lifting duties and, equally important, an objective pair of eyes to help you make the tough decisions about what to keep and what to throw away. If you're one of those people who finds it hard to part with your possessions, you'll find something nice about this process: By taking everything out of the garage for sorting purposes, your things are that much closer to the trash cans.

Use your driveway or an adjacent patio as a staging area, and divide it into zones for items you'll keep, discard, donate, and relocate. If you really have a jam-packed garage, consider PODS, or Portable On-Demand Storage (*www.pods.com*). A weatherproof and secure storage container is delivered to your home, enabling you to temporarily house belongings while you sort through the organizational process.

FACT

Sear, Roebuck & Co. introduced prefabricated garages and sold mail-order garage kits in the early twentieth century. Those early garages had windows for light and ventilation with doors that swung out like barn doors, instead of up. Some even had doors at both ends so that vehicles could enter from one direction and exit out the other side. No backing out necessary.

Start by getting rid of the obvious stuff that you can easily reach first. That'll help you clear out some space quickly. Then go through the remaining items one at a time. Follow this process:

- Donate anything your family has outgrown—either physically or interest-wise. The garage just isn't the place to hold onto sentimental favorites.

- Find a deserving home for tools that are still in working order but that you've replaced with the latest, greatest version.
- Say *adios* to anything that's been bested by time and humidity.
- Just say no to anything that doesn't belong in a garage.

One dutiful homeowner tried to get rid of the clutter. She'd regularly haul items to the curb for trash pickup, but then her husband would rummage through the piles after dark. The next morning, she inevitably found them right back in the garage.

On the day they moved out of their home, one family made two curious garage discoveries. The first was a pile of newspapers dated July 20, 1969, documenting the first moon landing. Unsurprisingly, after decades kept outside in unsuitable storage conditions, the historical papers were so brittle they disintegrated on touch and had to be tossed. The other surprise was finding a life-size cutout of the actress Tuesday Weld that had—for reasons unknown—been won at a church event years earlier. To paraphrase Forrest Gump, a garage is like a box of chocolates. You never know what you're going to get.

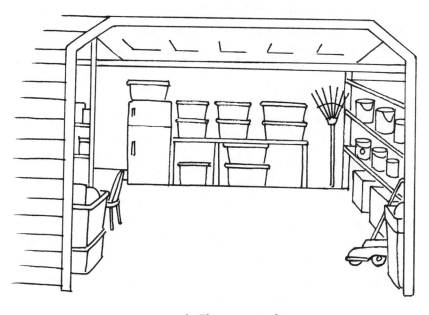

▲ The garage, after.

Stalled Plans

By being realistic about what you really need to keep, you've hopefully created an impressive pile for the next trash collection. But before you haul the keepers back into the garage, it's time to put an organizational plan in place.

The extent of your storage plan is predicated on how much stuff you have. Want another incentive to downsize? The less stuff you have, the less money you'll need to cough up for storage accessories. Make no mistake about it. The garage is one of the top areas in the home for storage and organizational product spending. It's typically the one place used by the entire family on a regular basis. As a result, consumers have begun making garage organization a priority to the tune of some $800 million in sales, representing about 11 percent of the total organization market. What's more, sales are predicted to grow by 12 to 15 percent.

ESSENTIAL

Consider this: What if the biggest piece of junk in your garage is actually your car? Some clunkers cost more to tow than they're worth on the open market. If that's the case, think about donating your vehicle to a charity. If your wheels are valued at more than $500, the Internal Revenue Service limits your deduction to the charity's actual selling price.

Don't think of your garage as a mere room, but as a multidimensional storage facility. You've got five sides to work with: the floor, two side walls, a back wall, and a ceiling. Consider location and accessibility when determining the best spots for your items.

Of course, let's start with a given. The sweet spots of a one, two, or even three-car garage are going to be reserved for—drum roll, please—your vehicles. Then subdivide the remaining space into dedicated zones for each major storage category or activity. Gardening, auto maintenance, home repair, sports, and outdoor entertaining are a few common examples.

Place the items you use the most in the easiest areas to access, making sure they don't interfere with the opening and closing of car or garage doors.

Haul Ways

Simple shelving, unobtrusive bins, and shallow closed cabinets can handle a moderate load, provided there are no hoarder types residing at your address. To maintain order, make sure each bin is clearly labeled and filled only with similar items. Dedicate separate containers for garden supplies, tools, sporting equipment, and maintenance products like tool sharpeners, oil, replacement parts, and so on. For more on gardening and yard equipment storage, see Chapter 12.

Pegboards are tried-and-true resources for housing tools—and then some. Have a board cut to size and then use it to hang wire baskets. It'll help you get protective sports equipment, pool accessories, and toys off the floor. Pegboards with wider holes and larger hooks can hold heavier gear. A simple solution for bulky items like soccer balls and baseball mitts is to place them in mesh bags and then hang them on a pegboard hook. Give new life to household discards by deploying old chests, cabinets, and even entertainment units that have seen better days in the garage for dust-free storage.

ALERT!

If you spend a lot of time in your garage doing projects, or if you store fragile items in there, an insulated garage door will provide better protection from extreme temperatures for both you and your possessions. You'll get the added advantage of soundproofing, too—something your neighbors will appreciate if you're on close terms with your high-decibel power tools.

If your garage reflects a busy household with family members who have lots of hobbies and all the equipment that goes along with them, it might be time to consider a garage system. Garage systems offer limitless storage possibilities. Some are budget-friendly; others demand more of a deep-pocket investment into the thousands of dollars, depending on the extent of the makeover.

◀ Sports equipment.

There are high-performance shelving systems with hooks, shelf baskets, and brackets that can be mixed and matched to suit your needs. GarageTek, the Long Island-based franchiser of garage systems, offers another type of garage scheme. The company installs custom-designed floors, cabinets, and shelves in an effort to transform garages into usable, flexible space. Slotted wall-storage panels that look a bit like retail-store displays allow you to hang up just about anything you can imagine. Many homeowners who use wall systems combine them with closed cabinetry to hide the less-presentable items. A company like GarageTek can remodel a two-car garage measuring twenty by twenty feet in just one or two days. The folks at Whirlpool have joined in this burgeoning consumer demand for garage storage systems, as well. Its line, called Gladiator® GarageWorks, is another alterative to the traditional peg-board scheme, offering component panels or slot-full wall system to reclaim valuable floor space. The company offers a free online tool called the Blueprint Estimator that allows you to design your own modular garage system. Visit *www.gladiatorgw.com/blueprint* for details.

If you live in a four-season climate, you'll probably want to rearrange your garage at least once or twice a year. Sure, it entails a bit of extra work, but, on the bright side, it also gives you additional opportunities to give your gear another once- or twice-over and determine what's worth keeping around. If you store your patio furniture inside for the winter, the ceiling rafters are an ideal place. Open, adjustable rafter shelves can be attached to the roof truss of your garage. Not only that, they can handle car seats, camping gear, and ski equipment, among other things, without getting in the way of your parked vehicles. If your garage is tall enough, you might even think about constructing a storage loft area using a bunk bed–style ladder to access it.

There are two main types of garage doors. A swing-up or tilt model is made of a single panel that pivots out and upward. Sectional roll-up doors, which are more expensive, are constructed of several sections that are hinged together and mounted onto a track with rollers.

Consider elevated platforms that lower to the ground for a motorcycle, scooter, snow blower, or lawn mower. A lift-and-pulley system is a useful floor-clearing device to get your bicycles out of the line of foot traffic. Another option is to mount bikes flush to the wall and add an additional rack for helmets and other accessories. If you're the tool-shy type, try an adjustable-tension design rack that can be secured to the walls or ceiling without any hardware or having to make any holes.

Getting the Most Mileage

There's never been a better time to get your garage into shape. Sales of garage storage products grew an astounding 40 percent in just five years, which means there are plenty of solutions on the market available to tailor a system to your lifestyle. How dramatic do you want to get? Do you prefer taking a do-it-yourself approach? Or would you rather hire a professional garage-makeover company? Your wallet, habits, and the importance you place on your garage's resemblance to a multifunctional new-car showroom will dictate your answer.

Whatever approach you take, there's no need to make permanent changes. In fact, you're better off with a system of shelves, cabinets, and units that can adjust and grow with your needs. The storage units you need now for all your kids' sporting equipment may be superfluous once they're out of the house and on their own.

FACT

The first overhead garage door was built by Overhead Door Corporation of Farmers Branch, Texas, in 1921. The company was also the first to manufacture an electric garage-door opener, just five years later.

Remember, the garage is a good place to repurpose old but still sturdy furniture—in moderation. Once you've got your system up and running, stick to it. The best storage system in the world won't last if you don't maintain it. A well-organized garage will pay you back many times over. Every time you hit the button on your garage-door opener, you'll feel good about the newly streamlined environment you've created and marvel at how easy it is to find what you need when you need it. And if it's been a while since your car has seen the inside of the garage, you've probably forgotten how nice it is not to have to clear snow off your vehicle in the winter or get into a sun-baked seat in the summer. Most important, your vehicle will be more secure and sport that coveted showroom-chic look a lot longer.

Chapter 14

Thanks for the Memorabilia: Collectibles

The collector's mantra: to preserve, to protect, and to keep amassing. But at what price? Is your home being overrun by every steal-of-a-deal you couldn't resist? Are you unwittingly harming your prized collectibles by displaying them in the wrong place and storing them under the wrong conditions? Not to worry. In this chapter, you'll learn the best way to showcase your goods, whether they're sentimental favorites or priceless heirlooms, and to avoid costly, and sometimes heartbreaking, mistakes.

Amass Appeal

Consider the sad tale of George, one lifelong Yankee fan. Over the years, he'd been lucky enough to collect baseballs autographed by three of the all-time greatest pinstripers: Mickey Mantle, Yogi Berra, and Phil Rizzuto. George bought three specially designed glass baseball-display cubes to protect them from fingerprints, dirt, and dust. He did everything right . . . right? He made just one error, but it was a biggie. He put his treasured trio on a desk that happened to be by a window in direct sunlight. Without realizing it, the ultraviolet rays faded the signatures over time to the point they were virtually unrecognizable. That Yankee fan still holds those autographed baseballs dear, but they're no longer the valuable assets they once were.

A good way to become better educated is to join a club or attend shows pertaining to your collectible. Whether you collect Steiff teddy bears, Hallmark Christmas ornaments, Depression glass, or baseball memorabilia, you'll have the inside track on current market prices and leads on reputable dealers.

Proper storage of your special collections, antiques, and figurines is about how and where.

Let's start with the how.

Crazy for Collectibles

America's gone collectible crazy, and it's easy to see why. Accessibility has never been easier. In the old days, amassing a collection involved sacrificing a certain amount of shoe leather to scout out stores, collectors clubs, thrift shops, and garage sales. But online auction sites—especially eBay—have given consumers an easy, exciting way to get their hands on any kind of item worthy of accruing, no matter how rare or obscure. You can find anything now with the click of a mouse, from ever-popular favorites like coins, Disneyana, bobble heads, and pottery to curious ones like ceramic string holders and airline menus. A history buff named Valero credits eBay along with actual brick-and-mortar auction houses like Sotheby's for his extensive collection of medieval weaponry.

If you can contain your collections to a manageable number, you're in good shape. If you've got lots of room in which to spread them out, so much the better. Many people, though, have massive collections—bigger than they could ever display. Or they've got multiple collections because, for so many, it all comes down to the thrill of the hunt. They enjoy the search so much that what they're actually collecting is almost secondary. The fun is in the perpetual pursuit.

E ALERT!

Condition is key to your collection. Buy the best quality you can afford. Take a pass on items with visible chips, cracks, or hairline fractures. And avoid excess handling. Depending on the item, it may hasten deterioration. Call a professional conservator if an item needs restoration. Never attempt to fix it yourself.

One television executive named Sue has been rebuying all the toys and books she loved as a little girl but that her parents threw away when she moved out of the house—Strawberry Shortcake, Poochie, and Alf dolls among them. She suspects it's an early midlife crisis at age thirty-two. Her husband, a neat and tidy type, claims (with a smile) she buys it all for spite. Then there's Joey, an eclectic collector who loves anything that sparks a memory: milk bottles that remind him of his childhood, record albums from the 1940s that harken back to his parents' generation, and Fiestaware that conjures up recollections of his grandmother's house. His nephew once called his home "Uncle Joey's Museum of Junk."

Controlling the Volume

When collections multiply like out-of-control rabbits, the pleasure you derive from them becomes overshadowed by their sheer volume. Displays become unwieldy or seemingly haphazard. One professional organizer said a client of hers would collect figurines from her world travels. The problem? The globetrotter had a small apartment, and the figurines were displayed anywhere and everywhere. The situation eventually got so out of hand she had to shell out money for a storage unit just to stow some away. It's a common story. Many organizing pros will confess that memorabilia is their greatest nightmare!

Some people wind up becoming accidental collectors. One Midwesterner named Tom, for instance, calls himself a "box-lot victim." Years ago, he attended an auction—in person, not the online kind—and put a winning bid on a box lot full of "junk." One valuable item that was part of the box—a cookie jar marked McCoy—happened to be highly coveted. From that day on, Tom became hooked on collecting McCoy pottery.

FACT

eBay was founded by Pierre Omidyar as a hobby in 1995. It's now the most popular online shopping Web site, with more than 100 million registered members from around the world.

Another accidental collector is Pat, who innocently picked up a Thomas Clark gnome on vacation out West. It was a few years later that she actually discovered it was considered a collectible and that her $18 purchase was now worth more than ten times her original investment. And then the barrage began. Every time another Christmas or birthday rolled around, some friend or family member would buy Pat another Thomas Clark gnome, turning an initial, casually made purchase into an out-of-control collection. Her moment of epiphany came when the collection started taking over shelves in her vacation home, too.

It's not an uncommon situation to have other people foist a collection on you. One woman who understandably wishes to remain anonymous says she's got a doll collection—but not because she wants to. She just doesn't have the heart to ask her mother to stop buying them for her.

Follow the lead of most experienced collectors and narrow your focus down to just a couple of categories. If you collect baseball cards, limit yourself to a particular team or era. Love anything to do with the military? Restrict yourself to a specific period in time. World's Fairs? Stick to one or two expositions.

Not many collectors take kindly to the idea of downsizing their trove, but it may be time to consider drastic action if the items exceed the space you have to store them in, plain and simple. Many people get possessive about their things, bordering on the obsessive. Others think the items are more valuable than they actually are or are convinced that one day they will be. Among baby boomers, in particular, there's a large group still smarting over the Barbie dolls and Hot Wheels their parents threw out ages ago, convinced that with them went a good chunk of their nest egg. As a result, they're determined to hang onto every childhood relic they've still got.

Cent-amental Value

Do a reality check and assess your situation. Are your collectibles overwhelming your living quarters? Are your possessions starting to possess you? Put bluntly, are they really worth the bother? Many collections are made up of items that hold sentimental value, such as ticket stubs or vacation souvenirs. But if your items have any kind of financial value, see if you can pare down your collection by bringing some pieces to market. Investigate the best avenue for selling your excess wares. Online auction Web sites like eBay, a free community forum like Craigslist.com, antique dealers, and consignment shops are venues that can turn your treasures into cash. You should keep in mind, however, that prices for items with chips or nicks take a nosedive.

What is a consignment sale?
A consignment sale is an arrangement in which merchandise is sold by an agent on the seller's behalf. Consignment shops differ from thrift shops in that a portion of the proceeds goes to the seller, rather than a charity.

When you're ready to put your collectibles on the market, do some homework to make sure you have an idea of what they're worth. Study the market, check auction prices, or contact a certified appraiser to determine the fair market value.

If cashing in is not part of the game plan, you can always pass your treasures on to family members or friends who may value the items as much as you do.

Aging Gracefully

The categories of collectibles run the gamut, from fragile glassware and priceless watches to postcards, snow globes, and precious stones. Many collectibles, like commemorative baseballs and pens, for instance, have special housing made to order. Since condition is key to maintaining the value of any type of collection, proper storage is important from both an aesthetic point of view as well as an investment perspective. Items in their original box command the highest prices. Spotting, discoloration, and age marks will work against you in the marketplace.

The market for collectibles is susceptible to reproductions and fakes. Arm yourself by reading some of the many value guides on the market. Counterfeits are made to deceive. Some items are even intentionally scuffed up, coated with dirt, or worn to simulate age. The better educated you are, the better armed you'll be against fakes.

In general, here are a few things to keep in mind:

- An enclosed cabinet, curio, or wall unit with glass doors will keep small items dust-free. As many a collector can attest, the worst part about collectibles is cleaning them.
- Ornamental glass vases are clever containers for small items such as matchbook covers, transit tokens, and medals.
- For silverware, slow down tarnishing by wrapping items in a silver cloth, available at jewelers and fabric stores, or in a zip-close plastic bag.
- Avoid using straight pins or safety pins on cloth items such as pennants, dolls, and stuffed animals. They can cause rust and corrosion.

Install high shelves around the perimeter of the room to spread out your collection without overwhelming it. This works well with any kind of decorative collection, like plates, vases, oil lamps, or vintage barware. But limit this method to items that don't need to be viewed up close to be appreciated. Delicate designs will lose their impact at a distance.

Here's a novel idea. *Use* your collectibles. If you collect teapots, say, liven up your everyday routine by putting them to good use. Rotate them from time to time. That way, you'll never get bored with your tableware. Recycling any collection adds dramatic impact and frees up surface space.

Heir Conditioning

Many items—not just autographed baseballs—should be kept away from direct sunlight. Teddy bears, dolls, artwork, wood, and textiles can all get bleached out by harmful ultraviolet rays. An option is to have window film installed to protect them from the sun's harsh effects. Speaking of windows, even if a collectible isn't in direct sunlight, displaying it near or below an open window could still prove detrimental. All it takes is a gentle breeze to sprinkle your beloved gems in a coating of dust, pollen, or other microscopic enemies.

Keep fragile things like crystal and china out of the reach of children. Consider a high shelf or a glass cabinet with a lock. Make sure display surfaces are sturdy, secure, and level and won't be affected by vibrations from nearby trains, vacuum cleaners, or the opening of an electronic garage door.

Do as museum experts do and add a touch of gummy wax to the bottom of figurines, glass pieces, and other delicate treasures to anchor them in place. The sticky wax is easily removed, leaving no damage to your precious objects or to shelves.

Did you know that wood and wood products can emit acids that cause metal to corrode? That's why you're better off keeping metal-based collectibles in metal cabinets or shelves instead of in wood units.

Glass expands and contracts when exposed to extreme heat and cold. Make sure your glass pieces are out of the direct line of air conditioners, radiators, and heating vents.

Beautiful objects deserve a place of honor in your home, but tempting as a fireplace mantel may be, resist. The smoke and soot from your fireplace will put your valuables on a fast track to ruin.

Humidity levels can play havoc on your collectibles—either too much or too little, depending on the item in question. Low humidity, for instance, will dry out leather goods, parchments, and baskets. High humidity can get the best of just about anything else. Bob, an enthusiastic collector of World's Fair memorabilia, keeps his pendants, pins, plates, coasters, and postcards in his finished basement where he can enjoy them. The basement is where his home office is and where he spends a good deal of his time, but it's not necessarily the ideal environment. Fortunately, Bob knows it. During the four to six-week period in the summer when humidity puddles up in the corners and the pipes drip with condensation, he keeps an extra vigil to make sure his rare treasures don't suffer.

Out of Sight

Before packing items away for seasonal or long-term storage, give them a good cleaning to rid them of dust and grime, and don't forget to pack items loosely so that air can circulate between pieces. Stack containers properly—don't just toss them on a shelf precariously where items can shift. And be sure to keep heavy items on the lowest shelves.

Head off potential dangers by wrapping fragile pieces with care—but not so fast with the newspapers and bubble wrap! Acid-free tissue is best. Newsprint contains acids that can leech onto the surface of your collectibles and mar their beauty, and bubble wrap can harbor moisture. Many items, including porcelain, artwork, and papers, are sensitive to temperature fluctuations and should be kept out of basements, attics, and garages. Give stored items a regularly scheduled eyeballing to make sure insects or mold hasn't crept in.

FACT

A conservator cares for, restores, and repairs collectible objects. For more information, contact the American Institute for Conservation of Historic and Artistic Works at 202-452-9545, or visit them online at *http:// aic.stanford.edu.* The organization can provide a free list of conservators in your area.

Properly mark your storage containers. A discophile named Eddie loves his record albums. Even though he also has a vast CD library, he has a longstanding rule in his home: Sundays are for playing LPs only. His record collection is populated with offbeat recordings like Soupy Sales' rendering of Motown songs and the *Best of Walter Brennan*. Unfortunately, in a move to Florida several years ago, Eddie dropped off the wrong milk crate of albums at the Salvation Army and lost some of his most precious titles. Today, he laments that someone else is enjoying *William Frawley Sings the Old Ones*.

Handle with Care

If only more die-hard collectors could be like the South Florida woman who says the only things she collects are memories of kindnesses and life experiences! You can bet she's one person who has no storage challenges.

There are collectors, and there are hoarders. If you spend weekdays on eBay sprees, weekends at garage sales, and your in-between time trying to find a place for it all, you're leaning toward the latter.

There's no question that some items anchor and comfort us. Possessions are a way of conveying our values and accomplishments or connecting us with good times. On the other hand, without even realizing it, some people amass bigger, better collections as a way of showing off and one-upping the Joneses. Their things empower them and affect their self-esteem. Understanding motives is a way of helping some people keep their collecting within reason.

Compile an itemized list of your most valuable keepsakes, and keep your list attached to photos and appraisals, if you have them. If possible, store the information off-premises in a safety-deposit box or with a relative.

Treasure your collections by caring for them properly. Do yourself and your investment a favor and act like a conservator. Know what the enemies are—both environmental and man-made—and learn how to combat them. Always opt for gentle cleaners, nothing abrasive. Call a professional to handle any serious damage.

If your collections are getting out of hand, change your mindset by thinking quality and not quantity. If your things are shoved in the back of a closet or boxed up in the basement and not enhancing your life in any meaningful way, finding them a new home where they'll be appreciated might just be the best storage solution of all.

Chapter 15

It's Only a Paper Boom: Ephemera

That paper disintegrates with age is no pulp fiction. Legal documents, autographs, certificates, important letters—in fact, all things paper—demand proper storage conditions and special protection for longevity. Find out how to hold the line against Father Time. In this chapter, paper-pushers will get no-nonsense ideas on archive-friendly storage solutions.

TeXt Marks the Spot

Remember when pundits predicted that the digital age would create a world of paperless homes and offices? Tick, tock, tick, tock. We're still waiting. Pamphlets, brochures, take-out menus, business cards—the incursion never stops. Despite the proliferation of data files, the ubiquity of e-mail, and the widespread ability to download documents electronically, papers are still piling up as quickly as they did in the old days of manual typewriters and carbon copies. It's one of the most common problems professional organizers have to deal with.

FACT

Paper is derived from the Egyptian word "papyrus." Papyrus was a form of paper produced in ancient Egypt as early as 3000 B.C. It wasn't until the nineteenth century that the process for producing paper was industrialized.

For one thing, many people still feel compelled to print out documents from their computer, be it an e-mail, a spreadsheet, or a word-processing file. There's something about the security of holding onto a hard copy that puts the mind at ease. It's a tough habit to break. Even among the most computer savvy, it's rare that all documents are exclusively filed electronically.

The Chief Culprits

A collective addiction to hard copies is not the only reason the paper situation has gotten so out of hand. You don't have to look far to track down the guilty parties:

- **Schoolwork:** Think homework assignments, permission slips, teacher's newsletters, and artwork. Have more than one child? Multiply the paperwork.
- **Media:** Catalogs, magazines, newspapers, and books—who's got the time to read them all, anyway?

- **Mail:** They call it junk mail and, yet, instead of junking it, we let it sit around until it creates a paper chokehold.

The pileups begin when these kinds of everyday items are tossed aside. It's the "I'll get back to it later" syndrome. And "later" comes only when the piles have gotten too big to ignore, and the paper trails start spreading from one room of the house to the next.

There's no point strategizing a storage system for your papers until you clear out what's already there. If you haven't already read Chapter 7, which discusses how to organize your home office, now's the time to take a look and launch into action. Remember, you need to be ruthless in going through your papers and make a clean sweep of things.

E ALERT!

Mail avoidance is a phenomenon that is particularly prevalent among people who suffer depression, financial problems, or both. If an individual is going through a difficult situation, the last thing he wants to do is open another past-due bill or letter that might contain more bad news.

Want to get rid of your magazines? Great. But don't use the pages as kindling for your fireplace. They actually contain toxic chemicals that may be released into the air if you use them to start a fire. Instead, drop old magazines off at your health club, recreational center, or laundromat for others to enjoy.

Collections

Are you an autograph hound? Have an interest in historical documents? Classic postcards? How about vintage magazine advertisements or theatrical playbills? Keep an eye out for paper shows, estate sales, and postcard fairs as well as auctions to add to your collection and your edification.

Books, autographs, love letters, clippings, concert stubs: Admit it, you've got a few such keepsakes stashed somewhere in your home. If the paper stuff has real sentimental value, save it. But if you're holding onto something because you think it's going to pay for your kid's tuition one day, do a little research to determine if it's really worth its weight in storage space. What might seem to have financial worth to you could generate a big yawn on the open market. A book's not valuable just because it's a first edition. A magazine isn't a collectible just because it's old.

Reamed Out

Reducing paper clutter is a matter of changing bad habits and adopting a few new ones. For items you face every day, the trick is not giving them a chance to take root. Deal with those things immediately.

Janet Groene, author of *Living Aboard Your RV*, says she can't live without books, newspapers, and magazines. It's not unusual, but it's also not easy when you live life the way Janet and her husband, Gordon, did. The couple lived in a twenty-one-foot motor home in summer and aboard a twenty-nine-foot sailboat in winter full time for ten years. Needless to say, paper was the couple's big bugaboo. They needed to establish strict rules to contain it. Newspapers went out the next day. Period. If they saved a newspaper clipping, it was cut out after they both finished with the page and then immediately filed. A pair of scissors was part of their reading equipment. Books? They limited their collection by starting a free lending library everywhere they went. All it took was setting up a cardboard box at a marina, laundromat, church basement, or campground with a supply of gently used books and a sign saying Take One, Leave One. Sometimes, Janet recalled, they returned months or even years later to find their book exchange program still in place and going strong.

FACT

Ephemera are items that were originally intended to be short-lived (such as postcards) that are now considered collectibles. The Ephemera Society of America is a nonprofit organization that was formed in 1980 to cultivate and encourage interest in ephemera and the history associated with it. The group actively promotes an understanding, appreciation, and enjoyment of ephemera for both personal as well as institutional collections.

Open the mail when it arrives and act upon it straight away, especially the junk mail. Don't let it take up even a few inches of precious surface space on your counters. Read the newspaper, and put it in the recycling bin. Stash magazines in a dedicated rack or basket, but don't hold on to any that are more than two or three months old. If you haven't gotten around to reading them in that time, you won't. Throw it out or pass it on. It's a smart idea to review your magazine subscriptions on a regular basis. Weeklies can be a killer. A busy few weeks, and suddenly your home looks like a publishers' convention. If you routinely find yourself falling behind on your reading, or if you're giving an issue only a brief once-over before tossing it aside, you should think about transferring your subscription to someone who might appreciate it more. On the other hand, if you're an avid reader who'd prefer to do without the clutter, see if your favorite magazines have an online edition you can subscribe to. Or visit your local public library. Chances are it has a large selection of popular publications on hand.

Stop unwanted catalogs before they arrive. Contact companies that send you catalogs that you have no use for, and ask to be removed from their mailing lists. Even the ones you do enjoy may have special editions you don't need, such as a baby line or travel line.

Out, Not About

For the catalogs you like to browse, you don't necessarily need to hold onto the whole issue. If you see something you like, tear out the page(s) and clip it to the back cover that has your customer information. Better yet, bookmark the company's Web site and toss the catalog entirely.

As far as other day-to-day papers, dealing with them immediately is the key. File what you need to save but don't need to act on. Use an in-box for action items. For more on filing systems, see Chapter 7.

If yours is a Hallmark-happy kind of family, greeting cards can get out of control quickly. Showcase them artfully on wire displays or posts so they're not overwhelming your countertops and shelves. One woman cleaning through the heaps in her home found a stack of birthday cards her son had received—from years past. As she went through the mound, she discovered several gift checks still tucked inside the cards. The unfortunate part was that the checks were way too old to cash.

QUESTION?

What is recycled paper?
Recycled paper is made of recovered paper products, collected from various sources such as excess newspapers, packing materials, and magazines. Recycled paper helps preserve forests by reducing the demand for wood. In addition, the production of recycled paper demands less energy use than the production of virgin paper.

For a clever display of vintage greeting cards and postcards, rotating carousels are available in tabletop and floor models.

Use everyday technology to save a tree or two. Instead of leaving notes all over the place, use voice mail and e-mail for little reminders. Paula, a freelance writer, has technology that combines both. She regularly uses her cell phone when she's on the road to leave messages for herself on her home phone machine. Special software allows her messages to be captured as audio files in her e-mail inbox that she can then forward electronically as needed.

Use a greeting-card organizer to not only record important dates like birthdays and anniversaries but also to hold cards you've bought in advance. Keep a supply of special-occasion, blank, and get-well cards on hand, and you'll never be left unprepared.

What's in Store

Every piece of paper worth saving needs a dedicated home, whether that home is a long-term folder, a lockbox, or an action file. Terri, from Fort Worth, Texas, admits to having spawned a huge clutter problem in a spare room of her home. That's where her sentimental papers have taken up residence in no fewer than six dresser drawers.

It's understandable why so many of us hold onto vestiges of our past. They connect us with loved ones or irretrievable moments in our lives. Be discretionary. Saving is one thing, but hoarding is another. Taken to extremes, hoarding creates stagnant energy and weighs down on you emotionally. That's no way to honor a memory. Devise a rating scale that allows you to evaluate the true importance of a given document or letter. Realize not everything holds the same emotional value. If you start to develop feelings of separation anxiety, taper off your collection in stages. No need to go cold turkey if it's just too painful.

FACT

The Computer History Museum, established in 1996 in the heart of California's Silicon Valley, is the world's largest institution for preserving and presenting the story of the information age and its impact. The museum houses more than 4,000 artifacts, including a Cray-3 super-computer and a computer-generated version of the Mona Lisa.

Many storage ideas have been addressed in Chapter 7. But within the province of pulp is a special category of documents you want to hang onto for the long haul. This kind of ephemera demands VIP treatment and includes such items as these:

- Diaries
- Wedding invitations
- Birth certificates
- Death certificates
- Vintage maps, postcards, and sheet music
- Personal letters, cards, and valentines

For just about the last century and a half, most paper has been produced from inexpensive and widely available wood pulp, rather than cotton fibers that had once been widespread. Added into the pulp mix are chemical acids, exactly the thing that causes paper to turn brown, break down, and turn brittle. Then there are the usual suspects, including insects, heat, humidity, and light. Suddenly, paper's got more enemies than Al Capone.

What's the lifespan of a piece of paper? How long before the disintegration begins? Well, there's no exact timetable, but there is a kind of pecking order. Newsprint, for instance, is usually the first to go. It's made of the cheapest paper available. Leave your recycling pile near a sunny window for a couple of days and you'll quickly see it start to yellow, a sure sign of deterioration. If a newspaper clipping or commemorative issue lasts ten or twenty years, it has lived to a ripe old age. Other paper, made of higher quality materials, will grow old more gracefully before showing signs of wear and tear.

ESSENTIAL

Want to frame a meaningful document or letter but afraid of how the light might fade it? Consider having a quality photocopy made of your original document, frame the copy, and keep your one-of-a-kind item well protected and under wraps elsewhere.

Recently, one of the largest private collections of letters accumulated from a single family was brought to light. The treasure trove dates back 200 years and numbers more than 75,000 documents. Historians called it a remarkable archive that chronicles the family's personal accomplishments—and scandals—and casts a light on American history. The letters filled hundreds of boxes that were stored in attics, sheds, and storage lockers; some still bore a coating of coal dust when they were discovered. Despite all odds, they managed to be in surprisingly good condition.

Can deterioration be contagious? Surprisingly, it can. Store a newspaper article, for example, with a greeting card and over the course of a few years, acid stains from the newspaper will discolor the card. It's a reaction known as acid migration.

Pulp Friction

In many ways, when working with delicate documents, you have to retrain yourself how to handle them properly. Metal paper clips can dent or tear precious papers and eventually leave rust marks. Ordinary envelopes can hasten deterioration. Only use acid-free alkaline envelopes and folders. Clear plastic is a good choice if you want to look at something but don't need to handle it directly. Make sure the plastic is made of materials like polyester, polypropylene, or triacetate. They go under the trade names Mylar D and Melinex.

The acids, oils, and dirt from your own fingerprints are a few more potential foes. Always wash your hands before handling documents, and make sure your hands are nice and dry, too. For particularly fragile items, wear white 100-percent cotton gloves.

If you're thinking about laminating an important document, think again. It's a big mistake. Instead of safeguarding it, lamination fuses the plastic film to the paper. The trouble with the process is that it's virtually impossible to reverse, and the plastic itself can shrink over time.

Keep important historical papers in low humidity areas. Experts recommend 35 percent relative humidity and temperatures below 72°F. Humidity can lead to spotting and mold growth. Not sure if a certain room is dry enough? It's easy to take the guesswork out of the equation by purchasing inexpensive humidity testing cards from specialty shops. Keep them in your storage boxes. If the humidity levels get too high, the card will turn color to let you know it's time to rethink your storage location. Try to avoid an area that experiences any kind of dramatic heat swings. It can destabilize the paper.

ALERT!

When handling your delicate papers, it's not enough to make sure your hands are clean and dry. That's a given. Look around to make sure there's nothing nearby—no uncapped markers, drinks, food, cleaning products—that could spill and permanently harm your documents.

Let there be light—but not near your papers! Ultraviolet light from the sun as well as from fluorescent bulbs is particularly destructive. The light will fade your documents and turn them yellow in a hurry. Minimize the exposure as much as possible. Keep framed documents away from sun-drenched walls and use filtered glass to reduce UV effects.

Greeting cards and old valentines, even those made from rag paper, are brittle. Store them away from the sun as well as moisture and direct sources of heat. If you frame a greeting card or postcard, use double matting to ensure that air circulates between the card and the glass. Don't paste them into scrapbooks. Adhesives of any kind are strongly discouraged. To help preserve their shapes, store cards as well as handbills flat, not folded, using archival backing board to prevent creases and tears.

ESSENTIAL

If an important document needs resuscitation, don't play paper doctor. You could easily make the problem worse. It's better to leave the patient as is and continue to store it under optimum conditions. If you really want to take 911 action, see a professional conservator to evaluate the situation.

Posters and maps are best stored rolled up and in archival, acid-free tubes. Never use adhesive tape to seal them in place. The tape will harm the paper. Leave off the rubber bands, too. They can pinch posters, compromising their shapes and even causing "burn" marks.

Scan Artists

Help! The plea is from Lori, a mother of three and a self-admitted clutter bug. Her biggest problem is figuring out what to do with all the school papers and drawings that have piled up over the years. She can't resist saving the many cute works of art and the English assignments that illustrate how her kids' handwriting has matured from kindergarten on up. It's hard to blame her. But is it any surprise then that she's got an old television carton, quite literally, filled with the stuff? What to do? Go digital.

The least effective (though very common) means of storage are shopping bags and trash bags. Items are tossed in and then forgotten about because you can't see what's in there.

Writer Moira Allen recommends backing up family treasures on your computer's hard drive. Scan small art projects and documents, and take digital photos of larger pieces. Moira burned her own family's creations onto CDs that she gave away as Christmas stocking stuffers to her relatives. You can even set up an account with a free online photo Web site that gives you the ability to archive and share digital images with friends and family members. By scanning and archiving, you'll be able to put an efficient filing system in place that will let you safeguard family treasures for the long haul. It's the best way of preserving delicate pieces. Just make sure your discs are properly labeled. Then go through the originals. If you can't bring yourself to discard it all, save just a few representative pieces.

Under Wraps

Face the paper heaps head-on, and deal with the ongoing onslaught daily. Don't put it off to another day. When it comes to deciding what to save and what to toss, be practical about it. Not all vintage documents are created equal. Age doesn't necessarily imbue anything with import.

Take special precautions when it comes to the handling and storage of your most important documents, books, letters, or works of art on paper. And make sure that out of sight is not out of mind. Monitor your precious documents on a regularly scheduled basis. Check for signs of damage due to pests, mold, dust, and other harsh environmental factors. If you're creating new documents you want to hold up for years to come, start with paper that's been age-tested and specially produced not to turn brittle or yellow the way stock made from mechanically ground wood pulp can. Generally you can rely on the fact that paper made from linen or cotton rags is more stable and will be able to survive the ages in better condition.

Chapter 16

Picture Perfect: Photographs

Photos, photos everywhere—in shoeboxes, drawers, cabinets—everywhere except where they should be. When you preserve your images, you preserve memories. The trouble is, we're so busy documenting every birthday, every vacation, and every milestone that we're too busy to organize them properly. In this chapter, you'll get the 411 on the best preservation, filing, and storage methods.

A Photo Finish

In 1888, a high school dropout by the name of George Eastman brought the Kodak camera to market with the slogan, "You press the button. We do the rest," ushering in the revolutionary era of snapshot photography.

It's no secret that photos accumulate. We never get rid of them—we just keep adding to the collection. In the old days—the *really* old days—before the advent of television and even film, having your photograph taken was big stuff, a luxury that cost dearly. A photograph was taken seriously and treated like an heirloom to be passed down through the generations.

E ALERT!

Your camera needs TLC just as much as your photos. Unless you've got a waterproof model, keep your camera away from spills, splashes, and raindrops. Store it in a protective camera bag, and if you don't use it often, remove the batteries so that battery acid doesn't leak inside.

Now images are everywhere because the technology is all around us—standard film cameras, disposables, Polaroids, digitals, and camera phones. How many cameras are in your home? We take pictures for granted and, as a result, have stopped giving them the respect they deserve. We snap some shots, get them developed, have a look and then add them to the photo heap. Even those folks who ordinarily run tight household ships suddenly lose momentum when it comes to their photograph collections. They've got piles of smiles tossed about with no rhyme or reason. Says one shutterbug who makes no excuses for himself, "I have a basket of photos that looks ridiculous in my living room, but I also don't have the inclination to sit down and put them in albums."

Another sharpshooter fesses up that she has photos in shoe boxes dating back decades, all the way to grammar school—unlabeled and unorganized. Still, she swears she's going to get her act together one weekend and make some sense out of it all.

Search and Destroy

Sometimes it takes a mishap to realize how much sentimental value photographs hold for you. A flood occurs, and all your high school prom pictures are washed away in minutes. Prints haphazardly stored in a basement turn memories of Christmas past into one of Christmas aghast after humidity does them in. How often have you seen news reports right after a natural disaster of families mourning the loss of their most beloved pictures? No question about it. Photos chronicle our personal history. Unfortunately, it takes far less than a natural disaster to do irreparable damage to what should be lasting memories. Poor handling and storage will do them in. Photos are a lot more fragile than you might think. The fact is that photographs have a finite life span. The best conservation efforts can slow the deterioration down, but they don't necessary halt it.

FACT

Matthew Brady, a pioneer in photojournalism, is one of the best known and most studied American photographers in history. His classic Civil War images remain some of the most powerful ever developed; his portraits include everyone from presidents and generals to poets and writers.

Before conservation, however, comes the culling of the collection. There's probably not a compilation in the world that can't use a little downsizing. If you keep in mind that quality, not quantity, is what counts most, you'll be amazed at the number of photographs you can discard.

Discard Without Fear

For some reason, we have an aversion to throwing photos away—no matter how bad they are. For the most part, that is. As one man says, he has no problem disposing of an awful photo of *himself*. But when it comes to his friends and family, he saves every picture, no matter how unflattering—from the eyes-wide-shut types to the mouths-wide-open variety. Is it superstition that stops us from chucking them in the trash? Is it guilt? Or is it the pure bother of it all? It's certainly a lot easier to throw pictures into a drawer than in an album or photo box. Professional photographers routinely take rolls and rolls of film on an assignment just to get a few good shots. Many hobby photographers do, too, but the difference is that they decide to keep every last one of them.

Poor-Quality Photos

Get tough and toss out unbecoming, poorly lit, out of focus, and damaged photos. If any pictures have lost their sentimental meaning, out they go, too. Janie might have been your best friend from summer camp, but now when you look at pictures of the two of you, you can't even remember her last name.

Decorating with framed photographs can create a dramatic focal point. Photos instantly personalize any location. Display them in a highly trafficked location where you, your family, and your guests can have the opportunity to enjoy them every day. Be creative in your display. A series of related pictures can work together to tell a story with high impact.

Plenty of people put their best photos in albums and file rejects in an envelope somewhere else. Hmmm. Well, if the rejects aren't good enough to make it into the photo album, think seriously about whether you really need to keep these substandard shots at all.

Double Prints

Oh, and then there are all those duplicates. When drugstores and photo-finishing shops started offering free double prints, customers went wild. But instead of doubling the memories, it just doubled the clutter problem. It seemed no one wanted to turn down the two-for-one offer, whether they had a use for the extras or not. It's finally time to deal with the doubles. Why not stick them in an envelope and mail them off to others who might enjoy them? Here's another idea: Have a photo swap party. Invite friends and family members over, and let everyone choose from the pool of spares. And don't be afraid to cast off whatever's left over.

Get rid of near duplicates as well. You know, those six shots of the Eiffel Tower all taken from practically the same angle. Or the series of beach shots that are all but indistinguishable from each other.

Developing Ideas

Now that you've weeded out the good from the bad and the ugly, organizing your photos is the next task at hand. What's your current storage method? A giant wicker basket? A series of shoe boxes? A gazillion envelopes stuffed in drawers and cabinets? Shopping bags loaded down with the stuff? Once you start down this slippery slope of sloppiness, it becomes a habit that gets harder and harder to reverse. Photographs bring us pleasure, but when they pile up and turn into a chore waiting to be tackled, it's something we go out of our way to avoid. There's no question that organizing a photo collection can seem overwhelming, especially if you've got years or even decades of picture-taking history behind you. Start by breaking the photos down into categories to make it easier to sort. Here are a few ways to do it:

- By date
- By special events: weddings, birthday celebrations, graduations, reunions, anniversaries
- By subject: family, friends, coworkers
- By subject matter or theme: landscapes, vacation, holidays, camp, home, pets, hobbies, work

You can inject some fun in the undertaking if you turn sorting duties into a family event. Gather up the kids, and they'll get a chance to hear some good family anecdotes and learn about their roots as the process goes along. If you choose to go solo, take it in short spurts or at least as long as you can manage it without getting overwhelmed by the sheer volume.

Box It Up

In the supermarket, cashiers will often ask you, "Paper or plastic?" For the bulk of your photographic storage, the question is "Box or album?" As long as you buy quality materials, there is no wrong answer. It's simply a matter of preference.

Photo boxes make organization easy. No arrangement is necessary—just stick them in, label the box, and you're good to go. Some boxes can hold 1,000 pictures, so it's certainly a space-efficient option.

ALERT!

Dirt, dust, and oils from your fingers can harm your photos. Make sure you hold photos—and especially negatives—on the outer edges only. If you're going to be wading through a thick archive of prints, put on a pair of white gloves made of lint-free material while you work. Remove dust with canned air only. Never blow on them. You'll wind up spraying tiny—but damaging—drops of moisture.

Not all photo boxes, however, are created equal. Be sure to purchase only those that are archival quality, made of acid-free materials. Check the labels to make sure. Standard boxes can release vapors that will damage photos and hasten deterioration.

Store boxes in a cool, dark closet. You might want to color-code them so they're easier to identify later on, using blue boxes for celebrations, red for vacations, yellow for family photos, and so on.

One caveat: Sometimes too much room is a bad thing. When using photo boxes, don't let the ability to very easily store a lot of photos dissuade you from tossing out the marginal ones.

In a Bind

Photo albums put pictures in context. They're a way of immortalizing important events or special times in your life. After all, you never heard of a new bride showing off wedding photos from a box, did you? The very presentation elevates and honors the subject matter. If you're the type who likes to show off your pictures for company or spend time enjoying them in your quieter moments, photo albums may be a better choice. Albums go back to the earliest days of photography, but when they started getting mass-produced, the quality of the materials used in the manufacturing went downhill. Ironically, the adhesives and paperboard were actually harmful to the photos.

Just as with photo boxes, you should buy and use photo albums that are made only of acid-free materials. Plastic materials like polypropylene, polyester, or triacetate are safe to use. On the other hand, take a pass on photo albums made of polyvinyl chloride or PVC. They're often the cheap versions available at drugstores and department stores. The worst are albums with sticky adhesive pages. Also, when putting your album together, avoid any use of rubber bands, paper clips, or everyday adhesive tapes. They can be photokillers.

Albums in the ring-binder style will allow you to add pages as needed. Bound albums made of archival paper with protective pH-balanced interleaving tissue between the pages are considered more formal and elegant. That's the reason professionals prefer them. Never use glue to adhere photos to the pages. Double-stick archival dots, which hold fast to both the photo and the page, are secure without being permanent. Then there are the good old photo corners to secure prints to the page. Sometimes, the old ways are the best ways. They've even been updated to give your albums a sleek design. Check out metal corners for an ultra sophisticated look.

Here's a word about envelopes. If you decide to store any photos in envelopes, again, make sure they're conservation-friendly. Standard envelopes don't meet the requirements for long-term photo storage. They're made with acidic adhesives, and the center seam can leave a permanent imprint on your images.

Battle Plans

It's time to move into preservation mode. Photographs decay with time, so it's crucial you give real thought to care and storage. Black-and-white photographic prints can last a century or more. Color photographs, on the other hand, are more susceptible to fading because of the many chemicals used to create the color. Instant prints, such as Polaroids, have been known to fade even more quickly.

Clearly, you can't create museum-quality conditions in your home, but you can combat the detrimental effects of humidity, temperature, and light. This three-prong environmental barrage can lead to fading, discoloration, and irreversible textural changes. Go ahead—frame your most prized photos and put them in a prominent place of honor. Just be sure to have them professionally mounted on acid-free boards and secured behind ultraviolet filtering glass. If it's nonreflective and shatterproof, all the better. No adhesives should ever touch the image.

ESSENTIAL

Select a frame that complements your picture and accents the room's furnishings—not one that distracts from or overwhelms the subject matter. A simple frame draws the eye to the image. Whether your photo is an accessory or a room's focal point, placement is critical. All elements of design—color, style, composition, and size—must work together to complete the decorative statement.

If you display too many framed photos, they'll just add to the tabletop and shelf congestion. Select a reasonable number to showcase, appropriate for the size of a given room. Can't decide? Rotate them regularly like an art gallery would. A long hallway is a great location in which to display your photos. Just rest framed prints on a thin strip of molding at around eye level. For added variety, create a 3D effect using a shadow box for your photos. Add mementos from a special celebration or memorable vacation.

Photographic paper sucks up moisture. To prevent the paper from warping, make sure your rooms are well ventilated. Hanging pictures on the interior walls of rooms is a better choice than on the damper exterior walls.

Avoid putting pictures up in steamy bathrooms and spill-prone kitchens. Sticking them on mirrors and under glass are also bad ideas.

The effects of direct light are cumulative, and ultraviolet light is the most damaging of all. If your photos are on shelves or walls in direct sunlight, close the curtains or blinds during the day. Try to remember to do so when you're away on vacation, too. Every once in a while, rotate the positions of your prints so they get an occasional break from light exposure. Keep the negatives of displayed photographs properly stored should you need to replace the prints at some point down the road.

ALERT!

Window film is another way to counter the damaging effects of ultraviolet rays on your favorite photos. Window film, which is thinner than even Saran Wrap and takes about a day to install in an average size home, can reduce harmful UV rays by as much as 98 percent. Window film also helps reduce fading of furniture, carpeting, and works of art.

Prints are fussy. They don't like heat or temperature swings. Keep them clear of radiators, stoves, portable heaters, and fireplaces. Even leaving them inside a hot car for any length of time is risky business. Storage of your photos in basements and attics is just asking for trouble. High humidity hastens deterioration and encourages mold. At the other extreme, exceedingly low humidity can cause photos to crack or curl. A cool, dark, and dry room is best.

Finally, don't store photos in a closet, pantry, or storage unit where they can be exposed to the harmful fumes of paints and cleaning supplies. Photographs have been known to respond unpredictably to the presence of chemicals.

Virtual Memories

Digital technology is changing the way we view and store images. Many people who have jumped the digital divide find they no longer make hardcopy prints at all. In fact, half of all photos are now taken with a digital camera. Most shots are stored on the hard drive and never even printed out. That's one good way to stem the flow of pictures around the house.

Free or inexpensive photo storage and display sites are becoming increasingly popular on the Internet. Three highly trafficked sites are Shutterfly.com, Snapfish.com, and Kodakgallery.com. They give users the ability to print, enhance, archive, and store digital images. Some sites even give you online editing tools so you can fix red eye as well as do some plastic surgery to other bloopers and blunders.

QUESTION?

How does a digital camera work?
A digital camera transforms images into data rather than recording them on film. Most digital cameras not only take photographs but have limited video capabilities as well.

Digital photography gives you endless options. You can refer friends to an online photo gallery, e-mail them individual images, or put your favorites on a disc to view on your TV. Of course, you can also print them out on a color printer any time you want. Digital backups are important as a preservation tool, as well. If you have irreplaceable, one-of-a-kind photos, it's a good idea to scan them into your computer for safekeeping. Writer Moira Allen launched a project to archive her old family photos—some images date back as long as fifty years—in a task she jokingly calls the "project that will never die." In addition to preserving these important photos, she says there's the added benefit of being able to restore photos that had become severely discolored with age. Now her electronically archived images are better than the originals.

Other digital storage considerations include the following:

- If you have a lot of digital images stored on your computer, think about using an external hard drive so they don't take up loads of memory.
- Protect your CDs by placing them in plastic jewel cases. If they get scratched, they can become unusable. A cool, dark storage place is best.
- Replace your backups every few years. Discs are long lasting but not infinite. It just takes a few minutes to burn a digital copy.

- Store copies of your most precious discs off-site at a safety deposit box or even a friend's house in case of a fire, flood, or other disaster.
- No digital camera? No scanner? No problem. Go to your neighborhood photo shop and have them create a CD of your favorite photos as a backup.

Make sure to label the back of your photos with date, location, and subject information, using an archival-quality pen or pencil, available at most art-supply shops or craft stores. A felt-tip pen can bleed through. It might be obvious to you who the subject is in a given shot, but think ahead. If your children, grandchildren, nieces, or nephews get hold of the pictures one day, they might be shaking their head wondering whom they're looking at. Good labeling goes for digital files, too. Space is limited, so try to be as descriptive as possible in a few short words.

Big Shots

The legendary photographer Diane Arbus once said, "A photograph is a secret about a secret. The more it tells you the less you know." That's one reason why they're endlessly intriguing, both as private history and as an art form. Quality counts, and it starts at the very beginning. Use the highest quality film, and opt for the best processing you can. A properly stored color photo that's been printed directly from a negative can last as long as seventy-five years. With new advanced photographic paper available, that life span nearly triples.

Photographs are arguably the most effective way we chronicle our lives. We not only frame them, we wear them, putting the cherished images we love in lockets and on charm bracelets.

The best photos communicate how we feel about ourselves, those closest to us, and the world around us. They can be an endless source of pleasure and comfort. When you take the time to preserve and properly store your photographs, you safeguard a bit of your personal and family history. By employing just a few simple measures and taking advantage of digital technology for storage and archiving, you can ensure the legacy of your irreplaceable images for the ages.

Chapter 17

Rooms and Boarders: Apartments

No basement. No attic. Fewer closets. Rarely a garage. Apartment dwellers don't have it easy. They need to make use of every square foot of space wherever they can find it. That means foraging for room in unlikely places and demanding that furnishings perform double or even triple duty. Fortunately, manufacturers are holding up their end of the bargain by offering smart solutions that take the sting out of stingy spaces. Don't believe you can beat the clutter in snug places? Keep reading.

Intimate Spaces

If there's one thing virtually all apartment dwellers can agree on, it's that there's just not enough storage space. You hear it from the person who lives in a three-bedroom duplex as clearly as the individual with the postage-stamp-size studio. Of course, it's a matter of perspective. For an empty-nest couple selling off their family home, downsizing into an apartment, no matter how big, is a cold splash in the face.

Eliminating apartment clutter is about matching quantity with space, making purchase decisions suited to the scale of your apartment, and considering how your existing furniture can be used to its best advantage.

Space is finite, even if your material possessions and desires aren't. Transforming your home into the inviting place you look forward to coming home to may mean making a few adjustments to fit the reality of your current situation. But it doesn't have to mean sacrificing. Quite the contrary. When you purge, you prosper. The effects of a well-organized and economically maintained home can diminish your stress and streamline your attitude, especially when you add in the other perks of a petite retreat:

- Things are always within arm's reach.
- You've got less household maintenance and cleaning to contend with.
- You're forced to be judicious in your purchase decision-making.

Apartments aren't just for renters. There are lots of small-living options. A condominium is an apartment owned by an individual or individuals. The common areas of the complex or building, including recreational room, lobby, parking lot, and so on, are jointly owned. Another type of apartment structure is a co-operative. In the case of a co-op, the apartment building or development is owned and managed by those who live in it. Members buy shares in the development, but they do not technically own the individual apartment they reside in. When done right, small-home living gives you a golden opportunity to weed out the waste and hang on to the best of the best.

Fit to Be Tried

The quandary is that many people move into apartments with all their old furniture, and that can pose two problems. For one thing, there's usually too much of it. They heap all their belongings onto the moving truck instead of taking the limitations of their new floor plan into consideration. Take the instance of a pair of newlyweds. On moving day, they were hauling furniture into their brand-new apartment when the landlord stuck his head out the window and shouted, "If I knew that you had this much furniture I never would have rented you the apartment!"

The second problem is the matter of buying furniture ill-suited to the apartment's layout. Pity Matt, a lawyer who stumbled across a handsome wall unit in a showroom he couldn't resist buying. He thought it would be ideal to house his stereo, CD collection, and television set. But once the unit was delivered, Matt realized it was all wrong for the space he set aside for it in his living room. It blocked access to his filing cabinets and obstructed the room's natural light. What seemed perfect in the showroom turned out to be a bad choice in practice.

QUESTION?

What does renters' insurance cover?
Apartment renters insurance covers two areas: property and personal liability. Take digital pictures of your most important possessions and save it on your computer or a DVD as a backup should the need arise to take advantage of your property insurance. Personal liability protects you in the event you're legally obligated to pay money to another person for actions caused by you, your family, or your property.

You may be guilty of such things yourself. Have you ever fallen in love with a gorgeous sleigh bed, turning a blind eye to the fact it was intended for a monster-size master bedroom? Did you ever buy a super-size treadmill as part of your New Year's resolution, which dominated your living room forever after? The key is working within the parameters of the space you have.

It's a Small World After All

The understandable reluctance of some renters to invest big bucks to alter their living spaces can create a feeling of impermanence. In her experience as a professional organizer, Misha Keefe discovered that people often compensate with clutter. They feel the need to clutter their homes with knick-knacks and pictures to diminish the sparse and impersonal feeling that many apartments convey. But a better method, she contends, is to keep the décor to a minimum and, instead, make it work within its environment rather than fighting it. Hang two or three large-format prints in sleek black frames rather than lots of small mismatched ones. Clean lines will provide a more dramatic feel and invite guests to look around and become interested and involved in the room.

Employ a few designer tricks to give your diminutive apartment a big-time feel. Use glass-top tables, which allow lots of natural light to filter in, and strategically place mirrors around your home to fool the eye and revitalize the space.

Be sure to make use of all the great vertical space your walls have to offer. Keeping everything low to the ground will only drag the eye horizontally and cause you to feel cramped, claustrophobic, and closed in. Installing wall shelves draws the eye upward. It not only gives a room more depth but allows you and your visitors to take in the room from all angles.

Clean Up Your Act

Want more space? Free up and throw out. Identify the most troubled area(s) of your apartment. Is it your closets? Your dining area? Your bedroom? Start by tackling the biggest offender. Once you clear up your most egregious area and see the dramatic difference it makes, you'll have the motivation to keep on going. And the nice part is that after you've gotten the hardest part out of the way, tackling the rest of your hot spots will be so much more manageable.

Don't try to take on the whole place at once, even if you're only dealing with a few hundred square feet. It's not about the size as much as the amount of stuff you've accumulated and how difficult it might be to maneuver in a limited space. Clutter can be deceiving. Having to go through a small pile of papers, for instance, may take longer than evaluating a bunch of big, bulky items in your cabinet.

FACT

An apartment in which each room is connected to each other in a straight line without a hallway is called a railroad flat. It takes its name from the way the floor plan resembles cars on a train. These units are often found in older walk-up apartment buildings.

Re-evaluate your possessions with fresh eyes—what's in your cabinets, your drawers, your closets, under your bed. If you've been living in one place for a while, that's not always the easiest thing to do. Do the little knick-knacks you bought long ago still have meaning for you? Have you been harboring stuff for the larger home you hope to own one day? Set limits.

Here's the cautionary tale of an accountant named Keith. He moved to an apartment in Manhattan and left an oversize club chair in his brother's attic that just couldn't fit into his new 750-square foot one-bedroom. A year passed. His brother moved, and Keith hired a van to move it again to a friend's unfinished basement and then, ultimately, to a self-storage facility. It's still there. Between the cost of the moving van rental and the monthly fees he's been paying for storage—and continues to pay—on the storage unit, Keith would have had a few more dollars in his pocket and less aggravation if he had sold the chair in the first place.

E
ALERT!

When purging your excess belongings, time it to take place just before trash collection day. Otherwise, leaving your castoffs to linger inside your apartment for a few extra days may be too tempting. The last thing you want to do is undermine your hard work by second-guessing your decisions.

Take action on everything, from the gifts you've received but never had a use for to the food in your kitchen cabinets that's remained unopened for months. One full-time mom was so overwhelmed by all the stuff she had in her puny apartment that she kept her kids' bicycles in one bedroom and turned the second bathroom into a clothes closet.

Good Things, Small Packages

In all but the largest apartments (you know, the kind with the maid's quarters), you'll need to prioritize your living areas. What are your hobbies? Your work and fitness habits? Usually, one or more rooms wind up being some kind of a hybrid, like the following:

- Living room/dining room
- Living room/office
- Bedroom/office
- Bedroom/gym
- Guest room/nursery
- Office/guest room

What's important to you? Do you frequently accommodate overnighters? Then guest quarters will be integral to your home plan. Do you spend a lot of time at your computer? Figure that an adequate and efficient office space will shoot to the top of your priority list. Then again, if cooking is your passion, you won't want to scrimp when it comes to the kitchen.

Hotel rooms, particularly those that target a business clientele, are good examples of the way a single room can be neatly zoned out to meet multiple requirements. Think about it: The best of those rooms can accommodate separate areas for entertainment (TV), work (desk), sleeping (bed), and socializing or relaxing (couch).

When you're crunched for space and trying to fit as much as you can into a limited area, the last thing you want is any obstructions to impede the works. Rub a little furniture wax paste or a bit of soap over a rough wooden clothes rod to get your hangers sliding back and forth more easily. Use the same approach on the gliders of your dresser drawers, too.

Use your accessories—and imagination—to create actual or perceived room dividers. Sheer curtains can create a soft wall to isolate your bed area. Freestanding open bookcases, floor plants, area rugs, and attractive screen panels are other quick and easy solutions for divvying up a room. Though it may seem counterintuitive, dividing up rooms into small subsections actually gives the perception of enlarging the space. And that's welcome news for the space deprived.

Furniture on Overtime

When a room is small, an important point to remember is not to overwhelm the space with too much furniture. So along with multifunctional rooms, think multipurpose furniture. An oversized ottoman can serve as a seat or as a coffee table. Opt for one with storage, and you've got a triple-crown winner. Try using wicker chests in varying sizes for side tables and coffee tables. Store occasionally used items, such as extra pillows, inside. Some pieces of furniture, like baker's racks and armoires, are like chameleons. They blend in effortlessly from room to room and job to job. For hidden storage, try a skirted end table or a stack of woven boxes for an artful side table.

Ever hear of a high-low table? It's a low-rise coffee table that rises up to dining table height with a few pumps of a foot lever. The table can also spin, like a lazy Susan, and roll on wheels for maximum flexibility.

Dining Furniture

As far as standard dining table options, you'll find no lack of innovative choices. There's a versatile three-in-one unit that starts out as a hall console and easily converts to a card table or a dining room table, as the need changes. Another take-off is a super space-saving table with a set of four chairs. When it's not in use, you simply fold up the chairs and nest them inside the drop-leaf table self-storage unit. One clever manufacturer offers a farmhouse table with sliding panels below the tabletop to store linens and silverware. When you need additional seating, slide in the leaves to accommodate an extra pair of guests.

Built-ins to Last

Many apartment dwellers are reluctant to have built-in storage created for their homes, and with good reason. It can be an expensive undertaking and one they're forced to leave behind for the landlord's benefit when they move. Under certain circumstances, though, these capital improvements might make sense—especially if it's someone else's capital. Talk to your landlord and see if she'll spring for the work. No go? Is it something you can take on as a do-it-yourself project?

E ALERT!

If you're lucky enough to have friends or family members who house some of your items in long-term storage, keep a master list of what's where. Then make it a point to inspect your things on a regular basis, checking for pests, mold, mildew, and other signs of damage due to the elements.

A shop owner named Roger struck out on both counts. His landlord had no interest in his storage-deprived plight, and as an inexperienced do-it-yourselfer, Roger couldn't tell a seesaw from a jigsaw. But he adored his long-time apartment and saw himself living there for many years to come. For him, it made sense to have built-in solutions for critical areas of his apartment.

Consider a built-in for your entertainment unit to bring your CD, DVD, and video game collection under control. A window seat makes good use of sometimes-awkward recessed spaces. Framing a doorway or window with bookshelves is a stylish way to recover wasted space. It's a mix of practicality with visual interest. Use extra-deep shelves and you can double up your books, two volumes deep. Though pricey, investing in a flat-panel wall-hanging TV monitor might make the difference between a room in a choke-hold and one that's got some breathing room. Got a sliver of space near your desk? Fold-down wall-mounted shelving, the kind you sometimes find in kitchens, puts narrow spaces to productive use. The shelf can hold and hide all your office supplies. Another versatile shelf idea? Replace standard windowsills with ones deep enough to be put to use. To showcase your prized keepsakes and collectibles without pilfering desk and countertop space, building niches between the studs in your walls is the way to go.

Kitchen Aids

Emily, an apartment dweller from Brooklyn, has a simple rule to keep her clutter under control. She leaves no more than three objects out on a non-working surface, such as the top of a dresser or nightstand, and absolutely zero objects on a work surface such as a kitchen or desktop. She says she initially thought sticking to the plan would feel like cruel and unusual punishment, but in fact once she cleared out all the unnecessary stuff on her kitchen counters, she discovered how much easier it was to work in there. And, she adds, after the initial shock wore off, she grew to love the look of the empty space.

Install shelves and built-in appliances as much as possible to free up that precious counter space. Just getting your microwave off the counter will make a big difference. Two-tier dish racks will help in your struggle for more workspace. There's a whole array of apartment-friendly appliances on the market, including thin-line compact refrigerators specially designed for tight spaces. KitchenAid's Briva is an in-sink dishwasher. It's sized to fit inside a forty-two- or forty-eight-inch cabinet and is a breeze for washing small loads. If you're not prepared to make a capital investment, countertop dishwashers are also available. To unclog cabinetry, pull out the prettiest of your space-hoggers, such as decorative dishes, mugs, and trivets, and put them on display on the walls instead.

▲ A kitchen island.

Think twice about whether you really need a standard kitchen table, particularly since there are so many interesting alternatives. How about a drop-down countertop that attaches to the wall? It's there when you need it and folds down and out of the way when you don't, for more floor space. You can take a heavy-duty wine rack, cabinet, or a sturdy stack of cubbies, lay a countertop over it, and you've created an instant kitchen table. Islands that double as tables and workstations are practical enough for the kitchen and chic enough for a dining area. Add a couple of stools, and you're good to go.

Slumber Parties

If you want more floor space in your bedroom, say the word: sleeper, futon, convertible lounger, Murphy bed, or daybed. Select a daybed with a trundle. It'll accommodate a spare mattress for guests. A variation of the traditional trundle offers bonus storage for bedding instead. Some convertible couches even have storage space for linens.

Loft beds aren't just for SoHo hipsters. Loft beds let you take advantage of otherwise wasted vertical space to free up "ground floor" real estate, perfect for a desk, chest of drawers, or low-rise entertainment unit.

There are times when a custom piece of furniture makes all the difference. One tenant ordered a bespoke captain's bed handcrafted to fit the exact specifications of his small bedroom. It wound up being the smartest decision he could have made. The mattress rests on a platform that houses five oversize drawers. The bed is big enough to eliminate his need for a separate dressing bureau—and eliminate his storage woes. That same tenant uses suitcases for storing his off-season clothing.

Create an instant guest room with an airbed. The newest generation of inflatable mattresses is quick to inflate and deflate with pillow-top comfort for durability. Plus, they're easy on the spine. When you're done, just roll them up and store them in their own carrying cases. Are you a camper? They're perfect for outdoor adventure, too.

You might also consider smaller-scale furniture. One newlywed couple may have been just starting out, but they were thinking ahead when they bought a three-quarter-size bedroom set in the teen department of a local furniture store. It was less expensive, and it fit their modest-size apartment better. What's more, they figured that in a few short years they'd be starting a family and would be able to move their mini-master bedroom set along into the child's room.

What is a Murphy bed?
A Murphy bed is a space-saving bed that folds up into a closet. It was invented in 1900 by William Lawrence Murphy of San Francisco; Murphy eventually formed the Murphy Bed Company of New York. The inventor patented his "In-A-Dor" bed in 1908, but he never did trademark the name "Murphy bed."

Curtains for You

Add by subtraction. In this case, thinking about subtracting the sliding closet doors in your bedrooms and replacing them with full-length curtains that match the fabrics in the room or even decorative beads instead. If you are replacing sliding doors, curtains give you unimpeded access to the full space. You eliminate the barrier where the two doors meet. Even for standard-size closet doors, open doors often eat into wall space that could be put to better use with a small dresser.

It's a Wash

Use a pop-up storage bag for laundry instead of a space-sucking hamper. No room in the closet for a full-size iron? No problem. Buy a portable tabletop ironing board or select one that's built into a cabinet and hung on the wall. Open the cabinet door and the ironing board swivels out, set up and ready to go. Apartment-friendly washers and dryers have been around a while. Now you can have both in one unit. Call it a "dwyer." It's a large-capacity unit that takes up half the space of a regular unit, so you can put your Laundromat quarters away.

Store and Order

Clutter will undermine your happy home unless you develop the ability to let go. It always boils down to one thing: You can't organize your living space properly if you have too much stuff for the size. Without a garage, attic, or basement, your storage options are limited, though some desperate souls have taken to using their cars and SUVs as makeshift self-storage units.

In the most crowded and expensive parts of big cities—like Manhattan, where a 250-square-foot studio doesn't raise an eyebrow—entire shops are devoted to the plight of space-challenged apartmenteers. There are even some professional organizers who specialize in all things small. It boils down to paring your world down to its essentials and using every available space in ways you might never have imagined. It could be built-in storage, portable storage, or a combination of both.

Organizing is about science: space versus matter. For every item that crosses your threshold, ask yourself these questions: Does it work? Does it enhance your lifestyle? Can you live without it? Never buy anything (even if it comes from one of those specialty boutiques devoted to small spaces!) without knowing exactly where it's going in your apartment and how it'll be used.

Chapter 18

Party On: Special Occasions

Some aspire to be the host with the most. Others hope to be the host with the least—the least anxiety and the least disorganization, that is. It comes naturally to a few. You know who they are. In this chapter, you'll get tips, strategies, and a game plan that will help you get the party started. Learn the tricks for being a cool, calm, and collected host. You can actually boost expectations by scaling back and simplifying. Bring on the guests.

The Wrong Stuff

There's the aunt who's always first in line to host every holiday dinner; the friend with the Type A personality who sends out "save the date" reminders a season early; the rah-rah neighbor who coordinates the annual block party down to the tiniest of details. Yet what may look effortless on the outside is actually the culmination of good planning and proper timing. If these enthu-siastic party planners always seem to have their act together, it's because they organize, utilize, and improvise.

ALERT!

Improper cooling of foods can cause illnesses. Avoid covering or stack-ing foods during the initial cooling stages. It prevents the heat from escaping. And don't leave cooked foods at room temperature for more than two hours. If you're not going to be digging into the goodies for a couple of days, put them in the freezer and stick a label on them identi-fying the dish and the date.

It's ten o'clock. Do you know where your guests are?
The doorbell rings. The first guests are here. Are you:

a. Still in your sweatpants and bedroom slippers?
b. Wondering where the good table linen is?
c. Searching for recipes for the evening's menu?
d. All of the above?

If your own soirees are more of an exercise in frustration than fun, it's time to go back to basics. For one thing, do you have too much of the wrong stuff taking up unnecessary space in your closets and cabinets? Take a run through this checklist and see how many of these situations apply:

- Mismatched glasses and dishes; two of this, three of that, but not a complete set in the bunch

- Lots of gadgets, appliances, and dishes that serve a single niche role—think olive dishes, caviar spoons, and frittata grills
- Recipes strewn about in cookbooks, notebooks, and kitchen drawers, with no logical filing system to keep them in order
- Tablecloths, placemats, and napkins that match the décor . . . of your last home
- Creased wrapping paper rolls and bags of crushed bows and ribbons
- Decorations celebrating long-ago milestones, like "Congratulations, Graduate!" napkins and "Happy 40th Birthday" paper cups
- Sets and serving pieces for every individual holiday and occasion

These are some sure signs that the countdown to each social gathering is fraught with inefficiency and stress.

FACT

In the publishing world, cookbooks have long been perennial favorites. One of the most successful cookbooks of all time was first published in 1896, when a woman by the name of Fannie Merritt Farmer took on the editorship of the *Boston Cooking-School Cook Book*. Farmer was the first to standardize the methods and measurements of her recipes, thereby assuring chefs a reliable outcome.

The other roadblock is lacking a sensible storage strategy for your special occasion items. Are the things you need for entertaining scattered in rooms throughout the house? Take Annie, a sometimes-happy hostess. She loves having her friends and family over for brunches and dinner parties but lacks a sane system for housing her partyware. She described preparations for one recent anniversary dinner that involved gathering special baking pans from a utility cabinet in the basement, table linens from a hall closet, and special china from the attic. And those were only the things whose location she could actually remember. She never did find the napkin rings.

Stock and Trade

Take stock of the items you cart out for special occasions and especially those you leave behind. They're the biggest space wasters of all. Throw out anything that's warped, chipped, broken, or stained, tempting through it may be to hold on to the tablecloth with the red wine stain you try to hide under the candlestick holder.

Some people like to mix and match different sets of plates or glasses if they don't have full sets, but if that's not your style, then move them out of your home and down to the neighborhood thrift shop or charity organization. Are you overstocked with more cake platters than a bakery and more cheese plates than a French bistro? Don't stockpile more items than you can reasonably expect to use. Find another home for the excess.

ESSENTIAL

Outdoor entertainment can keep a party going. Want to watch the big game on an HDTV while firing up the grill? Easily done. These days, outdoor home theaters are as elaborate as the state-of-the-art systems homeowners have in their media rooms. Weatherproof video systems can be hung from a valence or designed to pop up from the landscaping.

Often, homeowners are inundated with trays, platters, and serving dishes through no fault of their own. They're the recipients of dozens of anniversary, birthday, Christmas, and hostess gifts received over the years. Discard them? Heaven forbid. What will Aunt Lena think if her candy dish isn't prominently displayed? Take an inventory to see how many of these types of items you have squirreled away in your home. If it's more than a few, it's time to bite the bullet and devise an exit strategy. You do your generous gift-givers no favors by holding onto a present you never display or use.

Are you a "phase" chef? You know, someone who latches onto a specialty for a while and then buys up everything in sight to feed the fix? Four years ago it was your tart-jellyroll-cupcake baking phase, and you've still got every pan to prove it. But now that you've moved onto roasts for family fetes, the old baking gear has attained relic status in your cupboards. Clear them out and pass them on.

Attend to spills and stains right away. The longer they sit, the less chance you'll have of 100 percent success. Two of the biggest offenders are candle wax and red wine. To remove candle wax from a tablecloth, harden the wax using ice cubes, and scrape it off with a dull knife. For wine stains, act fast. Pour salt onto the stain, then blot the tablecloth with cold water. Wipe up water, too, especially on hardwoods.

Do you have items too good to toss but too much trouble to use? Think about your beautiful silver candlestick holders. The idea of all that polishing has you running straight for the low-maintenance crystal pair instead. Then there's the waffle iron, when the frozen toaster kind will do just fine. And how about the pasta machine when your family enjoys the good old reliable store-bought brands? These are the kinds of items that sound good in theory but that fall short when it comes to the realities of our time-constrained days. If you can't remember the last time you used it, move it out. Quite often we don't even realize how much of this special-occasion stuff we have because we rarely go in search of it. One woman had a fondue set. It was used exactly one time for company, but it took up the better part of a cabinet shelf for years on end. She just couldn't bring herself to get rid of something that was in "like-new" condition.

Rites and Wrongs

What about all the pretty heirloom dishes you hold on to out of guilt? It's a huge problem, according to Misha Keefe, an organizing guru. She says the guilt factor when doing any kind of purge of personal items is enormous. Keefe suggests passing on sentimental items to other family members. It might be more appropriate to their tastes or suitable for their needs; yet at the same time, you're still keeping it within the family. Not practical? If you inherited, say, your grandmother's china set and it's just sitting crated up in the basement, you're not doing her memory any honor by leaving it there. Take out one or two pieces and showcase them on a shelf. Then sell the rest. The key is detaching the sentimental value from the individual associated with it.

Mood lighting is one of the most undervalued elements of home entertaining. Marry the lighting to the task or tasks at hand. Use soft lights for an intimate dinner party and brighter lights for large-scale entertaining. For extra fun any time of year, snake a string of little white Christmas lights along the top of an entertainment unit or wrap the string around a large potted plant.

For years, Jessica had an ornate gold-trimmed cake platter a favorite cousin had given her just sitting in bubble wrap in her basement. As pretty as the platter was, it just didn't go with any of Jessica's décor. Finally—and reluctantly—she decided to sell it at a yard sale. Her guilt was palpable as potential customers neared. But the feeling instantly disappeared when a browser spotted the plate and became ecstatic over her discovery. As the sale transpired, Jessica realized her cousin's gift would be more cherished in another home.

Task Masters

The quantity of entertaining paraphernalia should have some relationship to the number of barbeques, bashes, and dinner parties you throw. If it's not a lot, reduce, reduce, reduce! Items reserved for infrequent guests shouldn't dominate, particularly at the expense of your everyday needs.

Need it? Yes. But do you have to own it? Not necessarily. Think twice about whether owning a twenty-four-cup coffee urn is necessary for that once-a-year book club meeting you host. One family of non–coffee drinkers simply buys "boxes" of java from their local doughnut shop whenever the need arises, instead of having a coffeemaker dominating a shelf year-round.

You can always borrow specialty cookware from friends, neighbors, and relatives. One woman who lives in a condo development borrows extra folding chairs from her development's clubhouse every year for her Passover seder. Rent appliances, china, chairs, and linens and more from party supply shops. You'd be surprised at the wide range of loaners available these days, everything from chafing dishes and chocolate fountains to barbecue grills and punchbowls. Of course, using paper plates and plastic cups will free up your storage space. If, however, the idea of throwaway place settings weighs on your conscience, there are companies that make disposable flatware and plates out of organic materials.

QUESTION?

How can I throw an environmentally friendly party?
Print invitations on recycled paper or tree-free materials such as hemp, organic cotton, or banana stalks. Instead of cut flowers, use a potted plant as a centerpiece that can be replanted later. For outdoor affairs, battle mosquitoes with fans and citronella candles instead of pesticide sprays. Find out about donating leftovers to a neighborhood food pantry or soup kitchen.

Simplify your tableware with fewer specialty items and more versatile ones that can serve a myriad of functions. The marketplace is flooded with items designed for niche purposes. Guess who benefits?

Do you really need turkey-decorated dishes that are just used for a single Thanksgiving Day meal? Or red, white, and blue drinking glasses for Independence Day? When it comes to dishes and plates, go the generic route. Instead of cartons full of entertaining pieces for every special occasion, maintain a set of adaptable dishes and multipurpose platters you can use over and over. But don't mistake basic for boring. Dress them up with seasonal herbs, garnishes, and even edible flowers.

If you insist on holding on to your holiday-theme dishes, bowls, and mugs, realize you'll need to take extra steps to be more organized because of them. Purchase large plastic tubs, separate them by holiday or occasion, and clearly label them: kids' birthdays, Valentine's Day decorations, New Year's Eve, etc.

In the case of storage tubs, bigger is better. If you store items in a lot of little containers, you'll have more difficulty keeping track of all you've got, and they're more likely to wind up strewn in various closets and cabinets throughout your home.

FACT

A pair of Kentucky sisters, Mildred and Patty Hill, are credited with one of the most famous songs ever, "Happy Birthday to You." The Hill sisters originally named the song "Good Morning to You," and published it in 1893 in a collection called *Song Stories of the Kindergarten*. Later, the song was republished in a songbook edited by Robert Coleman, in which the lyrics "Happy Birthday to You" first appeared.

Institute a system that flows naturally with your lifestyle by reconfiguring your storage to better fit your day-to-day requirements. For instance, if you regularly eat meals in your dining room, don't fill your china cabinet drawers with table linens that are used only on rare occasions for company. Make it work to suit your needs. See to it that the drawers house your everyday place settings. Your storage plan should be straightforward and intuitive. The less you use a given item, the farther it should be from your daily realm.

Group like items together. Keep all decorating items together, like garnishing tools and cake decorating tips. Store special baking items all in one spot. Do the same with "for-company-only" utensils and serving dishes.

Take the stress out of company cleanups. Line casserole dishes and pans with aluminum foil and baking trays with parchment paper. It's an easy way to say goodbye to caked-on grease and stubborn stains. Out of baking dishes? Use disposable aluminum trays, available at the supermarket, instead.

Serves You Right

Any reason for a celebration will do: birthdays, holidays, anniversaries, graduations. Do more with less. Use snack tables that have removable tops that can also be used as serving trays. Double-handled "gathering" baskets, made originally for gathering flowers from the garden, are ideal to hold breads or a smattering of little appetizer plates that can then easily be passed around from guest to guest. Some baskets are long enough and shallow enough to be used to hold place settings and napkins if you're hosting a buffet. Think vertically by using tiered plate holders that take up minimal table space with their elfin footprints.

FACT

Ninety percent of households in the United States buy greeting cards, purchasing an average of thirty-five cards a year, according to the greeting card industry. With cards ranging from 50 cents to $10, Americans generate more than $7.5 billion in retail sales every year. Who's doing most of the buying? Women. They purchase more than 80 percent of all greeting cards.

Have a table for six with no leaf expansion capabilities? No problem if you're planning dinner for eight or ten. Cut a sheet of plywood to size, throw on a tablecloth and you've got a custom table instantly proportioned for your affair.

Instead of buying more, simply reinvent. Here's how:

- Use elegant martini glasses to serve nuts or olives.
- Serve breadsticks in tall, slender parfait glasses.
- Repurpose pretty soup bowls for salsa and spreads.
- Carve out breads, tomatoes, and peppers to use as dip holders.
- Serve cheeses on wooden cutting boards.
- Display fresh flowers in pretty water pitchers.

Rethinking your furniture configuration is an often-overlooked aspect of entertaining. Make sure there are clear paths between rooms for guests to wander. Plant stands, chairs, statues, and other decorative pieces can wind up obstructing thresholds and cause traffic roadblocks.

Crystal-Clear Solutions

China, crystal, and fragile antique serving pieces deserve TLC, attention, and special storage consideration. If you house china in a cabinet, make sure to put felt pads or other cushioning material between layers to prevent scratches and chips. Stack cups no more than two high to avoid tumbling. Hanging them from small hooks is even better. If your china is behind closed doors, cushioned storage pouches will keep the pieces protected and dust-free. And don't forget the padded layers. Should you lose a piece in an accident, there's hope. The International Association of Dinnerware Matchers (www.iadm.com) is a group of independent dealers that can help you locate hard-to-find and even discontinued china, crystal, and flatware pieces.

Crystal and other delicate glassware should be stored stem-side down so there's no undue pressure on the rim. Keep a little "breathing" space between the glasses to head off accidental chipping. If possible, it's always a good idea to store fragile dishware in a cabinet that's segregated from your everyday, heavily used dishes so it doesn't accidentally get tussled about.

ALERT!

Not everything should go in the dishwasher. Wash delicate crystal and china by hand, especially those that are antique or have hand-painting or metal trim. When hand washing, put a rubber pad at the bottom of the sink as a cushion for extra protection. Dry immediately so you can put items away—and out of harm's way.

Food for Thought

When the next gathering comes around, you'll be more attentive to your guests if you economize your actions and scale down your party gear. Get rid of anything that's not pulling its weight. Sure, it's nice to have special dishes and accessories for company or to celebrate a holiday—it sets the day apart—but you never want so many that they intrude on the storage capabilities of your everyday things. Reframe how you think about those things. Separate the need-to-haves from the nice-to-haves.

Can't remember when you used it last? Lose it—fast. Keeping rarely utilized items or multiple sets of dishes, appliances, platters, and more is plain uneconomical and inefficient, even some items that hold sentimental value. There are better ways to pay tribute to a memory than keeping something boxed up in bubble wrap. Disassociate the thing from the person who gave it to you.

Hang on to host-and-hostess helpers that are most versatile, the accessories that will take you from season to season and celebration to celebration. The simple act of decluttering will calm you down and make time work in your favor.

Chapter 19

'Tis the Season: Holidays

Deck the halls . . . if you can find the decorations, that is. Christmas, Thanksgiving Day, Halloween—whatever the holiday, the celebration's not quite complete without all the trimmings to go along with it: the table settings, the specially designed baking dishes, and the indoor and outdoor ornamentations. Keep it all neatly under wraps with tailor-made stowaway solutions guaranteed to keep your holidays jolly.

Christmas Past and Presents

No matter how much you look forward to a holiday celebration, there's always a certain amount of stress and anxiety involved. Cleaning, shopping, decorating, sprucing up, hosting. The to-do lists are ever growing. What's more, they seem to start earlier every year. The proof? Before you can say "trick or treat," the shopping malls are already adorned in their jingle-bell finery. Before you can wish your neighbor a Happy New Year, the aroma of Valentine's Day chocolate truffles is wafting through the candy aisles. You might not be able to control the stepped-up timetable of the retail industry, but you can reduce some of the "holidaze" while increasing the enjoyment quotient by getting organized.

FACT

In the early nineteenth century, the American ambassador to Mexico, Joe Poinsett, brought home a plant that ultimately came to be named after him, the poinsettia. Less than a century later, the beautiful red and green poinsettia has become a widespread symbol of Christmas.

In the average home, a large chunk of closet, attic, and basement space is given over to holiday gear, and it just keeps growing. What might have been a few pretty ornaments, a tree stand, skirt, and some twinkling lights in the old days has now mushroomed into a full-blown North Pole spectacle. And that's just for Christmas. Move over, Santa. Cupid, the Easter Bunny, and the Great Pumpkin are approaching fast. Decorating the home has become a four-season sport.

Halloween is second only to Christmas as the biggest decorating holiday of the year. Some 60 percent of consumers go in for Halloween decoration purchases. Ghosts, goblins, scarecrows, black cats, and jack 'o lanterns of every size turn homes and gardens into funhouse displays. Trick-or-treating might be for the young, but Halloween is being increasingly embraced by the young at heart, and they're the ones pulling out all the stops.

It's a good thing for America's closets that other big holidays like Valentine's Day, Mother's Day, Father's Day, and Thanksgiving, as well as many religious holidays like Chanukah, Passover, and Easter, are centered on more transitory priorities such as food, flowers, and greeting cards. Jelly beans and chocolate bunnies may be responsible for piling on the pounds, but thankfully they don't create storage woes.

Christmas Countdown

There's always great anticipation to the start of every holiday season, a chance to gift-wrap your home in lights and make it a warm and welcoming place for friends and family to drop by.

Cheryl, a holistic health practitioner from Long Island, says her parents always made her childhood home a winter wonderland and, as an adult, she's happy to follow suit. But it isn't out of obligation. It just feels so good. Each silver candelabra, carved Santa statuette, and satin stocking has its own specialness, Cheryl says, and that's why every Christmas her home feels like a huge warm hug. The very act of decorating, adds her boyfriend Greg, is a constant that runs throughout the season. Among Greg's own traditions is wrapping gifts to a Robert Goulet CD soundtrack. It's a ritual Greg started thirty years ago—only then he was listening to the same recording on an LP.

Introduce rituals into your decorating activities to take out some of the drudge work. Put on a seasonal CD or a favorite holiday movie as a backdrop, like *White Christmas, It's a Wonderful Life,* or *Holiday Inn.* And don't put too much pressure on yourself by trying to decorate the whole house in a single day. Deck your halls over the course of a few days or even weeks so you don't feel overwhelmed. The measured pace will show in the details of your labor.

E ALERT!

If you have toddlers or pets that love to poke around the Christmas tree, decorate it with shatterproof ornaments. Although they look like glass, the ornaments are unbreakable because they're actually made of reflective resin. Any danger is averted, and you don't have to sacrifice style.

It's the lead-up to Christmas that leaves so many people unraveled. The picture-perfect family we imagine decorating the tree, placing candles in the windows and a wreath lovingly on the door—singing carols all the while—is the stuff of Hollywood fiction. Instead of "Ho-ho-ho," the exclamations are usually unprintable, and not very family-friendly. The reason for that can be directly traced to what happened at the end of the previous season. If last winter's cleanup ended with a get-it-over-with-it attitude once the festivities died down, you've set yourself up for a frustrating kick-off to another Christmas. Sloppy habits always come back to haunt you.

This year, plan on spending some extra time before and after the holidays reorganizing your Christmas wares. You'll shave off time and put the brakes on endless searches. It's guaranteed to make the next season brighter. Have an idea of what you want to do before you begin. You can always rearrange things later on.

Season Opener

Take out all your holiday items, especially the ones you haven't used in years. Look carefully through your closets and cabinets. Things like winter-plaid table linens, holly-decorated ice buckets, and berry centerpieces may be strewn in the far reaches of your home. One family rediscovered a box of holiday linens left ages ago in a storage alley in the attic only after embarking on an insulation project. Haul all your items to one central area, kind of like a Santa's workshop, for examining and sorting. Throw out any items that are chipped, faded, or damaged.

What you liked and how you decorated years ago might not match your tastes anymore. Even Christmas decorations go out of style. Instead of ignoring the things you're no longer interested in and letting them waste storage space, get rid of them. Donate them to a thrift shop to brighten someone else's home for the holidays, to a church, or to an individual just starting out in her own apartment.

If you have small decorative items too pretty to throw out, use them to dress up your gift-wrapping or greeting cards.

Consider selling valuable pieces you no longer have a use for either online or through a classified ad. Many Christmas villages and ornaments are highly collectible. One seasonal fan whose friends dub him Father Christmas sells off old pieces each year so he can continue adding new ones to his collection without clogging up storage space in his home.

Before buying those baking molds, specialty appliances, and cookie cutters you use only once a year, see if you can borrow what you need from a friend or neighbor. You can even start a new tradition of hosting a kitchen swap or organizing a lending library of seasonal goods that will save everyone money while giving you a good excuse to get together with pals.

Yuletide Wrap-Up

It's December 26. The presents are all unwrapped, the annual New Year's weight-loss resolution is just days away, and the houseful of Christmas paraphernalia is staring at you, waiting to be put away for another year. Before the packing begins, think strategically.

Get out a notebook and create a holiday organizer. In it you can do all these things:

- Keep tabs on presents bought and received. It'll prevent you from buying Aunt Martha yet another set of pajamas and dish towels next year.
- Note food preparations and what dishes you've made for company. What were the hits? What were the misses? And who was allergic to what?
- Inventory your holiday decorations. When next season rolls around, you'll know exactly what you've got. No chance you'll buy another set of silver snowflake napkin-holders by accident.
- Track your greeting card distribution: the people you sent cards, and those whose cards you received. One mom even saves a sample of the Chanukah picture postcards of her family she sends out each year as a special holiday keepsake.

Use color-coded storage containers so you can spot holiday stash more easily. Red and green will stand out from your standard storage tubs. Use orange and black for Halloween, brown for Thanksgiving, red for Valentine's Day, and so on. If you enlist personal elves to assist you with the task, your helpers will always know exactly just what boxes to reach for.

Label your containers clearly and be as specific as possible. Don't just write "Christmas." Jot down exactly what Christmas items are inside like "Baking dishes" or "Santa suit."

Avoid packing holiday candles away in attics. The heat will warp them. Find a cool area instead.

E ALERT!

If you save leftover holiday cards to use the following season or take advantage of after-Christmas sales to enjoy half-price card savings, store them in an area of your home that won't subject them to extreme temperatures or high humidity. One December, a woman discovered, much to her distress, that her stash of cards purchased the prior season was ruined because humidity had sealed the envelopes shut.

Have a rationale behind your storage approach to make subsequent set-ups a no-brainer. One strategy is to pack like items together. For instance, have all your lights in one box, all decorative figurines in another, and tree skirt, stand, and floor protector in a third. Another method is to pack by room. Somehow we seem to suffer amnesia from one year to the next. Where does the six-foot string of twinkle lights go again? In what room does the ceramic tabletop tree belong? That won't happen next year if you make your containers room-specific. That way all objects that go in the dining room, say, are together, and all outdoor objects are in another container. Go one step further. Attach little notes to each applicable piece before you tuck it away for the season reminding you where in the room it goes. If the white lights are designated for the bay window and the fuzzy snowman on the fireplace mantel, take an extra moment to note it.

Santa Claus is believed to be inspired by a bishop who lived in the fourth century named Saint Nicholas of Myra, now located in modern Turkey. The bishop was remembered for his generosity.

There are some items you may need to get to first, before the heavy artillery of decorations comes out. Place these in the most accessible areas, where they'll be easy to grab. Some people like getting an early jump on their baking, gift-wrapping, or card-writing, for instance.

Before you pack away ornaments, remove hooks to prevent scratches and mars.

If you have an artificial tree and tend to decorate it the same way year after year—and you have the room—you don't necessarily have to undecorate it at the end of the season. Throw a big plastic bag or tarp over it, and it'll be set up and ready to go next December. It's definitely the way to go for tabletop-size trees. The same thing goes with artificial wreaths, centerpieces, and garlands.

Going natural will really cut down on your storage needs. Buy a live tree and fresh greenery, and you won't have to think about off-season storage at all. Some communities even have programs in which trees are collected after Christmas and then chopped up into mulch, which is then offered free to residents. In New York City, for example, residents can drop off their trees and wreaths during "Mulchfest" at selected parks. Check with your local municipality to see if there's a similar program in your neighborhood.

Tailor-Made Solutions

Many Christmas items are oddly shaped or on the fragile side. Fortunately, tailor-made storage options are easy to find.

There's nothing more frustrating than dealing with a tangle of Christmas lights. Quell the chaos with specially designed plastic spools that make it kind when you unwind. For a more inexpensive option, wrap them around a piece of heavy cardboard or a wrapping-paper tube.

Invest in an ornament chest with thick, stable dividers to keep dust and pests out but protection built right in. Got leftover tissue paper? Scrunch it up and use it to cushion the layers. If your ornaments are particularly valuable, either from an investment or sentimental perspective, consider an archival quality chest that's made from acid-free materials. Chests made of standard cardboard can cause discoloration and deterioration of your ornaments over the long haul.

ALERT!

Keep your live tree watered. A dried-out Christmas tree is a major fire hazard, accounting for some 400 fires annually, according to the U.S. Fire Administration. A short in the electrical lights or a lighted candle nearby can ignite a dry tree in seconds. As a precaution, consider buying an automatic watering system. They're disguised as gift boxes and fit right under the tree.

Keep your most precious ornaments stored in their original packaging for the best protection. Food ornaments, like gingerbread cookies, should be double-sealed, first in plastic and then in a tin container to keep away pests with a sweet tooth.

Artificial wreaths and garlands keep their fresh-looking appearance and dust-free shapes longer when stored in boxes. Remove all wire and metal decorations before you pack them away. They could rust in high-humidity conditions. Another easy option is to hang wreaths on a wall of your basement or garage, then cover them up. It's also a good place to store holiday lawn ornaments.

Centralize all your wrapping paper and accessories. Upright plastic containers hold a season's worth of wrapping paper rolls without taking up much storage space. Other models are shaped to fit under a bed and are wide enough to hold gift boxes, too. Over-the-door hanging models have pouches to hold scissors, tape, ribbons, and bows.

For a Holly Jolly Christmas

One Santa wannabe says Christmas is part nostalgia, part fantasy for him. The sights and smells help to remind him of Christmases past—the people who've come and gone—while the newly added decorations give him something to look forward to for the following season.

Yet, experts say the holidays are the most stressful, anxiety-ridden time of year. There's so much to do, gifts to buy, parties to prepare, and every season, there's more pressure to surpass the year before. In some neighborhoods, decorating the home has turned into an extreme sport.

Want instant ambiance? Buy a DVD of a crackling fireplace and have it play in the background while you're decorating or entertaining. Some are so real you can practically feel the heat. You'll have all the charm of a Yule log with none of the ashes to clean up!

If you're the kind of person who'd rather enjoy a Christmas state of mind, instead of state of chaos, putting a storage system in place will do wonders for your private wonderland.

Put out only a few special items if the thought of doing a full-blown decorating redesign brings on an anxiety attack. Add some live strategically placed poinsettias and you'll cut down on your storage woes.

Once the holiday is over, concentrate on how you put things away. End-of-season inertia is often responsible for a slipshod get-it-over-with approach. Don't forget that nearly a full year will pass before you use these items again. If you don't do it right, next year will start off all wrong.

Chapter 20

On the Road: Travel

Seasoned travelers are always ready for anything, whether it's a globe-trotting long haul or an easy overnighter. Storage is as important when you're on the go as it is when you're home—maybe even more so. In this chapter, you'll get the lowdown on space-saving travel organizers and strategies that will leave you with enough room left over to cart home the souvenirs.

Mapping a Plan

They're the battle cries of classic overpackers who long for the days when enormous steamer trunks were still in fashion: "I might need it"; "I like having a choice"; "I want to be prepared for any situation"; "But what if I run out?"

In some ways, the advent of rolling luggage in the late 1980s, a development that revolutionized the luggage industry, enabled clotheshorses everywhere to feed their bad habits. You might think twice about dragging and lifting your suitcases through an airport and across a city, but if you can roll them along at a good clip, who cares what the scale says? Now virtually every type of bag is available on wheels, from backpacks and duffels to garment bags. Overpacking may no longer be tough on your back, but it could be tough on your wallet with the new, more stringent weight restrictions the airlines have set out.

Weight Woes

Go over a carrier's weight limitations, and prepare to pay the price. Did you know that using old luggage could potentially cost you money? Older models are made of heavier material. They can weigh ten or fifteen pounds empty, and that makes it more likely you'll be asked to cough up an overweight surcharge. Today's luggage manufacturers are producing bags of lighter, durable materials, knowing travelers are facing ever more stringent weight restrictions. Some luggage makers have even stopped making models with a lot of compartments. The reason? Built-in compartments tend to add a lot of weight to the bag.

If you lock your luggage when flying, be sure your locks are recognized and approved by the Transportation Security Administration (TSA). The TSA has a master device that will open the luggage when necessary for inspection, without having to cut the bag open or pry the lock off.

One thing to keep in mind is that weight is measured on a per-bag basis. Say you're allowed fifty pounds per bag and you've got two bags that total eighty pounds. You could still be facing a surcharge if one bag is sixty pounds and the other is twenty pounds. Make sure to balance the weight equally between the two. A luggage collection by Ricardo Beverly Hills comes with a built-in digital scale to instantly weigh suitcases and their contents.

With airlines strictly enforcing overweight surcharges, lightweight luggage and alternative organization cases are the solutions.

Packrat Problems

Cramming your bags could be tough on your psyche, too. Traveling is stressful, even under the best conditions. Packratitis means the decisions you've put off before your trip follow you to your destination. Consider the case of the fashionista whose hotel room in the Caribbean looked like a clothes shop gone bad inside an hour of her checking in. Shoes, shirts, slacks, and skirts were everywhere. Instead of a relaxing start to her tropical vacation, she was immediately surrounded with clutter.

Suit(case) Yourself

These days, you can buy luggage just about anywhere, but what's the right match for you? Before you buy, ask yourself the following questions:

- How often do you travel?
- What's your preferred mode of travel: air, car, train, bus, ship?
- Do you make frequent stops or unpack once and stay put?
- Do you typically travel with a tour group where someone else tends to your luggage, or do you go it alone?
- What's the typical length of your trips?
- What do you pack: casual? formal? business?

The kind of travel you do—whether for business, independent sightseeing, or family vacations—will affect the luggage style you choose. Backpacks and duffels are popular with the independent traveler crowd. Duffels are soft and seamless and can often slip under an airline seat. Models with expandability and telescoping handles make for easy packing and toting. On the other hand, it's harder to keep clothes organized in a duffel, so packing aids such as pouches and mesh bags may be needed. If you're a road warrior traveling from plane to meeting, garment bags make the most sense.

ALERT!

Be informed. When traveling to foreign destinations, check the U.S. State Department's Web site for any potential warnings as well as detailed information on health alerts and safety issues. Visit *www.travel.state.gov/travel.*

The frequency of your travel matters as well. If you rack up enough frequent-flier miles to be a million-air, durability is key. You need luggage that will go the distance.

If you are packing and unpacking frequently, or are likely to be doing all your own baggage handling, you should consider size and weight. Even though suitcases may be on rollers, there's still a fair amount of heavy lifting involved: on and off the luggage carousel, up and down the stairs, onto buses and trains, and so on. The more stops you make, and the more of an independent traveler you are, the more importance weight will have as you factor it into your decision. For a quick trip, an eighteen- or twenty-inch carry-on suitcase should do. Away a week? Think about a twenty-six-incher. Even longer? Try a twenty-nine-inch model.

Increasingly, airlines are making Internet service available in-flight, giving laptop users one more reason to haul their computers aboard the friendly skies. Look for light-frame laptop cases that have plenty of protective padding and snugly fitting inside straps.

For workspace while you're on the go, consider a business valise. It opens up to a portable desk that's as close to bringing along the whole office as you can get. The valise has swing-out pockets for storing magazines, writing pads, correspondence, and supplies (administrative assistant not included).

Route Causes

No need to reinvent the wheel for every trip. Some things you need to pack only once. Save time by keeping a toiletry kit filled and ready to go with sample sizes of the following:

- First-aid kit, including bandages, pain reliever, and antiseptic wipes
- Deodorant
- Shampoo and conditioner
- Disposable shaver
- Comb
- Soap

Pick a case with a built-in hook that lets you hang it from a towel hook or doorknob. The less stuff you have loitering around the bathroom sink, the better. A toiletry case with see-through plastic or mesh pockets will prevent you from having to rummaging around for your things. Replenish when supplies run out. The time to do that is at the end of each trip while it's still fresh on your mind.

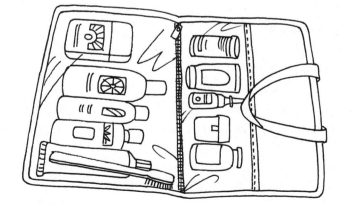

◀ A toiletry case.

Make a master list once and check it twice. Much of what you pack for one trip is the same stuff you need for subsequent trips: eyeglasses, medications, pajamas, socks, underwear, and razor. Keep a hard-copy list in your suitcase and another one on file in your computer and you'll never forget to pack something important.

FACT

The earliest trunks in America date back to the late 1600s and were made of woods and covered in animal hides. Demand increased as pioneers made their way west across the country by rail and stagecoach. In the late nineteenth century, new flattop styles were produced for steamship travel, and the "steamer trunk" was born.

Another idea to maintain control and stay organized during your vacation preparation phase is to establish a file for all your trip documents. You file should contain the following:

- Passports
- Airline tickets or e-ticket confirmations
- Travel books and articles related to your destination
- Rental car information
- Hotel confirmation
- Trip itinerary
- Important phone numbers

By having a dedicated place to store all your key papers, you'll never waste a moment scratching your head wondering where things are.

Lighten Up

Good principals of organization and storage apply at home and on the road. In both cases, less is more. A veteran travel writer manages to winnow her wares down to a single knapsack for every trip. You might not have it in you to go to that kind of austerity measure, but some easy rules will let you settle in a happy medium, somewhere between jam-packed and bare bones.

Pack your essentials, sure—medications, prescription eyeglasses, and so on, but don't pack for every "just in case" eventuality. Unless you're going to a desolate area, assume you can buy what you need at your destination. Many hotels have a gift shop on premises that carry the necessities.

Call ahead. Plenty of resorts, motels, and inns have hairdryers, travel irons, bathrobes, business offices, and even libraries in residence, so you can leave the heavy stuff behind.

ALERT!

For security purposes, avoid wearing flashy jewelry, even if it's costume. Potential thieves looking for a quick payday won't know the difference. When traveling to certain foreign destinations, wearing baseball caps, shirts, or even luggage with the logos of well-known American brands can make you an easy target. Stick with conservative attire that helps you blend in with the locals.

Think outside the box. When packing, take stuff out of the original packaging. De-box suntan lotions, snacks, medications, and cosmetics. Put anything that's liable to leak in a zip-close plastic bag.

Traveling with family members? This is one instance when "to each his own" should *not* apply. Don't pack multiple tubes of travel-size toothpastes, sample-size shampoos, and so on. Share toiletries whenever possible.

When it comes to clothing, pack the basics and build outfits around a few key pieces, using accessories to vary and spice up your look. Throw some lightweight scarves, belts, ties, and simple costume jewelry into your suitcase. And try to bring clothes that can take on more than one role:

- Sandals you can also wear as slippers
- T-shirt for casual daytime wear that can double as workout gear
- Camisole as undershirt or, later, for an evening top

Sporting equipment like bicycles and ski gear can be difficult to transport and may be subject to additional airline surcharges. Think about arranging equipment rentals at your destination instead.

When booking airfare, always check the airline's own Web site. You'll typically save $5 or $10 per ticket. Another way to save some money is by bringing your own food on the plane. With more and more airlines charging high prices for food service, you'll spend less if you BYOM— bring your own meals aboard.

Check weather reports and pack accordingly. Eva went to Ireland in the fall, ill prepared for an unseasonable heat wave. The thick woolen sweaters she brought went unworn. You can't always count on 100 percent accuracy, of course, but you can hedge your bets, especially when you're traveling to a dramatically different climate. If you're headed for Florida from, say, snowbound Wisconsin, it's hard to think of what you need for summer-like weather. That's when people tend to pack too much—usually four seasons' worth of clothing! Then there are the people who make the wrong assumptions. Sam, a first-timer to Las Vegas, packed shorts and T-shirts for his January vacation, not realizing how cold it gets at night in the desert. A little education can spare you a lot of aggravation.

On the Road

Why does it seem that the souvenirs we like best are the big, bulky, and impossibly fragile kind? If you spot an irresistible yet hulky keepsake, investigate the options involved in shipping it home. Another alternative is ordering it online once you get home so you don't have to deal with any packing hassles. Of course, you can also do as Ann, a veteran traveler, does. Instead of store-bought mementos, she brings home a small rock from every place she goes and then adds it to her collection, displayed in a vintage jar. She's like many who've discovered the joys of collecting easy-to-cart-home tokens, like these:

- Postcards
- Matchbooks
- Exotic stamps
- Jewelry
- Pens
- Magnets
- Key chains
- Ornaments
- Decals and patches
- T-shirts
- Music CDs

Some savvy travelers lighten their load as they move along. Judy, an avid reader, actually rips out pages of her books as she reads them. Stan leaves his books and magazines behind in common areas of his hotel for others to enjoy once he's done with them. He just might be the lightest packer around. Unlike most vacationers who gussy up when on the go, Stan packs his most tattered clothes and simply throws them away at the end of the trip. Needless to say, packing for the trip home is a breeze.

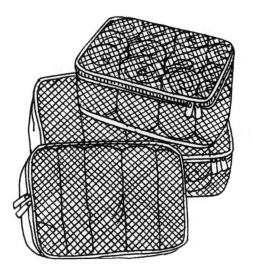

◀ Mesh packing cubes.

Instead of packing a separate outfit for every day, pack fabrics that are lightweight and quick-drying so you can rinse them out in the sink and get multiple wears out of each article of clothing you bring. Smart travelers often scout out a Laundromat where they can drop their clothes off in the morning and pick them up later in the day. Many hotels offer laundry service, too, though the bill has been known to turn frequent fliers into frequent criers.

Sort yourself. Before you pack up for the journey home, go through all the brochures, knickknacks, maps, and papers you've accumulated throughout your trip and throw out what you don't want. A lot of people toss everything into their suitcases to sort through once they get home and wind up loading down their bags unnecessarily. Business travelers, in particular, get bombarded by trade magazines, premium items, and fat information kits. Chances are most of that stash is unnecessary and unwanted, so why cart it home when you can leave it behind in the hotel's trash can? No need to introduce more junk into your house to deal with later. A frequent conference attendee who's up to his eyeballs in logo-inscribed T-shirts and branded tote bags gives his goodies to taxi drivers on his way back to the airport, along with their tips.

FACT

Airlines are enforcing luggage weight restrictions to save on fuel costs. Smaller regional carriers are particularly stringent. Call your airline to find out how many bags you're allowed and what the weight limitations are for each bag. Otherwise, you might be in for an unpleasant start to your trip owing to a hefty surcharge of anywhere from $20 to $70 per bag. Odd-size packages can be considered overweight as well.

When shopping around for souvenirs, don't buy first and then think second about the consequences. Make sure you have a place in your home to put it or someone in mind to give it to. Many mistakenly fall in love with an item in a gift store thinking a spot will magically open up in their home to accommodate it. Eliza bought a beautiful but oversize print during a trip to Barcelona. Two years later, it's still rolled up in a tube and lying somewhere in the back of a closet because she realized 6,000 miles too late it really didn't fit in her home. Another couple bought an exotic "rainfall" stick on vacation in South America. Trouble was, the three-foot-long instrument wouldn't fit in the suitcase and wasn't allowed on the plane. No doubt an airport employee in Chile is enjoying it about now.

Always on the go? Violight Travel is a toothbrush sanitizer housed in a sleek tubular storage unit that uses an ultraviolet bulb to eliminate germs and bacteria on toothbrushes. Place your toothbrush in the case and seven minutes later, 99 percent of the germs are gone.

Leader of the Pack

Wouldn't it be a relief if you could close your suitcase without having to sit on it? And wouldn't it be great if you didn't have to worry about straining the zipper to its bursting point? Imagine the embarrassment of one female executive waiting with her colleagues for her luggage at Kennedy Airport in New York. When the bag finally made its appearance on the luggage carousel, it had split open, and her lingerie was strewn all over the conveyer belt. So much for Victoria's secrets.

If you want to get to and from your destination with your bags in one piece, your items in shipshape condition, and your dignity intact, try packing smart:

- More than a few travel gurus recommend setting out your clothes for your trip—and then putting half back in your closet. You simply don't need all those shirts, slacks, shoes, and sweaters.
- Think in terms of thin layers of clothes, rather than bulky sweaters and jackets. It's more practical, too. It gives you the option of donning or shedding layers as needed to face a wide temperature span.

- Limit your footwear. Nothing eats up luggage space like shoes and sneakers. Speaking of footwear: Put shoes in a separate bag so they don't soil your clothes.
- Fill every crevice, right down to the hollows of your shoes. They're a great place for socks, underwear, swimsuits, sunglasses, and other small items that might otherwise get lost in your luggage.
- Reserve your bulkiest clothes and shoes to wear on the plane so they don't hog up space in your luggage.

Roll up socks, T-shirts, even trousers. Hold delicate silks in place by wrapping them in tissue paper or plastic bags from the dry cleaning shop. Hate the thought having to waste any time on vacation ironing? Wrinkles are the result of too much shifting in transit or overpacking that causes creases to set in. Find a middle ground by packing snuggly and using luggage straps to keep items in place. Bringing along a wardrobe of easy-wearing knits, Lycra, denim, and flannel is another tactic to keep you away from the ironing board.

ALERT!

It's always a good idea to make two copies of your important travel documents, including passport information, travelers' checks, prescriptions, credit card numbers, and emergency contacts. Be sure to store one copy in a separate compartment from your originals and leave the other copy home with a trusted family member or friend.

Take the last-in, first-out approach. If you're getting to your island getaway in time to hit the beach, make sure your bathing suit, sandals, and lotions are at the top of the pack. Arriving in time for dinner? Have your evening clothes within easy grasp.

Consider purchasing reusable vacuum-sealed travel bags that reduce bulk. They remove the air trapped inside your clothing. But keep in mind they wrinkle fabrics. Best to use them for your dirty clothes.

There are hundreds, if not thousands, of luggage variations, but you wouldn't know it by looking at the airport conveyer belt. Black, black, dark green, and black is about the standard. A New Jersey business executive named Ira probably wasn't the first traveler to make the mistake of grabbing the wrong suitcase. But you have to pity the guy. He discovered his error only after shlepping the wrong bag all the way home during a wild January snowstorm. Next stop for him? Back to the airport.

QUESTION?

What are noise-canceling headphones?
Noise-canceling headphones eliminate background noise and are a favorite accessory among frequent fliers. Headphones such as the NoiseBuster brand and Bose reduce engine din and enhance the sound and clarity of in-flight entertainment.

Brightly colored luggage may not be as dignified as blacks, greens, and grays, but it'll help you identify it more easily and prevent mix-ups. As an alternative, you can customize your bags with bold luggage tags, straps, or ribbons.

Auto-Matic

Clutter in your car is closer than it appears. Some people love road trips for the simple fact that they don't need to think about how they're going to pack. They simply toss everything in the car—suitcases, shopping bags, tote bags. The how's and where's don't really matter. Not so fast. There's a principle that seems to state that it takes no time to clutter up a vehicle but ages to clean it up again.

Sort through your maps and keep only the relevant ones. File the rest at home, but only if you think you'll need them again in the near future. John, a father of two, took his family on a ski trip to Vermont one time four years ago, and the roadmap detailing the way to Stratton Mountain is still in his SUV to this day.

Always keep a bag dedicated to trash, especially if you make frequent stops at the drive-through window. These days, one out of five restaurant meals is purchased from the driver's seat.

Organize your CD collection so it's not filling every nook and cranny of your vehicle. CD visor organizers keep your favorites within easy reach. Some storage visors have room enough to hold your vehicle registration card and glasses, too.

Don't leave home without a fully stocked emergency kit. Yours should include the following:

- Blanket
- Flashlight (with working batteries, checked periodically)
- First-aid kit
- Jumper cables
- Warning light or flare
- Ice scraper, depending on the climate

To keep the gang happy, invest in a back-seat organizer that has multiple pockets for storing magazines, water bottles, pens, iPods, audio books, and *more*.

For long trips, a collapsible trunk organizer will keep a bevy of small items, like umbrellas, books, and sporting equipment, neatly grouped in one central place.

Home Away from Home

The second-home market is booming. In part, the unprecedented growth in home equity has left many homeowners with cash to spend. But it's also that baby boomers are entering the peak buying years for second homes and using real estate to diversify their financial portfolios. According to the National Association of Realtors, vacation home sales rose nearly 20 percent in 2004, to 1.02 million, and industry insiders expect the second-home sales market to stay strong over the next decade. So what's the danger of having a beach house, ski resort, or chalet on a lake? "I look at my week-end house as a storage unit with a mortgage," says Barry of Manhattan and Connecticut. "I find every time I go I have to bring 'just this one little item' to leave there and that way it won't be taking up space in my closet in my New York apartment."

It's easy to fall into a bad habit of freeing up space in your primary residence but then turning your getaway retreat into a heap. Another caveat: For security reasons, don't store your antiques, valuables, or important sentimental items in your vacation home if it's used only sporadically.

On the Fast Track

Even when you're bound for a vacation of strictly beachside R&R, travel can be stressful, and not just in the preparation. Once you hit the ground at your destination, you've got new routines to contend with and weather to acclimatize to, not to mention the prospects of adjusting to new sleeping habits and an alien culture. So much is out of your power. That's why it's so important to manage the elements within your control.

Clutter isn't relegated to the home. It travels with you by plane, train, or automobile. Too much stuff is jammed into the suitcase, too many suitcases are jammed into the car. Can't you just see those sloppy mounds of clothes strewn all over the hotel room now?

FACT

Travel and tourism is a $1.3 trillion industry in the United States, according to the Travel Industry Association of America. The travel industry generates $100 billion in tax revenue for local, state, and federal governments and is one of the country's largest employers, with 7.3 million direct travel-generated jobs. The most popular domestic activity? Shopping.

In many ways, it's even more important to have a storage and organizational system in place when you're on vacation because space is at a premium. The basic principals of clutter-free living apply to clutter-free traveling. Do with less. Establish a dedicated place for everything. Put things where they belong.

Vacations are for recharging the batteries, whether that means powering down or a dawn-to-dusk agenda. Either way, bringing order to your planning and packing will pay off with a sense of calm and serenity when you need it most.

Appendix A

Glossary

archival quality
Conservation materials and techniques used in the preservation and storage of rare and old materials.

armoire
A tall cabinet, usually with drawers, shelves, and doors, used for storing clothes or household items.

baker's rack
A display unit, often made of iron, steel, or copper, that can serve as either decoration or as a functional piece for storage.

BookCrossing.com
A Web site dedicated to the practice of leaving a book in a public place to be picked up and read by others, who then do likewise.

captain's bed
A bed frame that accommodates a mattress, without a box spring, and features working drawers for storage within the frame.

clutter
A confusing or disorderly state.

Clutterers Anonymous
A twelve-step recovery program that offers help to the true clutterer, who is overwhelmed by disorder.

conservator
An individual who cares for, restores, and repairs collectible objects.

consignment sale
An arrangement in which merchandise is sold by an agent on the seller's behalf.

cosmeceutical
A term coined by the cosmetic industry that refers to cosmetic products that have medicinal or therapeutic effects on the body.

crawl space
The space between the ground and the first floor of a home, usually no more than a few feet high.

data (memory) card/Memory Stick

A device used to store data for digital cameras, camcorders, and computers. The Memory Stick is a proprietary Sony product and it is used by nearly all of Sony's products that use flash media.

dead storage

Storage reserved for items that are no longer needed for immediate use but that are still required for records.

digital

The method of storing, processing, and transmitting information through the use of distinct electronic or optical pulses that represent the binary digits 0 and 1.

digital video recorder (DVR)

A device that enables you to record and time-shift TV programs on a hard-disk drive for later viewing. Also known as personal video recorder.

DVD

A high-density compact disc used for storing large amounts of data, especially high-resolution audiovisual material.

eBay

An online shopping site with more than 100 million registered members from around the world.

ephemera

Documents published with a short intended lifetime.

external zip disk drive

A removable disk storage system.

feng shui

An ancient Chinese practice of living harmoniously with the natural elements and forces of the Earth.

flexispace

A space or room in the home that can be utilized for any function as needed

Freecycle Network (www.freecycle.org)

An online grassroots organization made up of communities around the globe that allows individuals to recycle their no-longer-wanted goods by offering them free to members.

garage system
A complete garage organization and storage plan.

home theater
A system of sophisticated electronic equipment for the presentation of theater-quality images and sound in the home.

International Association of Professional Organizers
An organization dedicated to setting and maintaining standards of excellence for professional organizers worldwide.

lazy Susan
A revolving tray typically used in the kitchen for condiments or food.

loft bed
A bunk bed in which the top of the mattress is more than 3 feet from the floor. Loft bunk beds, like other bunks, save space and add a creative element to a bedroom.

modular furniture
Furniture made up of independent units that can be combined into flexible formations.

mudroom
An anteroom to the house that provides a waterproof and weatherproof place for the removal and storage of rain or snow-covered clothes.

Murphy bed
A space-saving bed that folds up into a closet.

National Association of Professional Organizers (NAPO)
A nonprofit organization of organizing consultants, speakers, trainers, authors, and manufacturers of organizing products. Founded in 1985, NAPO is the largest national association of and for organizers.

niche
A recess in a wall (may be used to house decorative objects).

obsessive-compulsive disorder (OCD)
A neurobiological disorder characterized by recurrent, unwelcome thoughts and repetitive behavior.

online photo service

A Web site that provides users with the ability to print, enhance, archive, and store digital images. Popular sites are KodakGallery.com, Shutterfly.com, and Snapfish.com.

organic gardening

A method of gardening that uses only materials derived from living things, such as compost and manure for fertilization and pest control. In contrast to conventional gardening, the organic approach uses no synthetic chemicals at all.

peg board

A board perforated with regularly spaced holes into which pegs can be fitted that allow for hanging storage of tools and other accessories.

personal video recorder (PVR)

A device that enables you to record and time-shift TV programs on a hard-disc drive for later viewing. Also known as *digital video recorder.*

pocket door

A door that disappears into a specially built wall cavity.

PODS

Portable on Demand Storage

potting bench

A workspace and storage holder typically used by gardeners to pot or transplant plant material.

professional organizer

An individual who designs systems and processes using organizing principles to help clients take control of their homes and lifestyles.

purge housecleaning

The act of cleaning the rooms and furnishings of a house.

repurpose

Using an item for a different situation than was originally intended by the creator or manufacturer.

rewritable CD

A compact disc that allows users to read, write, and erase data.

R-value

A measure that indicates how well insulation resists heat flow. The higher the R-value, the better the insulation.

scanner

A machine that optically analyzes a two- or three-dimensional image and digitally encodes it for storage in a computer file.

self-storage facility

A property designed and used for leasing individual storage spaces. Charges are determined by the size of the room, per month.

shed

A building that is separate from a main building and usually used for storage.

thrift shop

A shop that sells secondhand goods at reduced prices.

ultraviolet light

Light lying outside the visible spectrum. The primary source of ultraviolet light is the sun. Ultraviolet rays can cause fading of paint finishes, carpets, photographs, art, and fabrics.

vertical space

The space above the head and high along the walls. Utilizing vertical space is an important element of storage planning.

window film

A protective coating designed to reduce the amount of solar heat transmission through window glass and prevent fading of furniture, artwork, and fabrics.

Appendix B

Additional Resources

Organizations and Government Agencies

American Institute for Conservation of Historic and Artistic Works
202-452-9545
http://aic.stanford.edu

Better Business Bureau
703-276-0100
www.bbb.org

Consumer Product Safety Commission
800-638-2772
www.cpsc.gov

Direct Marketing Association Mail Preference Service
212-768-7277
www.dmaconsumers.org

Federal Trade Commission
877-FTC-HELP
www.ftc.gov

Green Guide
212-598-4910
www.thegreenguide.com

Internal Revenue Service
800-829-1040
www.irs.gov

National Gardening Association
802-863-5251
www.nationalgardenmonth.org

National Pesticide Information Center
800-858-7378
www.npic.orst.edu

Poison Control Center
800-222-1222
www.poison.org

State Department
202-647-4000
www.travel.state.gov

United States National Arboretum
202-245-4523
www.usna.usda.gov

Organizational Consultants and Services

1-800-GOT JUNK
800-Got-Junk
www.800gotjunk.com

Ariane Benefit, Professional Organizer
973-429-2100
www.organizingforhealth.com
www.neatliving.org

Arranging It All
Barry J. Izsak, Professional Organizer
512-419-7526
✍*www.arrangingitall.com*

California Closets
888-336-9709
✍*www.californiaclosets.com*

Clutterers Anonymous
310-281-6064
✍*www.clutterersanonymous.net*

GarageTek
866-664-2724
✍*www.garagetek.com*

Gladiator GarageWorks
866-342-4089
✍*www.gladiatorgw.com*

HMG Organizing
Heidi M. Gaumet, Professional Organizer
631-803-7029
✍*www.hmgorganizing.com*

International Association of Professional Organizers
212-920-1440
✍*http://organizingtheworld.org*

Kitchen Solvers of Cincinnati
800-845-6779
✍*www.kitchensolvers.com*

Misha K.
Misha Keefe, Professional Organizer
202-256-7903
✍*www.mishak.com*

National Association of Professional Organizers
847-375-4746
✍*www.napo.net*

Retailers, Mail Order, and Online Storage Resources

Art Plasma
✍*www.artplasma.com*

Ballard Designs
800-367-2775
✍*www.ballarddesigns.com*

Bed, Bath and Beyond
800-462-3966
✍*www.bedbathandbeyond.com*

Brookstone
800-846-3000
✍*www.brookstone.com*

The Container Store
888-266-8246
✍*www.containerstore.com*

Crate and Barrel
800-967-6696
www.crateandbarrel.com

Design Within Reach
800-944-2233
www.dwr.com

Exposures
800-222-4947
www.exposuresonline.com

FridgeFile
www.fridgefile.com

Frontgate
888-263-9850
www.frontgate.com

Furniture.com
www.furniture.com

Get Organized
800-803-9400
www.shopgetorganized.com

Half.com
www.half.com

Hammacher Schlemmer
800-321-1484
www.hammacher.com

Hold Everything
888-922-4117
www.holdeverything.com

Holy Cow Cleaning Products
877-946-5926
www.holycowproducts.com

Home Focus
800-221-6771
www.homefocuscatalog.com

Hydra Design Tables
908-903-1997
www.hydradesigns.com

Improvements
800-642-2112
www.improvementscatalog.com

**Independent Association of
Dinnerware Matchers**
www.iadm.com

KitchenAid
800-422-1230
www.kitchenaid.com

Kodak Gallery
www.kodakgallery.com

Levenger
800-667-8034
www.levenger.com

Lillian Vernon
800-901-9402
www.lillianvernon.com

Linens 'n Things
866-568-7378
✎ *www.lnt.com*

L.L.Bean
800-441-5713
✎ *www.llbean.com*

Mama's Earth
800-620-7388
✎ *www.mamasearth.com*

Merillat Cabinetry
✎ *www.merillat.com*

Museum of Useful Things
800-515-2707
✎ *www.themut.com*

Organic Gift Shop
800-895-6045
✎ *www.organicgiftshop.com*

Pendaflex
✎ *www.pendaflexlearningcenter.com*

Petsmart
888-839-9638
✎ *www.petsmart.com*

Portable On Demand Storage
888-776-PODS
✎ *www.pods.com*

Pottery Barn
888-779-5176
✎ *www.potterybarn.com*

Restoration Hardware
800-762-1005
✎ *www.restorationhardware.com*

Rival Seal-a-Meal
800-557-4825
✎ *www.seal-a-meal.com*

Rubbermaid
✎ *www.rubbermaid.com*

Screen Dreams
800-625-9000
✎ *www.screendreamsdvd.com*

Sharper Image
800-344-5555
✎ *www.sharperimage.com*

Shutterfly
✎ *www.shutterfly.com*

Silicone Zone
212-997-9591
✎ *www.siliconezoneusa.com*

Snapfish
✎ *www.snapfish.com*

Stacks and Stacks
800-761-5222
✎ *www.stacksandstacks.com*

Wherehouse.com
✒ *www.wherehouse.com*

Whirlpool
866-698-2538
✒ *www.whirlpool.com*

Williams-Sonoma
800-541-2233
✒ *www.williams-sonoma.com*

Places to Sell and Donate

Big Brothers Big Sisters
215-567-7000
✒ *www.bbbs.org*

Book Crossing
877-468-4394
✒ *www.bookcrossing.com*

CoinStar
425-943-8000
✒ *www.coinstar.com*

CraigsList
✒ *www.craigslist.org*

eBay
✒ *www.ebay.com*

FreeCycle
✒ *www.freecycle.org*

Vietnam Veterans of America
800-VVA-1316
✒ *www.vva.org*

Travel Resources

Automobile Club of America
✒ *www.aaa.com*

Magellan's
800-962-4943
✒ *www.magellans.com*

Mapquest
✒ *www.mapquest.com*

National Passport Center
877-487-2778
✒ *www.travel.state.gov*

NoiseBuster Noise Canceling Headphones
800-468-8371
✒ *www.noisebuster.net*

TravelSmith
800-950-1600
✒ *www.travelsmith.com*

Violight Travel
888-882-2367
✒ *www.violight.com*

Appendix C

Further Reading

Leslie Plummer Clagett, *The Smart Approach to the Organized Home*

Rita Emmett, *The Clutter-Busting Handbook: Clean It Up, Clear It Out and Keep Your Life Clutter-Free*

Winifred Gallagher, *House Thinking: A Room-by-Room Look at How We Live*

Paige Gilchrist, *Stylish Storage: Simple Ways to Contain Your Clutter*

Cindy Glovinsky, *One Thing at a Time: 100 Ways to Live Clutter-Free Every Day*

Cindy Glovinsky, *Making Peace with the Things in Your Life: Why Your Papers, Books, Clothes and Other Possessions Keep Overwhelming You and What to Do About It*

Janet Groene and Gordon Groene, *Living Aboard Your RV*

Barry Izsak, *Organize Your Garage in No Time*

Claire Josefine, *The Spiritual Art of Being Organized*

Karen Kingston, *Clear Your Clutter with Feng Shui*

John Loecke, *Organizing Idea Book*

Christopher Lowell, *Seven Layers of Organization: Unclutter Your Home, Unclutter Your Life*

Martha Stewart Living, *Good Things for Organizing*

Julie Morgenstern, *Organizing from the Inside Out*

Lanna Nakone, *Organizing for Your Brain Type: Finding Your Own Solution to Managing Time, Paper, and Stuff*

Maxine Ordesky, *The Complete Home Organizer: A Guide to Functional Storage Space for All the Rooms in Your Home*

Jason Rich, *The Everything® Organize Your Home Book: Straighten up the Entire House, from Cleaning Your Closets to Reorganizing Your Kitchen*

Debora Robertson, *Making the Most of Storage*

Peri Wolfman and Charles Gold, *A Place for Everything: Organizing the Stuff of Life*

Index

A

Affirmations, for recovering clutterers, 144–45
Apartments, 217–29
    bedrooms, 227–28
    built-in storage, 224–25
    décor tips, 220
    dining rooms, 224
    furniture for, 219–20, 223–25, 227–28
    kitchens, 225–26
    laundry areas, 228
    prioritizing living space in, 22–23
    purging clutter, 220–22
    room dividers, 223
    small-space advantages, 218–19
Armoires, 48, 90
Attics, 135–45
    categorizing storage in, 141–43
    finding treasures in, 139
    finished, 143
    inventorying/purging, 140–41, 142
    permanent storage in, 137
    pests/critters in, 138, 141
    R-value, 138
    scheduling organizing of, 144
    storage in, pros/cons, 136–37, 138
    structural integrity of, 142
    taking things in/out of, 140–41
    types/feel of, 136–37
    what to put/not put in, 137–39
    zones in, 141–42

B

Basements, 123–34
    assessing, 124–25
    benefits of organizing, 134
    craft centers in, 132–33
    defining space in, 130–31
    as dumping grounds, 124–25, 134
    finished, 129–31
    laundry areas, 131–32
    lighting, 129
    mildew problems, 127
    sporting gear in, 133
    starting organizing, 126–29
    storage ideas, 128–29
    weeding out, 126–28
Baskets
    for audio/video media, 89
    for bathroom items, 76
    for breads, 239
    in entryways, 151
    for office accessories, 107
    for playroom/toys, 118, 120
    for steps, 152
Bathrooms, 69–81
    basket storage, 76
    bath and beauty products, 70–71, 78–79
    clearing areas out, 71–73
    clothes piles/hampers, 80
    discerning junk from usable items, 78
    excessive supplies, 70–71
    furniture in, 75–76
    guest baths, 80
    hairdryers/curling irons, 79
    inventorying/purging, 71–75
    kids' stuff, 79–80
    medicine cabinet, 74–75
    over-the-toilet shelving, 79

Bathrooms—*continued*
    powder baths, 80
    remodeling, 70, 79
    Shower-Shower cleansing system, 78–79
    small spaces/small things, 79
    storage products, 81
    suction-cup holders, 77, 78
    TVs in, 78
    vanity organization, 76, 77
    wall shelving, 77, 81
Bedrooms, 37–52
    apartment, 227–28
    bedside pockets, 48
    chests, 49–50
    clothes piles, 42–43
    commitment to organizing, 52
    convertible storage options, 48–49
    drawer organization, 44–46
    four-box segregation system, 40–42
    guest rooms, 51
    in- and under-bed storage, 44–45, 47–48
    inventorying/purging, 40–42
    kids' stuff, 50–51
    loose change piles, 45
    nightstands, 47
    reclaiming, as sanctuary, 38–40
    sleep importance and, 39–40, 47
    sock organization, 45–46
    See also Closets
Benches with storage, 151, 158
Bookcases, 25, 107–8, 120, 130

C

Car travel, 265–66
Chemicals, 163, 170, 175
Chests, 49–50
Christmas decorations, 244–51
    inventorying/purging,
        246–47

organizing/storing, 247–50
    reducing preparation stress, 245–46, 251
Closets, 53–67
    apartment, 228
    benefits of organizing, 54, 66–67
    causes of clutter, 55–56
    clutter effects, 54
    coat, 65–66
    commitment to organizing, 67
    curtains instead of doors, 228
    exaggerated-size, examples, 54
    inventorying/purging, 56–58, 66–67
    kids' stuff, 63–64
    linen, 64–65
    organizing clothes, 58–62, 63–64
    shoes in, 55, 56, 62–63
    special-occasion clothes in, 56
    storage systems, 55, 56, 58–61
Clutter
    balanced approach to, 5
    causes of, 2–3
    emotional effects of, 5, 98
    hiding, 6
    impact of, 5–6
    inventorying/purging, 10–11
    practical hoarding and, 3–4
    professional help for, 3, 4–5
    range of, examples, 11
    visitors/guests and, 5
    visual, 6
Clutter-busting. *See also* specific rooms
Clutterers Anonymous, 4, 144
Coat closets, 65–66
Coat hooks, 152
Collectibles, 183–92
    appropriate storage, 188–90
    caring for, 192
    controlling volume of, 185–87
    expanding interest in, 184–85

packing away, 191
paper items, 195–96
selling, 187–88
sentimental items, 187–88
See also Paper items; Photographs
Communications center, 155–56
Computer system/cables, 104–5. *See also* Digitizing
    to downsize
Consignment sales, 188
Cosmeceuticals, 75
Craft centers
    in basements, 132–33
    in playrooms, 117–18

D

Digitizing to downsize, 109–11
    CD/DVDs for, 109
    online bank payments, 103
    photographs, 213–15
    scanning papers, 109, 110, 202–3
    videotapes, 94
Donations, 10, 11
    clothing, 57
    electronic equipment/media items, 87
    garage items, 176
    kitchen items, 20
    places to give, 43, 280
    vehicles, 178
Drawers
    bathrooms, 76
    bedrooms, 44–46
    kitchens, 30–32, 33

E

Efficiency
    basic habits for, 7–8
    practical approach to, 5
Electronic equipment. *See* Media rooms
E-mail, clutter-control idea, 13

Emergency supplies, 30, 74
Entrances. *See* Hallways and mudrooms
Ephemera, defined, 196. *See also* Paper items

F

Family participation, 8, 14
Filing systems, 100–101, 108–11, 138, 198–99
First-aid kits, 30, 74
Furniture, 8
    in apartments, 219–20, 223–25, 227–28
    in bathrooms, 75–76
    in entryways, 151, 158
    flexible-sized, 92–93
    in garage, 182
    in office, 97–98, 104–8
    ottomans for media storage, 89
    outdoor (patio), 169, 181
    special occasions and, 239
    stand-alone, for storage, 48–49
    storage benches, 151, 158, 169
    storage chests, 49–50
    TV/electronics storage, 89, 90–94

G

Garages, 171–82
    cars out, junk in, 173–74
    ceiling storage, 181
    chemicals in, 175
    commercial storage systems, 179–80
    common uses of, 172, 173
    doors, insulating, 179
    evolution of, 172–73, 176
    gardening materials in, 164, 174, 179
    inventorying/purging, 175–77
    organization plans, 178, 179–81
    peg boards in, 179
    portable, 174
    seasonal rearrangement of, 180–81
    sporting gear in, 174, 179, 180

Garages—*continued*
 storage solutions, 179–82
 zones in, 178
Gardening materials, 161–70
 bulb storage, 169
 categorizing tools/equipment, 167–68
 chemicals, 163, 170
 identifying storage area, 163–64
 indoor plants/prep area, 164–65
 inventorying/purging, 162–63
 maintaining tools/equipment, 168
 open shelves vs. cabinets, 164
 organizing/storing, 167–69
 outdoor furniture, 169
 planting seasons and, 166
 PODS for, 164
 scheduling clean-up, 166
 sheds for, 164
Glossary, 269–74

H

Hallways and mudrooms, 147–59
 common clutter items, 148
 front entrances, 149–52
 furniture solutions, 151
 hooks in, 152
 keys/pocket necessities, 149, 151, 158
 maintaining order, 158–59
 mudrooms, 152–56
 pet areas and, 156–57
 secret spaces in, 157–58
 shoes in, 152
 space under stairs, 157–58
 storage benches in, 151, 158
 storage solutions, 151, 152, 153–55
Hoarding, practical, 3–4
Holidays, 244–45. *See also* Christmas decorations
Home offices, 95–112
 benefits of organizing, 111–12

books in, 107–8
computer system/cables, 104–5
desks in, 104–6
digitizing to downsize, 109–11
documents to keep, 102–3
evaluating needs of, 97–98
filing systems and, 100–101, 108–11, 138, 198–99
fireproof safes in, 108
hutches/cabinets in, 106–7
magazine articles and, 101–2
mail management and, 98, 103–4, 195, 197
multiple people using, 105
in non-office rooms, 111
organizers for, 106, 107
paper clutter in, 96–97
proliferation of, 96
purging piles and files in, 98–103, 107
reclaiming calm/focus of, 96–97
reducing paperwork in, 103
securing important documents in, 108–9, 199–200
using idle space of, 107
virtual, 111
Home theaters. *See* Media rooms

I

Identity theft, 102, 104

J

Junk removal services, 3, 11, 276–77

K

Keys/pocket necessities, 149, 158
Kids
 bathrooms, 79–80
 bedrooms, 50–51
 closets, 63–64
 See also Playrooms
Kitchen cabinets
 door storage, 29

drawers, 30–32, 33
high shelves, 25
junk drawers, 30–31
lazy Susans, 29
pantry, 25
rolling shelves, 25
under-sink, 27–28
Kitchens, 17–35
apartment, 225–26
baking items, 21
cold storage, 24, 26–27
cookbooks/periodicals, 24–25
cups and mugs, 23
donating things from, 20
herbs, 20
inventorying/purging, 19, 24, 34–35
layout and storage locations, 22–23
overhead storage, 23–24
plastics, 21–22
pots and pans, 23–24
sentimental items, 235–36
small appliances, 33
storage principles, 20–21, 22–25
using idle space, 24–25, 32–33
utensil storage, 31–32
wall storage systems, 30
See also Special occasions

L

Laundry areas, 131–32, 228
Lazy Susans, 29, 76
Linen closets, 64–65

M

Magazines
recycling, 195
reducing inflow of, 197
torn-out articles, 101–2
Mail management, 98, 103–4, 195, 197

Materialism, 2–5
Media rooms, 83–94
in apartments, 225
in basements, 130, 133
digitizing videotapes, 94
donating/discarding things, 87–88
equipment bonanza, 84
four-box segregation system, 85–89
inventorying/purging, 85–89
organizing "keeper" items, 88–89, 94
preserving items, 86
remote control storage, 93–94
storage products, 89, 90–94
trends with, 84–85
TV/electronics, 90–94
Mental health
affirmations for recovering clutterers, 144–45
clutter affecting, 5, 98
organizing affecting, 15
Motion and time, 7
Mudrooms. *See* Hallways and mudrooms

O

Offices. *See* Home offices
Organizational consultants, 276–77
Organizations/government agencies, 276
Organizing
approaches to, 6–7
basic habits for, 7–8
benefits of, 9–10, 15, 34–35
commitment to, 9, 14, 52, 67
family participation in, 8
four-box segregation system, 40–42
inventorying/purging, 10–11
place for everything, 7–8
products for, 8–10
relief with, 10
saving money by, 34–35
See also specific rooms

Ottomans, for media storage, 89
Outdoor (patio) furniture, 169, 181

P

Paper items, 193–203
    clutter from, 96–97, 194–95
    collections, 195–96
    ending hard-copy subscriptions, 197
    filing systems, 100–101, 108–11, 138, 198–99
    greeting card glut, 197–98
    handling/preserving delicate documents, 201–3
    mail management, 98, 103–4, 195, 197
    pulp/acids and, 199–200, 201
    recycling magazines, 195
    reducing clutter, 196–98. *See also* filing systems
    scanning, 109, 110, 202–3
    securing important documents, 108–9, 199–200
    See also Photographs
Peg boards, 179
Permanent storage, 137
Pet areas, 156–57
Photographs, 205–15
    digital, 213–15
    double prints, 208–9
    inventorying/purging, 207–9
    organizing/storing, 209–15
    poor-quality, 208
    preserving, 211–13, 215
    proliferation of, 206
Planning
    getting started, 13–14
    importance of, 13
    process makes perfect, 13
    setting dates, 13–14
Plants. *See* Gardening materials
Playrooms, 113–22
    considering child age/size, 121–22
    evolving requirements for, 118–20
    excessive toys, 114

    finding space for, 114–15
    inventorying/sorting, 115–18
    marking containers, 121–22
    sorting toys, 115–18
    storage principles, 119–20, 121, 122
    storage products/containers, 118–19, 120–21
    zones in, 117–18
PODS (Portable On-Demand Storage), 164, 176
Professional help, 4–5
    Clutterers Anonymous, 4
    full-service junk removal, 3, 11
    organizational consultants, 276–77
    organization industry size, 14

R

Relatives, storage for, 124, 140
Resources, 276–80
    further reading, 281–82
    organizational consultants, 276–77
    organizations/government agencies, 276
    places to sell/donate, 280
    retail/mail order/online storage, 277–80
    travel, 280

S

Safety deposit box, 108
Scanning documents, 202–3
Second homes, 266–67
Selling things
    benefits of, 9–10
    places/options for, 9, 280
    See also Donations
Sentimental items, 187–88, 235–36
Special occasions, 231–41
    china/crystal for, 240
    doing more with less, 238–39
    furniture configurations for, 239
    holiday-themed dishware, 237

inventorying/purging items for, 234–36, 240–41

owning vs. renting/borrowing items, 236–37

signs of inefficiency on, 232–33

storing items, 233, 237–38

Sporting gear, 133, 155, 174, 179, 180, 260

Stairways

baskets on, 152

using space under, 157–58

Storage principles

inventorying/purging, 10–11. *See also* specific rooms

like with like, 12

ongoing process, 13, 15–16

Storage products, 8–10

buying before needing, 43

converting items into, 48–49

general checklist, 10

recycling packaging for, 49

See also specific rooms

Storage units

PODS for, 164

renting, 12

self-storage industry size, 2

Suitcases

packing guidelines, 258–65

storage in, 49

storing, 128

for travel, 255–56, 262

T

Time and motion, 7

Travel

airline weight limits, 254–55, 262

by car, 265–66

checklist, 258

clutter free, 267–68

document checklist/organization, 258

lightening load as you go, 261

luggage for, 255–58, 263

overpacking, 255

packing guidelines, 258–65

resources, 280

saving on airfare, 260

second homes and, 266–67

with sporting equipment, 260

toiletry case for, 257–58

TV. *See* Media rooms

W

Wine storage, 24, 128–29

THE EVERYTHING SERIES!

BUSINESS & PERSONAL FINANCE

Everything® **Accounting Book**
Everything® Budgeting Book
Everything® Business Planning Book
Everything® Coaching and Mentoring Book
Everything® Fundraising Book
Everything® Get Out of Debt Book
Everything® Grant Writing Book
Everything® Home-Based Business Book, 2nd Ed.
Everything® Homebuying Book, 2nd Ed.
Everything® Homeselling Book, 2nd Ed.
Everything® Investing Book, 2nd Ed.
Everything® Landlording Book
Everything® Leadership Book
Everything® **Managing People Book, 2nd Ed.**
Everything® Negotiating Book
Everything® Online Auctions Book
Everything® Online Business Book
Everything® Personal Finance Book
Everything® Personal Finance in Your 20s and 30s Book
Everything® Project Management Book
Everything® Real Estate Investing Book
Everything® Robert's Rules Book, $7.95
Everything® Selling Book
Everything® **Start Your Own Business Book, 2nd Ed.**
Everything® Wills & Estate Planning Book

COOKING

Everything® Barbecue Cookbook
Everything® Bartender's Book, $9.95
Everything® Chinese Cookbook
Everything® **Classic Recipes Book**
Everything® Cocktail Parties and Drinks Book
Everything® College Cookbook
Everything® **Cooking for Baby and Toddler Book**
Everything® Cooking for Two Cookbook
Everything® Diabetes Cookbook
Everything® Easy Gourmet Cookbook
Everything® Fondue Cookbook
Everything® **Fondue Party Book**
Everything® Gluten-Free Cookbook
Everything® Glycemic Index Cookbook
Everything® Grilling Cookbook

Everything® Healthy Meals in Minutes Cookbook
Everything® Holiday Cookbook
Everything® Indian Cookbook
Everything® Italian Cookbook
Everything® Low-Carb Cookbook
Everything® Low-Fat High-Flavor Cookbook
Everything® Low-Salt Cookbook
Everything® Meals for a Month Cookbook
Everything® Mediterranean Cookbook
Everything® Mexican Cookbook
Everything® One-Pot Cookbook
Everything® **Quick and Easy 30-Minute, 5-Ingredient Cookbook**
Everything® Quick Meals Cookbook
Everything® Slow Cooker Cookbook
Everything® Slow Cooking for a Crowd Cookbook
Everything® Soup Cookbook
Everything® Tex-Mex Cookbook
Everything® Thai Cookbook
Everything® Vegetarian Cookbook
Everything® Wild Game Cookbook
Everything® Wine Book, 2nd Ed.

GAMES

Everything® 15-Minute Sudoku Book, $9.95
Everything® 30-Minute Sudoku Book, $9.95
Everything® Blackjack Strategy Book
Everything® Brain Strain Book, $9.95
Everything® Bridge Book
Everything® Card Games Book
Everything® Card Tricks Book, $9.95
Everything® Casino Gambling Book, 2nd Ed.
Everything® Chess Basics Book
Everything® Craps Strategy Book
Everything® Crossword and Puzzle Book
Everything® Crossword Challenge Book
Everything® Cryptograms Book, $9.95
Everything® Easy Crosswords Book
Everything® Easy Kakuro Book, $9.95
Everything® Games Book, 2nd Ed.
Everything® Giant Sudoku Book, $9.95
Everything® Kakuro Challenge Book, $9.95
Everything® **Large-Print Crossword Challenge Book**
Everything® Large-Print Crosswords Book
Everything® Lateral Thinking Puzzles Book, $9.95
Everything® **Mazes Book**

Everything® Pencil Puzzles Book, $9.95
Everything® Poker Strategy Book
Everything® Pool & Billiards Book
Everything® Test Your IQ Book, $9.95
Everything® Texas Hold 'Em Book, $9.95
Everything® Travel Crosswords Book, $9.95
Everything® Word Games Challenge Book
Everything® Word Search Book

HEALTH

Everything® Alzheimer's Book
Everything® Diabetes Book
Everything® Health Guide to Adult Bipolar Disorder
Everything® Health Guide to Controlling Anxiety
Everything® Health Guide to Fibromyalgia
Everything® **Health Guide to Thyroid Disease**
Everything® Hypnosis Book
Everything® Low Cholesterol Book
Everything® Massage Book
Everything® Menopause Book
Everything® Nutrition Book
Everything® Reflexology Book
Everything® Stress Management Book

HISTORY

Everything® American Government Book
Everything® American History Book
Everything® Civil War Book
Everything® Freemasons Book
Everything® Irish History & Heritage Book
Everything® Middle East Book

HOBBIES

Everything® Candlemaking Book
Everything® Cartooning Book
Everything® **Coin Collecting Book**
Everything® Drawing Book
Everything® Family Tree Book, 2nd Ed.
Everything® Knitting Book
Everything® Knots Book
Everything® Photography Book
Everything® Quilting Book
Everything® Scrapbooking Book
Everything® Sewing Book
Everything® Woodworking Book

Bolded titles are new additions to the series.
All Everything® books are priced at $12.95 or $14.95, unless otherwise stated. Prices subject to change without notice.

HOME IMPROVEMENT

Everything® Feng Shui Book
Everything® Feng Shui Decluttering Book, $9.95
Everything® Fix-It Book
Everything® Home Decorating Book
Everything® Home Storage Solutions Book
Everything® Homebuilding Book
Everything® Lawn Care Book
Everything® Organize Your Home Book

KIDS' BOOKS

All titles are $7.95

Everything® Kids' Animal Puzzle & Activity Book
Everything® Kids' Baseball Book, 4th Ed.
Everything® Kids' Bible Trivia Book
Everything® Kids' Bugs Book
Everything® Kids' Cars and Trucks Puzzle & Activity Book
Everything® Kids' Christmas Puzzle & Activity Book
Everything® Kids' Cookbook
Everything® Kids' Crazy Puzzles Book
Everything® Kids' Dinosaurs Book
Everything® Kids' First Spanish Puzzle and Activity Book
Everything® Kids' Gross Hidden Pictures Book
Everything® Kids' Gross Jokes Book
Everything® Kids' Gross Mazes Book
Everything® Kids' Gross Puzzle and Activity Book
Everything® Kids' Halloween Puzzle & Activity Book
Everything® Kids' Hidden Pictures Book
Everything® Kids' Horses Book
Everything® Kids' Joke Book
Everything® Kids' Knock Knock Book
Everything® Kids' Learning Spanish Book
Everything® Kids' Math Puzzles Book
Everything® Kids' Mazes Book
Everything® Kids' Money Book
Everything® Kids' Nature Book
Everything® Kids' Pirates Puzzle and Activity Book
Everything® Kids' Princess Puzzle and Activity Book
Everything® Kids' Puzzle Book
Everything® Kids' Riddles & Brain Teasers Book
Everything® Kids' Science Experiments Book
Everything® Kids' Sharks Book
Everything® Kids' Soccer Book
Everything® Kids' Travel Activity Book

KIDS' STORY BOOKS

Everything® Fairy Tales Book

LANGUAGE

Everything® Conversational Chinese Book with CD, $19.95
Everything® Conversational Japanese Book with CD, $19.95
Everything® French Grammar Book
Everything® French Phrase Book, $9.95
Everything® French Verb Book, $9.95
Everything® German Practice Book with CD, $19.95
Everything® Inglés Book
Everything® Learning French Book
Everything® Learning German Book
Everything® Learning Italian Book
Everything® Learning Latin Book
Everything® Learning Spanish Book
Everything® Russian Practice Book with CD, $19.95
Everything® Sign Language Book
Everything® Spanish Grammar Book
Everything® Spanish Phrase Book, $9.95
Everything® Spanish Practice Book with CD, $19.95
Everything® Spanish Verb Book, $9.95

MUSIC

Everything® Drums Book with CD, $19.95
Everything® Guitar Book
Everything® Guitar Chords Book with CD, $19.95
Everything® Home Recording Book
Everything® Music Theory Book with CD, $19.95
Everything® Reading Music Book with CD, $19.95
Everything® Rock & Blues Guitar Book (with CD), $19.95
Everything® Songwriting Book

NEW AGE

Everything® Astrology Book, 2nd Ed.
Everything® Birthday Personology Book
Everything® Dreams Book, 2nd Ed.
Everything® Love Signs Book, $9.95
Everything® Numerology Book
Everything® Paganism Book
Everything® Palmistry Book
Everything® Psychic Book
Everything® Reiki Book
Everything® Sex Signs Book, $9.95
Everything® Tarot Book, 2nd Ed.
Everything® Wicca and Witchcraft Book

PARENTING

Everything® Baby Names Book, 2nd Ed.
Everything® Baby Shower Book
Everything® Baby's First Food Book
Everything® Baby's First Year Book
Everything® Birthing Book
Everything® Breastfeeding Book
Everything® Father-to-Be Book
Everything® Father's First Year Book
Everything® Get Ready for Baby Book
Everything® Get Your Baby to Sleep Book, $9.95
Everything® Getting Pregnant Book
Everything® Guide to Raising a One-Year-Old
Everything® Guide to Raising a Two-Year-Old
Everything® Homeschooling Book
Everything® Mother's First Year Book
Everything® Parent's Guide to Children and Divorce
Everything® Parent's Guide to Children with ADD/ADHD
Everything® Parent's Guide to Children with Asperger's Syndrome
Everything® Parent's Guide to Children with Autism
Everything® Parent's Guide to Children with Bipolar Disorder
Everything® Parent's Guide to Children with Dyslexia
Everything® Parent's Guide to Positive Discipline
Everything® Parent's Guide to Raising a Successful Child
Everything® Parent's Guide to Raising Boys
Everything® Parent's Guide to Raising Siblings
Everything® Parent's Guide to Sensory Integration Disorder
Everything® Parent's Guide to Tantrums
Everything® Parent's Guide to the Overweight Child
Everything® Parent's Guide to the Strong-Willed Child
Everything® Parenting a Teenager Book
Everything® Potty Training Book, $9.95
Everything® Pregnancy Book, 2nd Ed.
Everything® Pregnancy Fitness Book
Everything® Pregnancy Nutrition Book
Everything® Pregnancy Organizer, 2nd Ed., $16.95
Everything® Toddler Activities Book
Everything® Toddler Book
Everything® Tween Book
Everything® Twins, Triplets, and More Book

PETS

Everything® Aquarium Book
Everything® Boxer Book
Everything® Cat Book, 2nd Ed.
Everything® Chihuahua Book
Everything® Dachshund Book
Everything® Dog Book
Everything® Dog Health Book
Everything® Dog Owner's Organizer, $16.95
Everything® Dog Training and Tricks Book
Everything® German Shepherd Book
Everything® Golden Retriever Book
Everything® Horse Book
Everything® Horse Care Book
Everything® Horseback Riding Book
Everything® Labrador Retriever Book
Everything® Poodle Book
Everything® Pug Book
Everything® Puppy Book
Everything® Rottweiler Book
Everything® Small Dogs Book
Everything® Tropical Fish Book
Everything® Yorkshire Terrier Book

REFERENCE

Everything® Blogging Book
Everything® Build Your Vocabulary Book
Everything® Car Care Book
Everything® Classical Mythology Book
Everything® Da Vinci Book
Everything® Divorce Book
Everything® Einstein Book
Everything® Etiquette Book, 2nd Ed.
Everything® Inventions and Patents Book
Everything® Mafia Book
Everything® Philosophy Book
Everything® Psychology Book
Everything® Shakespeare Book

RELIGION

Everything® Angels Book
Everything® Bible Book
Everything® Buddhism Book
Everything® Catholicism Book
Everything® Christianity Book
Everything® History of the Bible Book
Everything® Jesus Book
Everything® Jewish History & Heritage Book
Everything® Judaism Book
Everything® Kabbalah Book
Everything® Koran Book
Everything® Mary Book

Everything® Mary Magdalene Book
Everything® Prayer Book
Everything® Saints Book
Everything® Torah Book
Everything® Understanding Islam Book
Everything® World's Religions Book
Everything® Zen Book

SCHOOL & CAREERS

Everything® Alternative Careers Book
Everything® Career Tests Book
Everything® College Major Test Book
Everything® College Survival Book, 2nd Ed.
Everything® Cover Letter Book, 2nd Ed.
Everything® Filmmaking Book
Everything® Get-a-Job Book
Everything® Guide to Being a Paralegal
Everything® Guide to Being a Real Estate Agent
Everything® Guide to Being a Sales Rep
Everything® Guide to Careers in Health Care
Everything® Guide to Careers in Law Enforcement
Everything® Guide to Government Jobs
Everything® Guide to Starting and Running a Restaurant
Everything® Job Interview Book
Everything® New Nurse Book
Everything® New Teacher Book
Everything® Paying for College Book
Everything® Practice Interview Book
Everything® Resume Book, 2nd Ed.
Everything® Study Book

SELF-HELP

Everything® Dating Book, 2nd Ed.
Everything® Great Sex Book
Everything® Kama Sutra Book
Everything® Self-Esteem Book

SPORTS & FITNESS

Everything® Easy Fitness Book
Everything® Fishing Book
Everything® Golf Instruction Book
Everything® Pilates Book
Everything® Running Book
Everything® Weight Training Book
Everything® Yoga Book

TRAVEL

Everything® Family Guide to Cruise Vacations
Everything® Family Guide to Hawaii

Everything® Family Guide to Las Vegas, 2nd Ed.
Everything® Family Guide to Mexico
Everything® Family Guide to New York City, 2nd Ed.
Everything® Family Guide to RV Travel & Campgrounds
Everything® Family Guide to the Caribbean
Everything® Family Guide to the Walt Disney World Resort®, Universal Studios®, and Greater Orlando, 4th Ed.
Everything® Family Guide to Timeshares
Everything® Family Guide to Washington D.C., 2nd Ed.
Everything® Guide to New England

WEDDINGS

Everything® Bachelorette Party Book, $9.95
Everything® Bridesmaid Book, $9.95
Everything® Destination Wedding Book
Everything® Elopement Book, $9.95
Everything® Father of the Bride Book, $9.95
Everything® Groom Book, $9.95
Everything® Mother of the Bride Book, $9.95
Everything® Outdoor Wedding Book
Everything® Wedding Book, 3rd Ed.
Everything® Wedding Checklist, $9.95
Everything® Wedding Etiquette Book, $9.95
Everything® Wedding Organizer, 2nd Ed., $16.95
Everything® Wedding Shower Book, $9.95
Everything® Wedding Vows Book, $9.95
Everything® Wedding Workout Book
Everything® Weddings on a Budget Book, $9.95

WRITING

Everything® Creative Writing Book
Everything® Get Published Book, 2nd Ed.
Everything® Grammar and Style Book
Everything® Guide to Writing a Book Proposal
Everything® Guide to Writing a Novel
Everything® Guide to Writing Children's Books
Everything® Guide to Writing Research Papers
Everything® Screenwriting Book
Everything® Writing Poetry Book
Everything® Writing Well Book